# Governing
# the Ungovernable City

Barbara Ferman

# Governing
# the Ungovernable City

## Political Skill, Leadership,
## and the Modern Mayor

Temple University Press
Philadelphia

Temple University Press, Philadelphia 19122
© 1985 by Temple University. All rights reserved
Published 1985
Printed in the United States of America

Library of Congress Cataloging in Publication Data

Ferman, Barbara.
    Governing the ungovernable city.

    Bibliography: p.
    Includes index.
    1. Mayors—United States.    2. Municipal government—United States.    I. Title.
JS356.F47    1985        352′.0083′0973        84-16375
ISBN 0-87722-376-9

# Contents

# Contents

# Tables and Figures

# Preface

The idea for this book grew out of the contradiction between the dim predictions for mayoral leadership in the 1970s and the powerful administration of Boston's Kevin White. Believing that strong mayoral leadership is necessary and intrigued by the exception that Kevin White represented, I decided to investigate his administration. Although this single case study produced many interesting findings, a study comparing two municipalities seemed more likely to lead to broad conclusions about mayoral leadership.

After a preliminary analysis of more than twenty cities, I elected to study mayoral leadership in San Francisco. Both cities have nonpartisan, reformed political systems, competitive political environments, ethnic and economic diversity, and similar problems and issues. Within these similar contexts, however, there are important differences; San Francisco's political structure and its informal arrangements are more fragmented than Boston's and its electorate is more issue-oriented. Further, San Francisco's political culture has a strong reform ethos as compared to the more private-regarding ethos in Boston.

Most significant, however, Boston and San Francisco provide a good representation of the obstacles to mayoral leadership. They are tough cities: tough in the sense that they contain the full range of political, economic, demographic, legal and social problems that mayors in all major American cities encounter. And, since many of the topics addressed in this book apply to all levels of government, the study teaches us about executive leadership, political behavior, and organizational development at the state and national levels as well.

The conclusions in this book are based primarily on interviews with politicians, government officials, journalists, and academic observers, and secondarily, on documentary research. In all, 123 interviews were conducted—65 in Boston and 58 in San Francisco—during 1980 and 1981; the research covers the period between 1967 and 1979.

As often happens in social science research, I began with a primary concern and, during the course of the analysis, stumbled upon other interesting, and sometimes disturbing, phenomena. My first interest was in how a mayor acquires power in a time of dwindling resources. My examination of the various strategies for governing, however, revealed the problem of costs. Power is necessary to govern, but developing that power often has a price. Many of these costs seem to result from the structure of urban institutions. Municipal reforms tend to weaken, and in many cases, remove, the institutional checks on power. This weakness, combined with the mayor's need to acquire power, often leads to power being developed for its own sake. The fine line between necessary power and self-aggrandizing power is lost and there are no institutional mechanisms to reinstate it. Many have argued that this was the tragic flaw in Kevin White's administration: the power to improve the quality of public service was replaced by an obsession with power.

The issue of limits is clearly important in a study of executive leadership. In the book I do explore the costs of strong leadership as well as the costs of weak leadership. However, the primary focus is on acquiring power; we learn what the limits should be when we see how power is exercised; we learn which institutions to strengthen when we see how they actually operate. By examining the dynamics of mayoral leadership, this book addresses these issues and offers recommendations for improving the quality of that leadership. These recommendations are not a cure-all; in fact, they are only a beginning. The study identifies many problem areas; the recommendations identify some potential solutions. But most important, the findings and the conclusions underscore the need for more scholarly work in urban politics. It is my deepest hope that the issues raised in this book will stimulate the type of analysis that is needed to improve the working of local government.

# Acknowledgments

A work of this scope must draw on the intellectual and moral resources of a variety of persons and institutions. My first debt is to the Politics Department at Brandeis University. In particular I thank Martin A. Levin for teaching me the importance of urban government and executive leadership. His ideas, encouragement, and constructive criticism on earlier drafts significantly improved the quality of this book. Christopher Leman's comments on earlier drafts forced me to reexamine my ideas, broaden my scope, and tighten my arguments. Robert Binstock made important comments on portions of an earlier draft. Conversations with Thomas Glynn from the Heller School gave me a fuller understanding of Boston city politics. Paul Rulisun and Bill Vogele provided the appropriate blend of interest, ideas, and humor that a project such as this requires.

Sharon Krefetz of Clark University read an earlier draft. Her comments, as well as her own work on San Francisco city government, provided important insights for this book. Aaron Wildavsky's comments on portions of the manuscript were helpful in final revisions.

I thank Michael Harrington of Queens College for teaching me the importance of political ideas. A special thanks goes to Harvey Burstein of Queens College for convincing me to pursue those ideas.

My family and friends gave me constant encouragement, confidence, and moral support. Dr. Natale Cipollina offered intellectual support as well, never failing to answer my many questions. His own work on New York City politics provided many valuable insights. My deep appreciation goes to Gary Apotheker for allowing me to make his home my home in San Francisco.

Special thanks goes to the James M. Gordon Foundation for their financial support and for their commitment to improving the quality of local government.

Lisa Robinson from the Politics Department of Brandeis University provided valuable administrative support and always with a smile. Rita Oriani from Simmons College typed an earlier draft, putting up with the frantic time crunches like a trooper.

I wish to thank the many people in Boston and San Francisco who generously provided the information I needed to write the book. While space and confidentiality prevent listing them individually, I would particularly like to thank those whose candor and questioning reflect their commitment to effective government. Special thanks to John Rothmann for giving me access to his library files in San Francisco.

Michael Ames, Doris Braendel, Jennifer French of Temple University Press, and Murdoch Matthew did an excellent job as editors and in production.

Thanks are due to *Policy Studies Review* for permission to reproduce parts of my article, "Beating the Odds: Mayoral Leadership and the Acquisition of Power" (vol. 3, no. 1 [Summer 1983]: 29–40). Thanks to Daniel Pool for permission to reproduce his table "Changing Contribution of Boston Vote to Statewide Totals in Gubernatorial Elections, 1910–1970." Thanks also to REALTOR NEWS® and the NATIONAL ASSOCIATION OF REALTORS® for permission to reproduce their tables "Total Monthly Housing Costs" and "Average Price of Existing Homes Sold."

Again, my heartfelt thanks to every individual, named and unnamed, who helped me to grow along with my work. I alone, of course, am responsible for the conclusions.

# Introduction

# ONE

# Mayoral Leadership
# in the Nonpartisan City

Given its present political organization and decision-making process, the city is fundamentally ungovernable.[1]

As formal head of the city, the mayor is caught between the high demand for action and the low supply of political resources. In recent years this gap has widened as federal intervention increased, local tax bases declined, and civil service unions, minorities, neighborhood and reform groups became more powerful and vocal. The inability of most mayors to bridge the gap convinced many observers that the prospects for mayoral leadership were dim.

In Boston, however, something exceptional occurred. During a time of dwindling resources, Kevin White was able to acquire a significant amount of power. The first question of this study is, "How did he do it?"

## THE PROSPECTS FOR MAYORAL LEADERSHIP

Mayors of all styles and strategies face a common dilemma: gaining and maintaining political authority.[2]

The dilemma of gaining and maintaining political authority has worsened because of structural and political changes at the local and national levels. The decline—in many cases, elimination—of local political parties has removed an important source of mayoral campaign support, patronage, insulation, and conflict management. Whereas mayors like Richard Daley in Chicago, David Lawrence in Pittsburgh, James Tate in Philadelphia, and Richard Lee in New Haven could dispense patronage in exchange for political support and had precinct workers to act as buffers with the electorate, the mayor in the nonpartisan city lacks these mechanisms. As a result, more demands come directly to the mayor's office. But other structural reforms have weakened the mayor's ability to deliver. Civil service reforms removed still another source of patronage and, more important, sharply curtailed the mayor's control. The city of Boston does not control its major parks and roads or its water system and must go to the state legislature to create sources of revenue. Until 1962, the mayor did not even control the city's police department. San Francisco's Public Works and Public Health Departments are under the jurisdiction of the Chief Administrative Officer (CAO), a mayoral appointee with a ten-year tenure. (Before 1975, the CAO had lifetime tenure.)

Even when a mayor does have formal control over a department, it is limited to a few individuals at the top—the department head or commissioners. But as Michael Lipsky pointed out, it is often the "street level bureaucrat" who implements policy, not the department head.[3] The mayor's ability to bridge this gap between formal control and actual control is severely limited by the civil service protection of street level bureaucrats.

The creation of public authorities and special districts further limits the areas of mayoral control. Boston's public transportation system and its port and airport activities are controlled by regional authorities (Massachusetts Bay Transportation Authority and Mass Port, respectively). In San Francisco, portions of the transportation system are under the control of a regional district (Bay Area Rapid Transit District) and many activities involving the San Francisco Bay are under the jurisdiction of the Bay Area Air Pollution and Control District. In many cases, public authorities have been headed by strong leaders who rivaled the mayor's power. In New York City, five mayors were forced to make important concessions to Robert Moses, the powerful head of the Triborough Bridge and Tunnel Authority.[4]

The result of these reforms was the creation of "functional islands of autonomy" and a weakening of mayoral resources.[5] As Theodore Lowi argued,

> the legacy of reform is the bureaucratic city state. Destruction of the party foundation of the mayorality cleaned up many cities but also destroyed the capacity for sustained central, popularity-based action. This capacity, with all its faults, was replaced by the power of professionalized agencies. But this has meant the creation of new bases of power . . . the bureaucracies . . . are the New Machines.[6]

Exacerbating this fragmentation was the nationalization of local politics. The weakening of political parties encouraged national candidates to appeal directly to local voters. Emphasizing broad social issues and sponsoring major federal programs, these candidates helped to politicize various groups within the cities—minorities, reform groups, neighborhood groups. Moreover, the issues around which those groups organized—busing, desegregated housing, decentralization, affirmative action—led to major conflicts at the local level. The scattersite housing and school decentralization issues in New York, for example, helped to destroy the coalition of liberal Jews and blacks that had been built up over many years. The organizing activities of these new groups were strengthened by the resources provided through federal programs. In Oakland, Jeffrey Pressman showed how federal programs pulled power away from the center, thereby increasing the obstacles to mayoral leadership.[7]

The difficulties created by the federal presence were intensified by the media. By focusing intensively on these conflicts, the media increased their saliency and encouraged the pattern of "street fighting pluralism."[8] Moreover, their emphasis in the 1960s on charismatic and innovative leaders often encouraged mayors to accommodate and support the protest activities of many of these groups. But the mayors' "crusading" leadership strategies merely reinforced the conflict behavior. From his experience in the Lindsay administration, Douglas Yates discovered that "the best way for a community group to get a bureaucratic response to an ordinary service problem was to make an emergency call to City Hall and announce that a riot was just about to break out."[9] The 1960s were not called the era of protest politics without cause.

The proliferation of issue politics at the local level brought another force into city politics—the courts. In Boston, the courts made important policy decisions on busing (they monitored the entire system and assumed receivership of one of the high schools) and city revenues, and assumed jurisdiction of the public housing authority. In San Francisco, the courts were involved in redevelopment and affirmative action issues, including a ban on hiring of police. The court presence in local politics often resulted in externally imposed decisions that were highly controversial within the city and were beyond the mayor's ability to resolve.

Finally, mayors face challenges to their power from the more traditional sources: local legislative bodies, independent school boards and committees, regional, state, and federal agencies, other elected officials, and the business community.

The mayor's job is further complicated by the anti-power bias in the American political culture. Although the electorate expects the executive to handle all problems that arise, they are reluctant to give the formal tools with which to accomplish this. This obstacle merits special attention.

First, the anti-power bias is a major obstacle to the acquisition of power at *all* levels of government. Second, the anti-power bias among many political scientists has tended to draw attention away from the politics of leadership.[10] The Pluralist school of thought, for example, sought to deny the importance of executive leadership and the acquisition of power. As a result, it offered only a limited understanding of a complex and necessary field. Third, the anti-power bias has influenced many of our leaders as well. Further, it has often been blended with an anti-party and anti-politics approach. John Lindsay entered the mayor's office as a good government reformer who was going to wipe out backroom politics. Michael Dukakis came to the governor's office in Massachusetts in 1974 as a managerial leader seeking to streamline state government and make it more honest. And Jimmy Carter went to the White House believing that the federal government could be run on the principles of rationality and scientific management.[11] They were all unsuccessful and, consequently, they were all defeated.[12] Moreover, their experiences illustrate the difficulties today of acquiring power at any level of government.

## OBJECTIVES

This study seeks to identify the factors that contribute to strong executive leadership at the local level. The analysis builds on earlier theories of executive leadership while transcending some of their limitations. Two major difficulties have been in methodological and conceptual areas. Although powerful leadership is not quantifiable, some writers have offered operational definitions. Andrew McFarland defined it as "unusual influence"—the ability to alter behavior in ways desired by the executive.[13] Building on this idea, Jeffrey Pressman suggested that successful leadership involves the setting and achievement of goals.[14] These concepts imply certain observable features; successful mayors are able to persuade others, control policy arenas, extend their influence within city government, implement priorities, and mobilize support for electoral and nonelectoral goals.

While the development of these criteria has been an important contribution to the field of leadership analysis, their usefulness is limited by their almost exclusive emphasis on outputs.[15] This emphasis raises several methodological problems. First, many outputs are difficult to identify. Subtle outputs (such as behavioral changes) or symbolic outputs may completely elude the analyst. Second, a performance-based approach does not give sufficient attention to whether the performance is actually what produces the results. Things may occur—or not occur—regardless of what the mayor does. Third, there is danger that performance analysis will become totally divorced from the structural context in which the leader is operating. That is, by underemphasizing the context, we cannot predict what the result of a given action will be in different settings. Finally, the performance-based approach gives insufficient attention to the power of non–decision-making. Bacharach and Baratz have demonstrated the power of this tool in leadership success.[16]

A major conceptual problem lies in the realm of model building. The earlier attempts to develop models of mayoral leadership ultimately rest on different styles of leadership—entrepreneurial, broker, crusader, manager, etc.[17] These models are useful for distinguishing between different types of mayors. The major flaw, however, is their failure to view style as another political skill or as the culmination of various skills. Consequently, they assume a fixed rigidity that takes each style as mutually exclusive. The incompatibility between certain models, such as the power broker and the crusader, limits the explanatory power of this approach. By contrast, when we view style as a political skill, we can integrate the major components of each of these models. In the White administration, for example, there were elements of the crusader, the entrepreneur, and the power broker. In fact, his skill in projecting these diverse styles was a major factor in his ability to acquire resources.

Earlier model-building attempts are also limited, according to Charles Levine, to the extent that they assume a pluralist political system. In his critique of this literature, Levine argued that these model builders overlook the impact of sharp community cleavages on mayoral strategies because the studies were conducted in communities characterized by "political pluralism and low or moderate degrees of conflict."[18] Indeed, the definition of mayoral effectiveness produced by these studies has limited applicability; it applies only in pluralist political settings.

Levine's attempt to overcome these limitations through a contingency theory of mayoral leadership makes a significant contribution to leadership analysis. His emphasis on the need for integrative frameworks that examine the dynamics of mayoral leadership is a sharp and necessary departure from the one-dimensionality of many earlier works. My analysis agrees with Levine's critique and makes a broader attempt to overcome the limitations that he cites. Whereas Levine examines the impact of racial conflict on mayoral leadership and strategies, my study considers the impact of a wide range of varied contexts on mayoral leadership, allowing us to examine the full gamut of opportunities and constraints in which the mayor operates. Moreover, by examining a variety of cleavages (divisions within the electorate), this study poses an even more fundamental challenge to the pluralist model. I argue that, in the absence of a strong center, the pluralist competition for resources does not alter the distribution of those resources.

This study attempts to overcome the limitations of the performance-based approach by examining not only the achievements of mayors but also how they establish the conditions necessary for achieving their goals. I define success as actions that yield immediate resources as well as actions that help the mayor to acquire future resources and to implement subsequent policies.

In my study, I consider three major variables—political skills, political systems, and political culture. By focusing on political skills in general, the inquiry is able to avoid the rigidities of earlier model-building attempts. Giving attention to political systems and culture provides a context for analyzing the constraints on and opportunities for mayoral leadership. This consideration of the context also allows us to explain events more usefully. Tracing the relationship between political skills and political systems enables us to identify the types of strategies most appropriate in different settings and to predict outcomes more accurately.

Fortunately, for our purposes, Boston and San Francisco differ greatly in their political systems and political cultures, offering a wide scope for testing the relationship between the three variables. My study will focus on the administrations of Kevin White in Boston and of Joseph Alioto and George Moscone in San Francisco. I will show that the political system and the political culture influence the resources and opportunities of a mayor, but that an executive may succeed or fail according to how skillfully he or she manipulates the political context.

### Political System

The political system influences the resources and strategies available and, hence, the opportunities for executive leadership. The key features are the degree of formal fragmentation, the nature of other actors within city government, and the organization of the electorate.

A less fragmented political system provides greater opportunities for strong executive leadership. There is a greater opportunity to centralize control within city government through formal tools. Once acquired, this control gives the mayor resources with which to influence others. This was the approach taken by White in Boston and his strategies increased his power. In highly fragmented political systems like San Francisco, mayors have to rely more on informal mechanisms such as personality, bargaining, persuasion, and image. The dispersion of authority within the formal arena often leads to strategies that seek to pull power from the sides to the center. Such strategies can offset some of the obstacles posed by fragmentation, but the expenditure of resources that it requires makes it difficult to accumulate political capital.

The orientation of the actors within city government helps to shape the resource opportunities and strategies available. Highly political actors will be more receptive targets for an exercise of political skills than less politically oriented actors. The first situation characterizes Boston's city government and the second characterizes San Francisco's government.

Finally, resource opportunities and leadership strategies vary with how politics are organized. During Alioto's administration, powerful groups within the electorate provided the basis for a coalitional politics that gave Alioto a measure of insulation. Moscone and Feinstein faced a fragmented and issue-oriented electorate that strained their ability to manage conflict. White faced an electorate characterized by low levels of organization and political activism and oriented toward material benefits. This created opportunities for a patronage-based politics and for co-optation strategies.

## Political Culture

A city's political culture helps to shape the resource opportunities and the strategies available. I use the term *political culture* in the narrow sense to distinguish between a public-regarding or reform ethos and a private-regarding or nonreform ethos. A reform political culture is *not* synonymous with, nor necessarily related to, a reformed political system. The latter term refers to the structural arrangements—nonpartisan, at-large elections; the holding of local elections at times when there are no state or national elections; extension of the merit system; reduced size of local legislative bodies.

A reform political culture, however, is a matter of the electorate's conception of politics and government. Reform culture is usually found among middle and upper middle class populations and professional classes. Its major characteristics are a view of politics as a form of public service that benefits the whole community; a conviction that the public interest should prevail over private interests; a belief that this public interest can be discovered and, hence, "good government" achieved through the application of management techniques (rationality, long-

9

term planning, broad objectives); a belief that these management techniques should be executed by professional administrators and experts; and an emphasis on procedure. The emphasis on procedure rather than outcomes and on government as an administrative or business-like operation produces a low tolerance for the traditional types of political behavior—patronage, deals, and backroom politics. The perception of government as an instrument for social change often results in a preoccupation with issues. The professional and upper class bias of reform usually produces a fairly liberal climate of opinion, most notably on social issues. These characteristics create obstacles to the exercise of political skills, to policymaking, and to conflict management.

By contrast, a private-regarding or nonreform political ethos— which, as Boston shows, can coexist with a *reformed* political structure—is found among working class and ethnic populations. It is characterized by a view of politics as a competition among private interests; a conception of government as a "source of power to be used for individual, rather than social, ends";[19] an emphasis on material and solidary incentives for political participation; a tolerance of corruption and "backroom politics"; an emphasis on ethnic and personal loyalty; and an emphasis on pragmatism and tangible rewards or outcomes. The emphasis on outcomes produces expediency and a high tolerance for open politicking. The view of government as a mechanism for achieving the individual's well-being often facilitates a patronage-based politics. The working class character tends to generate a conservative bias on social issues. This ethos creates a favorable climate for the exercise of political skills, which reduces some of the obstacles to policymaking and conflict management. The major expression of this ethos at the local level was the urban political machine.

### Political Skills

The influence of the political system and political culture on the mayor's resources makes effective political skills a necessity. Formal tools and informal resources must be manipulated in such a way that the mayor establishes the conditions for increasing executive power. Broadly, we can view the relationship between political skills and the acquisition of resources as a combination of selection, interaction, and concealment.

First, the mayor must perceive the opportunities to increase resources, select appropriate strategies, and choose the arena in which to operate (see Figure 1). Since some strategies are more effective in some arenas than in others, this is a crucial step. Conflict, for example, is a

FIGURE 1: Power Acquisition Model

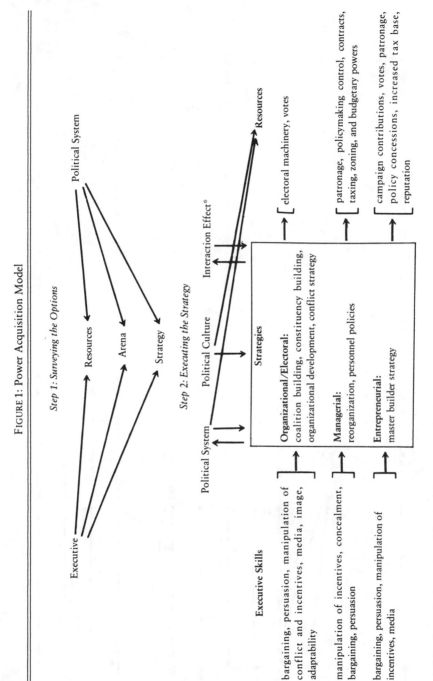

*Step 1: Surveying the Options*

Executive

Political System

Resources

Arena

Strategy

*Step 2: Executing the Strategy*

Executive Skills

Political System    Political Culture    Interaction Effect*

Strategies

**Organizational/Electoral:** coalition building, constituency building, organizational development, conflict strategy

**Managerial:** reorganization, personnel policies

**Entrepreneurial:** master builder strategy

bargaining, persuasion, manipulation of conflict and incentives, media, image, adaptability

manipulation of incentives, concealment, bargaining, persuasion

bargaining, persuasion, manipulation of incentives, media

Resources

electoral machinery, votes

patronage, policymaking control, contracts, taxing, zoning, and budgetary powers

campaign contributions, votes, patronage, policy concessions, increased tax base, reputation

* This refers to the interaction of the particular strategy with other strategies, actors, institutional arrangements, and goals.

# FIGURE 1 (CONTINUED)

*Step 3: Pyramiding Resources*

|  | |  |
|---|---|---|
| campaign contributions | → | get re-elected |
| votes | → | |
| electoral machinery | → | manage conflict, support other candidates |
| patronage | → | co-opt and defeat opposition |
| budgetary power | → | create new programs and jobs, protect old programs, enforce policy priorities, reward and discipline actors |
| policymaking control | → | implement priorities, achieve goals, gain media endorsement |
| taxing power | → | discipline actors, bargain for additional resources, influence economic development |
| zoning power | → | |
| contracts | → | implement priorities, influence economic development, bargain for additional resources |
| increased tax base | → | improve services, attract media attention |
| policymaking concessions | → | achieve goals |
| reputation | → | attract federal resources, attract new development |

viable strategy for mobilizing support within the electoral arena but often is too divisive to use as a governing strategy. The choice of arenas is also important because the resources they contain vary. Ideally, the mayor wants to direct strategies toward those arenas where the resources are the greatest.

Interaction is an important component in the exercise of political skills because strategies are not executed in a vacuum. Rather, they interact with other strategies, other actors, and resources. The first type of interaction means that a mayor's ability to pyramid resources is often a function of the outcomes of his or her previous strategies. Effective strategies enable a mayor to pyramid resources, whereas ineffective strategies tend to pyramid obstacles. When the latter occurs, the mayor's ability to take action is diminished. I call this the "downward spiral" of the weak mayor. When strategies designed to accomplish one goal interact with other actors and with institutional arrangements, they can create difficulties for a mayor in other areas and become another obstacle to mayoral leadership. The interaction between strategies and resources makes adaptability a necessary component of mayoral leadership. Resources and the mechanisms for acquiring them change. Thus, the mayor must shift strategies in order to maximize opportunities to acquire resources. This theme is very prominent in White's administration and helps to explain how he was able to acquire power in a time of dwindling resources.

Further complicating the use of political skills and the task of acquiring resources is the anti-power bias in the American political culture. To overcome this obstacle, mayors often must develop power without appearing to do so. Thus, concealment is a crucial tool of strong mayoral leadership.[20]

## ORGANIZATION OF THE STUDY

Chapter 2, following, examines the demographic, economic, and political characteristics and differences of Boston and San Francisco in order to provide a context for the study's major themes. The chapter also contains a sketch of each mayor.

The remainder of the study examines the mayors' strategies. The material is organized to illustrate the relationship between strategies, resources, and arenas. Chapter 3 examines the use of conflict strategy and mayoral visibility to mobilize support in the public arena. The focus here is on the differences between electoral and governing coalitions; the relationship of conflict to political organization, political orientation, and target of appeals; and the relationship between the composition of city government and the scope and arena of issues.

Chapters 4 through 6 explore mayoral strategies in the formal arena of city government. Chapter 4 examines the use of personnel strategies to develop an infrastructure. Comparing the centralized control and consolidated influence approaches to accumulating power, the chapter shows how centralization results in a hierarchical structure that reduces the executive's costs in acquiring additional resources. The second approach, which involves pulling power from the sides to the center, requires a larger expenditure of resources and, when the sides are fragmented, hinders the mayor's ability to manage conflict. Comparing the two approaches highlights important themes concerning organizational development, coalition building, constituency and issue-oriented politics, and liberal appeals and innovative mayors. Chapter 5 looks at the use of reorganization strategies to overcome the obstacles posed by bureaucracy. The advantage of this strategy is that it can be justified on managerial grounds and so conceal the executive's attempt to acquire power. The chapter also examines the dilemmas and opportunities of avoidance behavior. When practiced by bureaucracy, avoidance impedes policymaking and service delivery but also leaves the way open for mayors to exercise leadership in those neglected areas. Avoidance behavior by mayors is a way to conserve resources, but it carries costs for certain segments of the electorate. Chapter 6 looks at the defeat of charter reform policies in Boston and San Francisco. As an example of an unsuccessful strategy, it emphasizes the mayors' need to be politically astute enough to develop power without appearing to do so.

Chapter 7 reevaluates the mayor's role in the federal arena. Contrary to the widely held belief that mayors and cities are prisoners of the federal leviathan, this chapter shows how the skillful mayor manipulates federal programs to gain advantage. The cases also demonstrate that, in the absence of mayoral control, the federal presence has a disruptive effect on the local political system.

Chapter 8 compares White and Alioto's use of the master builder strategy to acquire power in the private sector arena. This is a complex strategy because it requires the mayor to operate effectively in many arenas. When these arenas collide, we see the significance of the interaction effect, the difference between pyramiding and dispersing resources, and the importance of choosing arenas.

Chapter 9 analyzes the themes developed in the study and their implications for theory building and policymaking. It looks at the requirements for strong executive leadership, the costs and desirability of that leadership, and the costs of weak leadership. It then makes policy recommendations for developing, and limiting the costs of, strong executive leadership.

# TWO

# A Tale of Two Cities:
# Boston and San Francisco

Urban life, a subject of fervent interest to the young, to environmentalists, to politicians, and to many academics, is still an enigma to most. We have in the past few generations chosen to move away from the city's complexities or resolved not to go near them. As a result, many of the subtle intricacies of the "urban style" are still hidden shadows of behavior that are poorly understood and easily misinterpreted.[1]

Although 3,000 miles apart, Boston and San Francisco have important political, economic, demographic, and physical similarities. Politically, both cities are heavily Democratic and have reformed, nonpartisan, at-large electoral systems, mayor-council forms of government, and civil service bureaucracies.[2] Economically, both cities have developed from major shipping and industrial centers into financial and service headquarters. The populations and land areas of the two cities are roughly the same size. Both are ethnically diverse and have relatively small black populations. Both cities blend distinct ethnic neighborhoods and a larger cosmopolitan flavor; both support long-standing cultural institutions.

Despite these similarities, Boston and San Francisco have important differences that have influenced their political systems. The most important factors are the strong influence of labor on the political system in San Francisco compared with a negligible impact in Boston, and a strong reform ethos in San Francisco compared with a more private-regarding political ethos in Boston.[3] Furthermore, important changes in San Francisco's demographic makeup during the 1970s resulted in an even stronger reform ethos and an increasingly fragmented, issue-oriented, and hyperpluralistic electorate.

## POPULATION AND ECONOMY

On 46 square miles, Boston, the capital of Massachusetts, has a population of 636,725 people. Of almost equal area, San Francisco has a population of 664,520 on 45.4 square miles (see Table 1). Both cities have the traditional ethnic mix of Irish, Italian, Jewish, and black, but San Francisco's population of Asians and Hispanics has increased since the late 1950s.[4] Thus, where the Irish are the leading ethnic group in Boston, the Asians lead in San Francisco. In addition, San Francisco's white population (57 percent of total population) is significantly smaller than Boston's (82 percent of total population). In contrast to some of the older industrial cities, Boston and San Francisco have relatively small black populations. In 1970 blacks comprised 16.3 percent of Boston's total population and 13.4 percent of San Francisco's, compared with 38.3 percent in Cleveland, 33.5 percent in Philadelphia, 46.4 percent in Baltimore, and 20.2 percent in Pittsburgh.[5] The political significance of this is that blacks in Boston and San Francisco have not developed effec-

TABLE 1: Socioeconomic Characteristics: Boston and San Francisco

| Characteristic | Boston | San Francisco |
|---|---|---|
| 1975 population | 636,725 (Rank, 19) | 664,520 (Rank, 16) |
| 1970 population | 641,071 | 715,674 |
| Foreign stock | 37.0% | 44.3% |
| Leading country of origin | Ireland | China |
| % of foreign stock | 21.8 | 15.3 |
| Black population | 16.3 | 13.4 |
| Hispanic population | 2.8 | 14.2 |
| Asian population | 2.4 | 15.0 |
| Jewish population | 5.0* | 10.0† |
| White population | 82.0 | 57.0 |
| Sixty-five and over | 12.8 | 14.0 |
| Twenty-five and over | 54.7 | 69.0 |
| Four years high school or more (persons over 25) | 53.5 | 61.8 |
| Per capita income | $4,157 | $ 5,990 |
| Median family income | 9,133 | 10,495 |
| % families earning $15–25,000 | 14.8 | 20.0 |
| More than $25,000 | 3.3 | 7.1 |
| Below poverty level | 11.7 | 9.9 |
| % employed in manufacturing | 17.5 | 11.7 |
| retail and wholesale | 19.4 | 20.4 |
| government | 17.5 | 19.1 |

Source: 1970 Census, U.S. Department of Commerce, County and City Data Book (Washington, D. C.: Government Printing Office, 1977). All data is 1970 except where noted, because most of the cases in the study were around 1970.

* This is an approximation extrapolated from neighborhood data.

† American Jewish Yearbook (Philadelphia: Jewish Publication Society, 1970).

tive political organizations as have their counterparts in these other cities.[6]

The ethnic diversity within the two cities has helped to maintain strong neighborhood identifications. In Boston, this neighborhood orientation largely resulted from the city's geographical makeup and was enhanced by ethnic and economic factors; East Boston is an island and predominantly Italian working class; South Boston and Charlestown are peninsulas and predominantly Irish working class. The other major ethnic areas of the city include Roxbury, Mattapan (black areas), South End (primarily black, but changing now as a result of gentrification), and Dorchester (Irish working class and partly black).[7] In San Francisco the major ethnic areas are Chinatown, Japantown, the Mission District (Hispanic), North Beach (Italian), Fillmore, Hunter's Point/Bayview, and the Western Addition (black).

As in many older cities, Boston and San Francisco's populations declined during the 1970s. In contrast to Boston and many cities of the U.S. Northeast, San Francisco's black population decreased by 10 percent from 1970 to 1980.[8] During that time, Boston's black population increased by 20.6 percent.[9] Possible explanations for San Francisco's decline include the high cost of housing in San Francisco,[10] the displacement of blacks by redevelopment in the 1970s, the influx of Asians, the loss of shipping to Oakland,[11] and the broader shift in the city's economy from blue-collar industries to service industries and financial headquarters.

The decline in San Francisco's black population reflects a larger and more important difference between the two cities. Boston is primarily a working class city and San Francisco is primarily a middle class city. Politically, San Francisco, like the rest of California, developed a strong reform ethos and an issue oriented electorate. These two factors strongly influence the political system and, hence, mayoral leadership. The neighborhood orientation in San Francisco often supports issue-oriented or ideological concerns that become citywide conflicts. By contrast, Boston's working class neighborhoods tend to concern themselves with issues of basic service delivery and material concerns that can be dealt with within the neighborhood (see Chapters 3 and 4).

With a reputation as a tolerant, liberal, and exciting city, San Francisco attracted a younger, more professional, and wealthier population than Boston. This trend has intensified in the last two decades as San Francisco had an even larger influx of young and single individuals. The Haight-Ashbury scene in the 1960s and the rise of the gay community in the 1970s attracted many people seeking alternative lifestyles. As in other cities, many working and middle class families migrated to the suburbs. The replacement of working and middle class families with middle class and professional individuals helped to shift the political emphasis from basic services to salient issues.

San Francisco also has a larger Jewish population than Boston that has been very active and influential in the city's economic, cultural, and political life. Disproportionately represented on institutional boards and in political associations, San Francisco's Jewish community, like its counterpart in New York City, contributed to the liberal climate and reform ethos of the city.

Since the earliest days of California state politics, Jews held elected and appointed positions in San Francisco, including the office of mayor (Adolph Sutro, 1894–1896). Jewish influence in the city's political system was especially prevalent in the period between the 1930s and the mid-1960s when Jews filled 25 to 30 percent of the board and commission positions. During that same period in Boston, Chicago, Philadelphia, and Baltimore, Jews figured in less than 10 percent of mayoral appointments.[12] A more unusual phenomenon was Boss Abe Reuf, a Jewish machine politician who founded the Union Labor Party in San Francisco in 1901. Few other cities have had Jewish bosses (Cleveland had Bernstein and Maschke; Chicago had Jacob Avery).

In addition, San Francisco's Jews were, and still are, important campaign contributors and fundraisers in city, state, and national elections. Among the most important from the 1950s onward were Cyril Magnin, Walter Schorenstein, and the late Ben Swig.[13] Swig was national campaign manager for Adlai Stevenson in 1956, co-chairman of Edmund Brown's Democratic gubernatorial campaigns in 1958 and 1962, and a delegate to four Democratic national conventions. Walter Schorenstein, the nephew of a Tammany boss of Brooklyn, is a multimillionaire land developer and one of the principle Democratic fundraisers in California. In 1968, he raised half a million dollars for Hubert Humphrey.[14] Cyril Magnin, financier and owner of a major department store, was a personal friend and confidant of Presidents Kennedy and Johnson and one of the most important fundraisers in California and San Francisco.

Although historically many San Francisco Jews joined the Republican party, they tended to support liberal candidates and progressive issues.[15] The Jewish community strongly identified with the liberal Republicanism of California Governor Earl Warren (1943). Moreover, they did not support conservative Republican Harold Dobbs when he ran against Alioto in the 1967 mayoral election, even though Dobbs was Jewish (just as many New York City Jews voted for the liberal, progressive John Lindsay over the conservative, but Jewish, Abe

TABLE 2: Per Capita Income Ranking of the Thirty Largest Cities, 1929, 1959, and 1975

| Rank | 1929 | | 1959 | | 1975 | |
|---|---|---|---|---|---|---|
| 1 | $5,169 | San Francisco | $5,436 | Chicago | $7,754 | Washington, D.C. |
| 2 | | New York | | San Francisco | | Denver |
| 3 | $5,121 | Boston | | Washington, D.C. | | San Francisco |
| 4 | | Washington, D.C. | | Cleveland | | Chicago |
| 5 | | Chicago | | New York | | Houston |
| 6 | | Cincinnati | | Newark | | Cleveland |
| 7 | | St. Louis | | Los Angeles | | Seattle |
| 8 | | Newark | | Seattle | | Los Angeles |
| 9 | | Denver | | Indianapolis | | Newark |
| 10 | | Detroit | | Milwaukee | | New York |
| 11 | | Milwaukee | | Cincinnati | | Atlanta |
| 12 | | Cleveland | | Denver | | Dallas |
| 13 | | Philadelphia | | Houston | | Pittsburgh |
| 14 | | Los Angeles | | Dallas | | Milwaukee |
| 15 | | Pittsburgh | | Pittsburgh | | Indianapolis |
| 16 | | Indianapolis | | Buffalo | | Detroit |
| 17 | | Buffalo | | Atlanta | | Cincinnati |
| 18 | | Baltimore | | Detroit | | Nashville |
| 19 | | Houston | | San Diego | | Kansas City |
| 20 | | Seattle | | Kansas City | | San Diego |
| 21 | | Dallas | | Philadelphia | | Buffalo |
| 22 | | Kansas City | $4,080 | Boston | | Philadelphia |
| 23 | | San Diego | | St. Louis | | Phoenix |
| 24 | | New Orleans | | New Orleans | | Memphis |
| 25 | | Atlanta | | Baltimore | | Jacksonville |
| 26 | | Jacksonville | | Phoenix | | New Orleans |
| 27 | | Nashville | | Nashville | $5,570 | Boston |
| 28 | | Memphis | | Jacksonville | | Baltimore |
| 29 | | Phoenix | | Memphis | | St. Louis |
| 30 | $2,322 | San Antonio | $3,312 | San Antonio | $5,112 | San Antonio |

Source: Data from BRA Research Department and U. S. Bureau of Economic Analysis, in *A Decade of Development in Boston*, a report of the Boston Redevelopment Authority, May 1979, p. 22.

neighborhood and ethnic character of the city. As a result, San Francisco has an inflated image as a liberal city. While the socioeconomic composition of San Francisco makes it a more liberal city than Boston, it still contains a large conservative population that is usually underestimated by observers. The 1975 mayoral election demonstrated the force of that conservative element, as we shall see.

Despite these recent economic developments in the two cities, they face similar sets of issues and problems faced by many older cities—

crime, housing, transportation, jobs, education, fiscal constraints, and recent decreased federal revenues.[28] Two issues that merit special attention are the housing issue in San Francisco and the race issue in Boston, which is considered in a separate section later in this chapter.

Like many parts of California, San Francisco has undergone a soaring inflation in its housing market. With the median cost of a dwelling at $129,000, San Francisco had the highest cost of housing in the continental United States in 1980 (see Tables 3 and 4).[29] This factor—combined with the .5 percent vacancy rate in San Francisco,[30] the shortage of available land for housing construction, and the stringent zoning regulations—has made housing one of the most volatile issues in San Francisco.

## GOVERNMENT AND POLITICS

The institutional arrangements in Boston and San Francisco are the result of reform charters in 1949 and 1932 respectively. The different objectives of the reformers in the two cities, however, contributed to shaping two different governmental structures (see Figures 2 and 3). The impetus for reform in Boston was the ethnic cleavage between the Irish and the Yankees. The Yankees sought to maintain control over Boston's affairs by limiting the city's jurisdiction. They succeeded. The charter created a strong mayor form of government while limiting the areas in which the mayor could exercise authority. By contrast, San

TABLE 3: Average Price of Existing Homes Sold

| City | 1978 | 1979 | 1980 | 1981 | Rank by 1981 Price |
|------|------|------|------|------|--------------------|
| San Francisco | $94,700 | $99,500 | $120,200 | $133,900 | 1 |
| Los Angeles | 82,900 | 93,200 | 110,800 | 120,100 | 2 |
| Washington, D.C. | 68,300 | 82,200 | 91,700 | 100,900 | 3 |
| Houston | 63,400 | 76,000 | 82,900 | 95,000 | 4 |
| New York | 68,700 | 76,200 | 85,000 | 93,600 | 5 |
| Minneapolis | 59,900 | 67,500 | 76,300 | 82,300 | 6 |
| Milwaukee | 58,500 | 65,000 | 76,000 | 78,200 | 7 |
| Chicago | 63,900 | 68,500 | 71,100 | 77,200 | 8 |
| Atlanta | 53,300 | 59,200 | 67,500 | 75,900 | 9 |
| Baltimore | 53,200 | 59,000 | 63,800 | 72,100 | 10 |
| Boston | 54,700 | 59,300 | 65,400 | 71,200 | 11 |

*Source:* Federal Home Loan Bank Board and the National Association of Realtors, *Realtor News,* 17 Aug. 1981.

TABLE 4: Total Monthly Housing Costs*

| City | 1978 | 1981 § | % Change |
|------|------|--------|----------|
| San Francisco | $839 | $1,731 | 106.3 |
| Los Angeles | 807 | 1,441 | 78.6 |
| New York | 700 | 1,371 | 96.9 |
| Washington, D.C. | 761 | 1,310 | 72.1 |
| Houston | 568 | 1,166 | 105.3 |
| Boston | 682 | 1,163 | 70.5 |
| Minneapolis | 606 | 1,102 | 81.9 |
| Milwaukee | 595 | 1,073 | 80.3 |
| Chicago | 594 | 1,000 | 68.4 |

Source: National Association of Realtors, Realtor News, 17 Aug. 1981.
*Total of principal and interest, property taxes, utilities, and hazard insurance.
† Estimates.

Francisco's reformers sought to end corruption in city government. They therefore gave the city more control over its internal affairs but created a highly fragmented political structure.[31]

## The Formal Setting: Boston

The battle between the newer Irish immigrants and the older established Yankees, who represented the reform segment of the state electorate, culminated in Boston in 1949 with the creation and adoption of the new city charter. Aimed primarily at James Michael Curley and his personal style of politics, this charter attempted to separate politics and government. Political parties were prohibited in local elections, at-large elections were established for city councillors and school committee officials, and a strong mayor-council form of government was created.

Behind this façade of good government reform, as we have seen, lay the deeper cleavage between the Irish and the Yankees. When the former gained control over the local political machinery in Boston, the Yankees retreated to the State House and attempted to run the city from there. Through their control over the legislature, the Yankees limited the areas in which the Boston mayor had formal power, thereby maintaining their control over the city. Thus, while the charter gave the mayor strong formal powers, it sharply limited the areas in which they could be exercised.

By virtue of its charter, "Boston is one of the strongest of the strong

FIGURE 2: Boston City Government

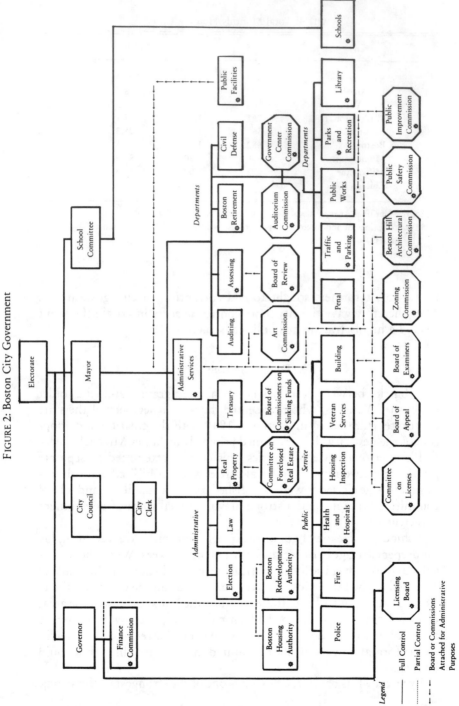

mayor governments in the country."[32] Most department heads are appointed directly by the mayor, with very few requiring council approval, and most city departments are run by a single commissioner. Although the mayor shares some budgetary power with the council, the council can only decrease, not increase, appropriations. In addition, there is no Board of Estimate as in New York City and no life-appointed controller as in San Francisco.

Despite these powers, there are many areas in which the Boston mayor has no formal authority. The major parks and roads are under the control of the Metropolitan District Commission (MDC); the public welfare system (since 1968) and the public transportation system are controlled by the state; the public schools are under the jurisdiction of an elected school committee; and the power to raise revenue lies with the state.[33]

The city council primarily has budgetary and personnel powers: it can decrease appropriations and approve certain appointments. The school committee has fiscal autonomy and is responsible for selecting a superintendent, thereby giving them influence over educational policy.

As in other nonpartisan cities, the removal of political parties from Boston city politics removed an important mechanism for recruiting leadership. In the absence of such a mechanism, electoral politics has been characterized, as Key predicted, by a high degree of factionalism.[34] The most important consequences of this factionalism have been the introduction of media campaigns, which lead to a politics of personality, and the high cost of such campaigning, which gives the advantage to the incumbent.

Unless candidates are independently wealthy or have the backing of strong, organized financial interests, they have to rely on their own resources to generate support. In the absence of a party, the resources within city government—such as patronage, contracts, and tax abatements—fall into the purview of elected or appointed officials, thereby giving them the advantage over the opponents. In the 1979 mayoral election, Kevin White spent $1.2 million,[35] a significant portion of which came from individual city workers and the business and development communities, all of whom thought it to be in their interests to contribute.

The factionalism created by the at-large electoral system has reduced the sources of potential opposition; there are few stepping stones to higher office in Boston. Since city councillors and school committee officials are elected at-large rather than by district, they do not build up a district constituency that could help them to move to higher office. Running against one another in at-large elections, no single candidate

FIGURE 3: San Francisco Consolidated City and County Government

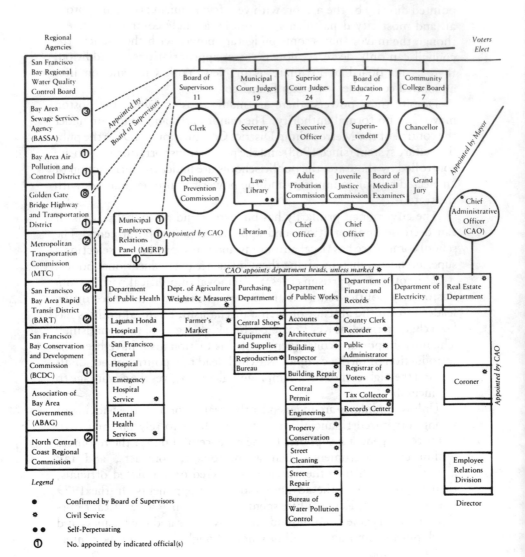

Regional Agencies

Voters Elect

San Francisco Bay Regional Water Quality Control Board

Bay Area Sewage Services Agency (BASSA) ③

Bay Area Air Pollution and Control District ① ①

Golden Gate Bridge Highway and Transportation District ① ⑧

Metropolitan Transportation Commission (MTC) ②

San Francisco Bay Area Rapid Transit District (BART) ② ②

San Francisco Bay Conservation and Development Commission (BCDC) ①

Association of Bay Area Governments (ABAG)

North Central Coast Regional Commission ②

*Appointed by Board of Supervisors*

*Appointed by Mayor*

Board of Supervisors 11 — Clerk — Delinquency Prevention Commission

Municipal Court Judges 19 — Secretary — Law Library — Librarian

Superior Court Judges 24 — Executive Officer — Adult Probation Commission — Chief Officer

Board of Education 7 — Superintendent — Juvenile Justice Commission — Chief Officer

Community College Board 7 — Chancellor

Board of Medical Examiners

Grand Jury

Chief Administrative Officer (CAO)

Municipal Employees Relations Panel (MERP) ① ① ① *Appointed by CAO*

CAO appoints department heads, unless marked ✿

| Department of Public Health | Dept. of Agriculture Weights & Measures ✿ | Purchasing Department | Department of Public Works | Department of Finance and Records | Department of Electricity ✿ | Real Estate Department ✿ |
|---|---|---|---|---|---|---|
| Laguna Honda Hospital ✿ | Farmer's Market | Central Shops ✿ | Accounts ✿ | County Clerk Recorder ✿ | | |
| San Francisco General Hospital | | Equipment and Supplies ✿ | Architecture | Public Administrator | | |
| | | Reproduction Bureau ✿ | Building Inspector ✿ | Registrar of Voters ✿ | | Coroner ✿ |
| Emergency Hospital Service ✿ | | | Building Repair ✿ | Tax Collector ✿ | | |
| Mental Health Services ✿ | | | Central Permit ✿ | Records Center ✿ | | |
| | | | Engineering | | | |
| | | | Property Conservation ✿ | | | Employee Relations Division |
| | | | Street Cleaning ✿ | | | |
| | | | Street Repair ✿ | | | Director |
| | | | Bureau of Water Pollution Control ✿ | | | |

*Appointed by CAO*

Legend

● Confirmed by Board of Supervisors

✿ Civil Service

●● Self-Perpetuating

① No. appointed by indicated official(s)

Source: San Francisco City and County Government.

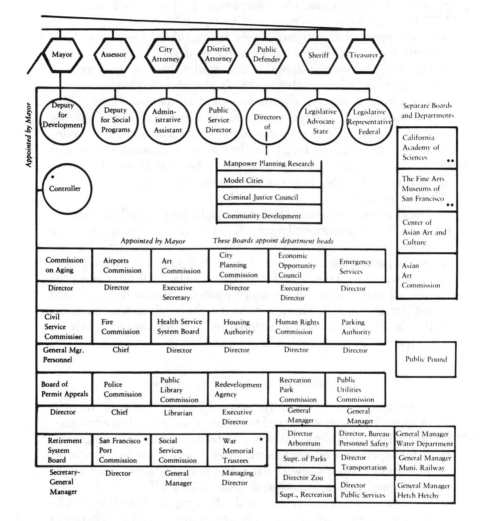

Appointed by Mayor

**Top row (hexagons):** Mayor · Assessor · City Attorney · District Attorney · Public Defender · Sheriff · Treasurer

**Second row (circles):** Deputy for Development · Deputy for Social Programs · Administrative Assistant · Public Service Director · Directors of · Legislative Advocate State · Legislative Representative Federal

Controller

- Manpower Planning Research
- Model Cities
- Criminal Justice Council
- Community Development

Separate Boards and Departments

- California Academy of Sciences ••
- The Fine Arts Museums of San Francisco ••
- Center of Asian Art and Culture
- Asian Art Commission
- Public Pound

Appointed by Mayor    These Boards appoint department heads

| Commission on Aging | Airports Commission | Art Commission | City Planning Commission | Economic Opportunity Council | Emergency Services |
|---|---|---|---|---|---|
| Director | Director | Executive Secretary | Director | Executive Director | Director |

| Civil Service Commission | Fire Commission | Health Service System Board | Housing Authority | Human Rights Commission | Parking Authority |
|---|---|---|---|---|---|
| General Mgr. Personnel | Chief | Director | Director | Director | Director |

| Board of Permit Appeals | Police Commission | Public Library Commission | Redevelopment Agency | Recreation Park Commission | Public Utilities Commission |
|---|---|---|---|---|---|
| Director | Chief | Librarian | Executive Director | General Manager | General Manager |

| Retirement System Board | San Francisco • Port Commission | Social Services Commission | War • Memorial Trustees | | |
|---|---|---|---|---|---|
| Secretary-General Manager | Director | General Manager | Managing Director | | |

| | | | | |
|---|---|---|
| Director Arboretum | Director, Bureau Personnel Safety | General Manager Water Department |
| Supt. of Parks | Director Transportation | General Manager Muni. Railway |
| Director Zoo | Director Public Services | General Manager Hetch Hetchy |
| Supt., Recreation | | |

requires a large percentage of the total vote. Further minimizing their need for votes is the number of candidates who run and the low voter turnout in these elections. The voter turnout for the council election in 1977 for example, was 34 percent.[36] Thus, it is more effective to capture the support of a small part of the electorate then to build up a large constituency. And, there is no incentive to develop a stable constituency. A councillor may appeal to one small portion of the electorate in one election and to another interest in the next election.

The electoral process also makes for disunity and vulnerability within the council. The fact that councillors run against one another every two years precludes their developing long term alliances. A councillor is not in office very long before beginning to campaign again, and the other councillors are potential threats rather than allies. This makes all of them vulnerable to divide-and-conquer tactics, a strategy that White often used.

The electoral process has also encouraged a lot of headline grabbing by councillors. Some council members have received substantial media coverage, but the things for which they received it only served to decrease the public's already low esteem for that body. All this helped to move power toward the executive, if only by default. While many people argued that White had too much power, very few recommended giving it to the council. Through its own actions, which were triggered by the electoral pressures of a factionalized politics, the council eliminated itself as a serious contender for power in the city.

### The Formal Setting: San Francisco

In an attempt to sweep corruption out of city government, voters in 1932 approved a charter designed to promote honest and efficient government. The establishment of a nonpartisan system and at-large elections for supervisors on a staggered basis were similar to the reforms brought in by Boston's new charter. The major difference was in the plans adopted and the subsequent results. Where Boston adopted a strong mayor form of government and other cities adopted the council-manager plan or commission form of government, the 1932 charter in San Francisco compromised among all three types. The result was a high degree of fragmentation with several potential centers of power. The CAO (Chief Administrative Officer), the controller, the board of supervisors, the regional agencies, the commission system, and the electorate all have formal powers that, if exercised, can be obstacles to mayoral leadership.

Although the mayor has the formal authority to make most commission appointments (approximately 120), supervise budget requests for city departments, veto board decisions (these vetoes can be overridden), and nominate school board members (a power not held by the Boston mayor), authority is shared with others who are not under the mayor's formal control. In addition, the San Francisco mayor is limited to two successive terms in office.

Formally, the CAO's office is a powerful one; jurisdiction includes the Departments of Public Health, Public Works, Government Services, and Special Projects, representing approximately a third of the city budget.[37] The exercise of these powers depends largely on who fills that office. Although the mayor appoints the CAO, the mayor's control is diluted by the CAO's lengthy tenure; lifetime before 1975 and ten years after. As a result, many mayors inherit their CAO, as did Alioto, Moscone, and Feinstein.[38]

The controller is also a partner in executive power. The appointment is made by the mayor, but the position is held for life. Removal from office must be for cause and requires the approval of two-thirds of the board of supervisors. Thus, the person responsible for the city's fiscal affairs, one of the most important areas of city government, is virtually free of formal control. This is not to say that the mayor cannot exert influence but rather that the mayor will have to rely on *informal* mechanisms in order to further his or her priorities.

Unlike Boston, San Francisco is both a city and county government. Thus, in addition to the municipal boards and commissions, there are nine regional agencies (see Figure 3). With only a few exceptions, these appointments are made by the board.[39] This translates into a form of indirect influence over policy decisions, since these agencies often rule on policies. The board also has formal responsibility for adopting the budget, setting the tax rate, and enacting local laws.

Although supervisors are limited by the part-time nature of the job (they are paid $9,600 annually, compared with Boston councillors' $32,000), they tend to be more active in substantive areas than their counterparts in Boston. One explanation is the composition of the board and their constituents. Before elections were by district, board members came disproportionately from middle and upper middle income areas and represented middle and upper middle class homeowners. (see Table 5). Thus, while supervisors had the same incentive for headline grabbing as Boston councillors the type of appeals that gained the most political mileage concerned tax issues and basic services. (These appeals also existed in Boston but often in conjunction with issues of corruption, patronage, and personality.) By dealing with such appeals, the board maintained a more responsible image than did the Boston city

TABLE 5: Socioeconomic Characteristics of Supervisors' Neighborhoods*

| Description | % in Outer Sunset | % in West of Twin Peaks | % in City |
|---|---|---|---|
| White | 82 | 84 | 57 |
| Earning more than $15,000 | 33 | 54 | 27 |
| Earning more than $25,000 | 6 | 23 | 7 |
| Managerial/professional | 23 | 42 | 25 |
| Owner-occupied housing | 72 | 84 | 31 |
| Single-family units | 95 | 88 | 68 |

Source: Coro Foundation, *The District Handbook: A Coro Foundation Guide to San Francisco Supervisorial Districts* (San Francisco: Coro, 1979). Information is for 1976, except earnings, which are for 1970.

*Before district elections, supervisors were disproportionately drawn from Outer Sunset and West of Twin Peaks (*Bay Guardian*, 14 Aug. 1980).

council and they have maintained their power better than has the Boston city council.

As in Boston, at-large elections have favored incumbents and proved a disadvantage to minorities. Only one black, one Hispanic, and two Chinese have served on the board. All four first secured their position through appointments and three won in subsequent elections running as incumbents.[40]

The system of at-large elections also made campaigns very expensive. Supervisors rely on contributions from business and labor and so have been sensitive to their interests.

San Francisco's commission system is another potential center of power. A combination of structural factors (term appointments for most boards and commissions, and restrictions on removal)[41] and cultural factors (the strong reform ethos that inhibits overt executive interference with the commissions and departments) results in the commission's enjoying a significant amount of autonomy in policymaking and a measure of insulation from elected officials.

While not part of the formal apparatus, the electorate must figure in a description of San Francisco's government. Under the current charter there are seventy-four elected officials (not including the mayor), compared with twenty-three in Boston.[42] Thus, the San Francisco electorate has a much larger say in the composition of their government. And, the areas in which elections occur are significant: monetary (treasurer, which includes tax collection), legal (sheriff, district attorney, city attorney, public defender, municipal judge, superior court judges), revenue (assessor), and education (board of education; the mayor nominates, the electorate approves). Thus, the electorate is an important factor in financial, legal, educational, and crime policies.

The San Francisco electorate also has the formal power of the referendum. Designed as a direct protection against corruption, the referendum has led to the proliferation of issues and has politicized various groups within the electorate. Every election, local and national, usually includes more than twenty propositions on the ballot. The issues range from important to mundane; questions have dealt with rent control, labor relations, the awarding of city contracts, federal military spending, and the Vietnam War. Certain issues, such as district elections, have mobilized city-wide campaigns.[43]

## Communications

Boston and San Francisco are major communications centers with diverse television and radio broadcasting operations. Both cities have publicly owned and independent broadcasting stations, which provide a wide variety of national and local news and imaginative and community-oriented programming. WCVB in Boston, which began in 1972, has been cited by *T.V. Facts and Figures* as providing the most innovative and extensive local programming of any commercial station in the country. The broadcasting media in both cities also provides extensive educational and ethnic programming.

The press in Boston and San Francisco are less similar. The newspapers in Boston, particularly the *Boston Globe*, have better journalistic reputations and tend less to sensationalism than the San Francisco papers. In both cities, the newspapers have influence, however difficult it is to measure. As in other non-partisan cities, the newspapers wield a disproportionate amount of influence as shapers of public opinion and as cue givers. Further, the press influences the local political agenda by the amount of attention it gives to an issue. This is probably more important in San Francisco because of the strong issue-orientation of the electorate. Finally, as major carriers of advertisements for local merchants, the newspapers deal with important actors in the informal arena. Thus, the press itself is an actor that must be considered by local executives. In elections, the press can influence the electorate, but it is not decisive. Alioto and Moscone both won mayoral elections without the endorsement of a paper. Before 1967, the *Boston Globe* did not endorse candidates for local office.

Currently, Boston has two major dailies, the *Boston Globe* and the *Boston Herald American* (although, in the early 1970s, the city also had the *Herald Traveler* and the *Record American*), and a weekly newspaper, the *Boston Phoenix*. The *Globe* is more reserved than the *Herald*, which tends toward sensational journalism. The *Globe*'s coverage of local and national news is fairly well regarded. A noteworthy feature is its "Spotlight Series," which provides exhaustive exposés on topical issues such as the Boston public schools and the Boston police. These periodic stories are compiled by a team of reporters and usually run over seven to ten days. In addition to the daily citywide newspapers, most neighborhoods have their own local newspaper, which focuses on issues and events of concern to the neighborhood. Their amount of influence varies from neighborhood to neighborhood.

Like Boston, San Francisco has two major daily newspapers, the *Chronicle* and the *Examiner*, and an underground-type weekly, the *Bay Guardian*. The two major dailies jointly issue one Sunday paper, share a library and clipping files, and are located on the same block. The *Examiner* is owned by Hearst and tends to be more conservative than the *Chronicle*, which is not very liberal. Neither of these papers is noted for high journalistic quality, a factor which probably diminishes their influence. As in Boston, most San Francisco neighborhoods have local papers that deal with neighborhood issues and events.

## Informal Arrangements: Boston

A combination of historical, political, economic, and demographic circumstances have helped to give Boston a set of informal arrangements that is weak and uncoordinated.

## Labor

In contrast to the experience of cities like San Francisco, Detroit, and New York, labor has not played an important role in Boston politics.[44] A possible explanation for the different historical developments is the police strike in 1919, when Governor Calvin Coolidge systematically fired all of the strikers. Many observers of Boston city politics and labor relations suggest that the memory of this incident influenced the behavior of the police union and other unions in Boston until the present.[45]

To the extent that organized labor does play a role in city politics, it has not been confrontational as in New York City under Lindsay or disruptive as in San Francisco. With wages comparable to those of their counterparts in other cities and, from the 1960s onward, a high level of services in the city, Boston's public employee unions have grown up in a favorable climate.[46] And, unlike Mayor Lindsay, neither Mayor Collins nor Mayor White antagonized the unions.


## Business

Boston's economic history, combined with the political battles between the Yankees and the Irish working class, resulted in business taking a less direct role in the city's politics than did its counterparts in San Francisco, New York City, Detroit, Baltimore, and Philadelphia.

When the local machinery of the city's political system passed to the Irish, corruption and attention to corruption increased. This discouraged involvement by many businessmen, especially the older established ones, who by-passed the city and forged economic and business alliances with other business interests on the state and regional levels.[47]

The distaste and distrust with which many businessmen approached Boston city politics was intensified by Mayor Curley. During Curley's administration, with its emphasis on the "little guy," public expenditures soared and business was asked to pick up the tab. There is a colorful story of Curley pointing to a downtown building and saying to one of his aides, "I want $10,000 more out of those bastards next year."[48] Curley's abrasive and devious ways toward business people discouraged new business from locating in Boston. After Curley reneged on his promise to the John Hancock Life Insurance Company not to raise the negotiated assessment, construction of new office buildings in Boston came to a halt for twenty-five years.[49]

The hiatus ended in 1961 when the Prudential agreed to locate in Boston—but only after the state agreed to protect them against discretionary taxing by city politicians.[50] Since then, many new businesses have located in the city and the business community has come to play a more direct role in the city's politics. This increased activity has been encouraged by the politicians, especially Mayor Collins, who established the Vault—the group of businessmen, bankers, and others who had access to city hall—and Mayor White.

This point merits special consideration. City politics is composed of various arenas of power, each of which requires different strategies. In non-partisan cities, business has come to play an increasingly important role in the informal arena. The fact that business constituted a less powerful force in Boston when White was elected than in San Francisco when Alioto and Moscone were elected is important to understanding the different strategies employed.

Although business has increased its role in Boston's political system

33

during the Collins and White administrations, its role is still limited. Its most important contribution is financial. As in other non-partisan cities, electoral campaigns in Boston are expensive, so that contributions from the business community are highly sought after.

## Blacks

Boston's black population has not had a significant impact on the city's political system. In contrast to cities like Detroit and Cleveland, Boston is not likely to elect a black mayor. Among the impediments of the black community are its relatively small size and low voter turnout, the at-large system of elections, and its geographical isolation. Most important, however, are the absence of a local party system, the absence of a liberal population, and racism.

Voter registration among Boston blacks has long been low; between 1951 and 1975 black voter registration trailed white voter registration by 15 percentage points.[51]

The electoral behavior of blacks is largely attributable to the non-partisan electoral system, which tends to depress minority participation.[52] The absence of a party also removed a mechanism for integrating blacks into the political system. In Chicago, the party machinery performed this function and also produced a powerful black leader—the late William Dawson. In Cleveland's 1967 election, the Ford Foundation performed a similar function; their intensive voter registration efforts, combined with a black candidate (Carl Stokes) on the ballot, resulted in a black turnout 15 points higher than the white turnout in the primary.[53] In contrast, in Newark's 1970 mayoral election that also featured a black candidate—Kenneth Gibson—but no mechanism for registering black voters, the black voter registration rate was approximately 15 points lower than the white voter registration rate.[54]

Organizational development within Boston's black community also has been hindered by the system of at-large elections for city councillors and school committee officials. Requiring only a small percentage of the total vote to win, these candidates have no incentive to appeal to the minority community. In fact, Boston's extreme racism has discouraged minority appeals altogether. Voting data from school committee elections has shown that the traditional cleavage between the Irish and the Italians disappeared when a black candidate, or a white candidate sympathetic to blacks, was running. Even more interesting is the Jewish vote. In contrast to New York, where the large Jewish vote was often in alliance with the black vote, in Boston the small Jewish population joined with the Irish and the Italians when a black threat surfaced.[55]

This last factor is very significant for black political development in Boston. The small size of the Jewish community and its voting behavior removed an important source of support for blacks. In New York City, for example, blacks were able to compensate for their size through their alliance with the large liberal Jewish population.[56] In Boston, the black community had no allies within the city. Since the adoption of the 1949 charter, only two blacks have been elected to the city council (1967 and 1981) and one to the school committee.[57]

Standing alone politically, blacks also stood alone geographically. Like their counterparts in many other cities, blacks lived in segregated housing. In addition, the physical makeup of the city, combined with the physical threat to blacks in white areas during the past ten years or so, often worked to keep black people within the black community.

The Boston public school system was another limitation on black physical mobility. Boston maintained a racially segregated public school system until 1974 when, under federal court order, it began to desegregate. By this time many cities outside the South had already integrated their public schools; some (Baltimore, St. Louis, and Pittsburgh) had begun as early as 1968.[58]

Boston's delay in desegregating its public school system was an aspect of the larger race issue in Boston, a factor which must be addressed in any analysis of Boston city politics.

Race largely became an issue in Boston city politics with the proposal for racially balanced schools (1961–1963) and was magnified with the state's passage of the Racial Imbalance Act (RIA) in 1965. This measure required local public school systems to achieve a racial balance in the individual schools. In Boston, this set off a fierce reaction, which was probably the biggest Northern backlash to desegregation. This opposition was exploited and reinforced by school committee officials who used the act to gain political mileage. Non-partisan systems tend to generate a need for issues among candidates; the Racial Imbalance Act offered school committee candidates an excellent target and a safe one. The politically weak black community was not likely to be able to retaliate electorally. Although the school committee took no steps to implement the RIA, they kept the issue alive through constant attacks on it, which intensified racial tensions in the city.

Louise Day Hicks rose to citywide prominence through her firm opposition to the RIA. In her first campaign for the school committee in 1961, Hicks used nonracial appeals. She secured a seat, coming in third with 38.4 percent of the vote. In her re-election campaign in 1963, Hicks attacked the NAACP's proposal for desegregated schools. She finished a strong first with 68.8 percent of the vote. Observers attributed this sharp increase in support to the use of racial appeals.[59] Gaining national attention as well, Hicks was asked by George Wallace to be his vice-presidential running mate in 1968, but she declined.

Another candidate who took advantage of the race issue was Kevin White in the 1967 mayoral election. In contrast to the school committee, however, White fashioned a pro-civil rights platform and maintained that position during the early part of his administration. His position represented an extremely liberal stance for Boston city politics. White did not get the support of some of the more conservative areas of the city, like South Boston, but he did win the election.[60]

Between 1969 and 1973 the intensity of the race issue fluctuated as other issues (such as a highway controversy and airport expansion) temporarily overshadowed it. In 1974 the race issue came to the fore once again when Federal District Court Judge Arthur Garrity ordered the Boston public schools to desegregate immediately or lose all federal money. The order was carried out in two stages—accompanied by violence, large demonstrations, major boycotts, and a severe decline in the schools' white population.[61] The resurgence of racist feelings continued for some time after and, although race has not been the chief issue in Boston politics for the last few years, it has emerged as a major concern on several occasions. Moreover, Boston's experience with desegregation gave the city a national reputation as an extremely racist city.

## Suburbs

Beginning in the 1960s, the suburbs acquired important influence over Boston city politics. As statewide population shifts increased the relative importance of the suburban vote, state officials became more responsive to suburban concerns (see Table 6). The impetus for the Racial Imbalance Act and its passage in the State House came from the suburbs.

The suburbs have also increased their influence through the ambitions of Boston mayors. Both Collins and White had aspirations for higher state office and their policies and approaches were influenced by the desire for suburban backing. However, the suburbs are everything that Boston is not. The voters in Newton, Brookline, Cambridge, and Wellesley—the major suburbs around Boston—are predominantly white middle and upper middle class and disproportionately professional.[62] These characteristics translate into an electorate that is public regarding: issue-oriented and liberal on social matters. As this study suggests, the dichotomy between the suburbs and the city presented problems for Mayor White.

TABLE 6: Changing Contribution of Boston Vote to Statewide Totals in Gubernatorial General Elections, 1910–1970

| Year | Total Boston Vote | Total State Vote | Boston Vote as % of State Vote |
|------|------|------|------|
| 1910 | 85,249 | 440,831 | .19 |
| 1920 | 161,335 | 960,697 | .16 |
| 1930 | 209,099 | 1,250,114 | .16 |
| 1940 | 348,829 | 2,062,403 | .16 |
| 1950 | 309,809 | 1,947,071 | .20 |
| 1960 | 297,694 | 2,495,504 | .11 |
| 1970 | 191,076 | 2,043,287 | .09 |

Source: Commonwealth of Massachusetts, Report of Secretary of State, Election Statistics, in Daniel Pool, "Politics in the New Boston" (Ph.D. diss., Brandeis University, 1974).

## Informal Arrangements: San Francisco

In discussing San Francisco's informal arrangements, it is tempting to treat it as two different cities. In the mid-1970s, a combination of changes in labor's position in city politics and demographic changes contributed to a shift. Before, the most important difference between Boston and San Francisco was the role played by labor in San Francisco city politics. This lent an organizing force to the electorate that did not exist in Boston and is one explanation for the different strategies adopted by Alioto and White. The most important differences between Boston and San Francisco after the mid-1970s were the more fragmented and issue-oriented electorate in San Francisco and the strong reform ethos. These structural and cultural factors partly explain the different leadership patterns of White and Moscone and Feinstein.

## Labor

Developing as a port and manufacturing city, San Francisco had a large concentration of blue collar workers. Like the rest of California, San Francisco experienced a growth in the political involvement of organized labor and a great many strikes as well (see Tables 7 and 8).

Called a "union town par excellence," San Francisco contained some of the strongest unions and union leaders in the country.[63] The International Longshoremen's and Warehousemen's Union (ILWU), a predominantly black union, was very active and wielded significant influence on local and national levels. Their former leader, Harry Bridges, was viewed as one of the most powerful union leaders in the

TABLE 7: Work Stoppages by State, 1967–1970

| State | Number in 1967 | Number in 1968 | Number in 1969 | Number in 1970 |
|---|---|---|---|---|
| California | 300 | 354 | 368 | 343 |
| Illinois | 289 | 317 | 448 | 413 |
| Indiana | 166 | 236 | 214 | 220 |
| Massachusetts | 157 | 169 | 172 | 184 |
| Michigan | 283 | 354 | 305 | 313 |
| New Jersey | 214 | 217 | 225 | 280 |
| New York | 484 | 488 | 521 | 570 |
| Ohio | 536 | 573 | 672 | 632 |
| Pennsylvania | 480 | 472 | 655 | 636 |
| West Virginia | N.A. | 170 | 245 | 313 |

Source: Bureau of Labor Statistics, *Analysis of Work Stoppages*, 1967–1970, Annual Bulletin nos. 1611, 1646, 1687, 1727 (Washington, D.C.: Government Printing Office, 1969–1972).

country.[64] The ILWU had an historic reputation as one of the most progressive labor unions in the country; it strongly supported civil rights movements and strongly opposed the Vietnam War. The San Francisco Labor Council was very active and influential in the city's politics. Before 1932, organized labor had its own political party, the Union Labor Party. Although a charter change in that year removed political parties from local elections, the unions still remained a powerful force in local politics, acting in many ways like a surrogate party; they provided formal endorsements, campaign contributions, and campaign workers. More recently, in the late 1960s, the city workers unions (especially the Service Employees International Union or SEIU) became active, vocal, and at times, militant in city politics.

During Alioto's eight years in office, labor enjoyed a cozy relationship with city hall, increasing its power. Through favorable wage settlements engineered by Alioto and appointments to major boards and commissions, organized labor exerted strong influence over the city's decision-making processes.

## Business

Although influence is difficult to measure, certain factors suggest that business was both more organized and more active in San Francisco politics than its counterpart in Boston. Certainly, there is a widely held perception in San Francisco that business is very influential in the city's politics.

In contrast to regional-level business organizing as in Boston, the

TABLE 8: Work Stoppages by SMSA, 1967–1970

| SMSA* | 1967 | | 1968 | | 1969 | | 1970 | |
|---|---|---|---|---|---|---|---|---|
| | Number | Workers‡ | Number | Workers | Number | Workers | Number | Workers |
| Baltimore | 46 | 26.0 | 41 | 20.5 | 57 | 33.0 | 66 | 29.6 |
| Boston | 64 | 18.9 | 63 | 32.7 | 79 | 49.6 | 86 | 28.8 |
| Newark | 59 | 16.7 | 66 | 23.2 | 68 | 16.2 | 96 | 49.3 |
| New York City | 201 | 162.0 | 191 | 204.4 | 218 | 96.0 | 215 | 199.2 |
| San Francisco† | 82 | 37.6 | 152 | 47.8 | 121 | 24.8 | 129 | 58.5 |
| San Jose | 21 | 6.3 | 35 | 7.7 | 26 | 5.6 | 22 | 6.5 |

Source: Bureau of Labor Statistics, Analysis of Work Stoppages, 1967–1970, Annual Bulletin nos. 1611, 1646, 1687, 1727 (Washington, D.C.: Government Printing Office, 1969–1972).
* SMSAs picked for comparable size.
† SMSA includes Oakland.
‡ In thousands.

San Francisco Chamber of Commerce and the Downtown Association were and are organized on a citywide level. Another contrast to Boston was the powerful concentration of money and status among businessmen. A few key individuals within San Francisco's financial community were very active in political campaigns and the city's politics. Ben Swig raised $203,500 for Alioto's 1967 campaign in "exactly 45 minutes."[65] The different routes that urban renewal followed in the two cities also indicates the different roles played by business. In Boston, the effort was initiated by Mayor Collins, who then persuaded the business community. In San Francisco, the initiative came from members of the business community, who then had to persuade the mayor's office.

The different roles played by business in the two cities largely resulted from cultural and historical factors. San Francisco's reform ethos stimulated business participation, supporting Banfield and Wilson's suggestion that political and civic involvement of business increases in reform cities.[66] Even in a partisan city like Chicago, Daley encouraged business participation to appeal to reform-minded segments in the electorate as well as to business itself.

In addition, San Francisco was never abandoned, as was Boston, by monied interests because of widely publicized deep ethnic cleavages. Moreover, San Francisco had no Mayor Curley whose dealings with business discouraged investment. San Francisco had Republican mayors from 1948 to 1964—Elmer Robinson and George Christopher—who provided a favorable climate for business.

As in Boston, however, business participation in local politics is most evident when the high costs of nonpartisan campaigning must be met. In the 1979 mayoral election, for example, Dianne Feinstein spent $830,966.[67] Thus, in both cities, the business community is an important source of campaign contributions.


## Minorities

Taken together, blacks, Hispanics, and Chinese make up more than one third of San Francisco's population. Each group has had a member on the board of supervisors. Nevertheless, none of these groups have had a significant impact on the city's political system, either individually or collectively. Structural, numerical, cultural, and economic impediments have prevented them from organizing individually, presenting an obstacle to collective action. Furthermore, as minorities, these groups often compete with one another for scarce pieces of a shrinking pie, another factor inhibiting concerted action or coalition building.

BLACKS    Black voter registration rates in San Francisco trail those of whites by approximately 13 percent.[68] As in Boston, black participation in the city's political system has been limited by their small numbers and the absence of a party to integrate them. The ILWU, a predominantly black union, could have served as a vehicle for organization within the black community, in the fashion of the UAW in Detroit. This did not happen, however, possibly because of social and economic factors.

In earnings, black ILWU members are in the top one-half of 1 percent of their racial category.[69] Thus, there is an economic gap between the union members and the poorer segments of the black community. In addition, many union members were more closely associated with the conservative and established members of the black community, most notably the ministers. Finally, there was more to be gained through cooperation with city hall. This was especially true when Alioto was mayor, since his ties were largely with the more conservative blacks. His close ties with the ILWU resulted in substantial plums for that union and its locals. Thus, the split within the black community between the potential leaders and the led was reinforced by Alioto's policies.

The political position of the black community under the Feinstein administration seems little changed. The obstacles to organization and strong leadership appear still to exist. Although Moscone, Alioto's successor, drew support and appointments from the more liberal and militant segments of the community (such as the Rev. Jim Jones) this was a short term development. The absence of a party or similar vehicle to organize the black community, the relatively small size of the black population, and the termination of many federal programs, which in other cities provided an impetus for organizing (e.g. New York), remain as impediments to political development.

HISPANICS    The Hispanic population, which is slightly larger than the black population, has had less impact on the political system. Although Robert Gonzales, a Mexican American, was elected to the board of supervisors in 1973 (after being appointed by Alioto in 1971), voter registration rates for Spanish-speaking people in San Francisco trail the rate for blacks by 6 percentage points and the rate for whites by 19 points.[70] Like the black community, the Hispanic community has a strong union that could serve as an organizing force. The Centro Social Obrero, the caucus of Local 261 of the Laborer's International based in the Mission district, has been important in past elections. But the impediments to organizing within the Hispanic community are even more severe than in the black community. First, there is a language barrier. Second, many members of the community are illegal aliens who cannot vote and avoid attracting notice. Third, there is the traditional emphasis on the "barrio," which leads to relative isolation. In San Francisco, the Mission district is the Hispanic community's barrio. These factors suggest that the lack of Hispanic impact on the city's political system is not likely to change in the near future.

CHINESE    The Chinese community, despite its large concentration in San Francisco, has not had a significant impact on the political system, either. Although Chinese voter turnout is now 5 percent above the city-wide average, the voter registration rate is significantly lower than the Hispanic and black rates.[71] At 44 percent, the Chinese voter registration rate trails the Hispanic rate by 14 percentage points, the black rate by 20 points, and the white rate by 33 points.[72] As with the Hispanic community, there is a language barrier, a cultural separation, and a fair amount of segregation. The Chinese community is confined primarily to Chinatown, which is overcrowded, has a severe housing shortage (.5 percent vacancy rate), and rundown housing.[73] Most of the community cultural and social activities and a substantial number of the economic transactions take place within Chinatown.

   In contrast to the Hispanic community, however, the Chinese community has shown some potential for influencing the city's political system. Many of the younger Chinese who were born in San Francisco have moved away from the more stringent cultural practices of their parents. In the Chinese American Democratic Club (CADC), for example, a split has developed between the older, more conservative members and the younger, more liberal members.[74] Gordon Lau, a member of the latter wing, was appointed by Moscone to the board of supervisors. What impact these developments will have on the city's political system is difficult to determine. It is clear, however, that there is more political activity in the Chinese community than in the Hispanic community and that it is in a process of transition.[75]

## The Shift in Informal Arrangements

While organized labor is still important in the city's political life, its influence declined during the mid-1970s, contributing to the fragmentation of the electorate. As San Francisco's economy continued moving in the direction of finance and service, many blue collar workers moved out of the city. The Labor Council, which had more than 100,000 registered voters in 1967, had only 92,341 in 1979.[76] The containerization movement in the shipping industry led to a decline in the ILWU's membership from about 20,000 in 1967 to about 17,000 in 1980.[77] Further, only about half the 1967 members lived in San Francisco. By 1980 Oakland's quick move to containerization made it a growing center for shipping and many workers followed.

In addition, the public mood was changing from pro- to anti-union. This phenomenon was common to many cities in fiscal difficulties. In New York, the unions became the scapegoat for the city's fiscal woes. In San Francisco, the media helped to shape public opinion by portraying city workers' wages as high and emphasizing the cost of their contracts to taxpayers.

The anti-union sentiment came to a head in the police and fire strike in 1974, which was a watershed issue for organized labor. Alioto ended the strike by declaring emergency powers and granting the unions' demands. The events that followed this settlement, which included the passage of anti-union legislation, altered labor's influence in San Francisco and helped change the balance of the city's politics. The craftworkers strike (1976) was perhaps the best indication of labor's decreased influence. Where unions had won favorable wage settlements under Alioto, this strike lasted thirty-four days with no demands won. Thus, when the political system was most in need of manageability and stability, the unions were at their weakest.

Demographic changes also affected the city's politics in the mid-1970s. San Francisco's Asian population increased by 50 percent between 1970 and 1980. This broad category includes Chinese, Japanese,

Korean, Filipino, Cambodian, and Vietnamese. During this same period, San Francisco lost 10 percent of its total black population.[78]

In addition to ethnic fragmentation, San Francisco received an influx of young, single, professional people. According to recent census data, approximately 37 percent of San Francisco's population is between the ages of fifteen and thirty-four. By contrast, this age group accounts for 29 percent of the population in New York, 29 percent in Baltimore, 29 percent in Chicago, and 28 percent in Cleveland.[79] Politically, San Francisco's age distribution manifests itself as an excessive burden. Whereas families tend to be concerned with basic services like police, fire, and education, single people tend to be more issue oriented. The most important difference, for leadership, is that the demands of families largely fall into the category of disaggregatable benefits and the demands of singles often fall into the area of confrontational politics.

The gay community is a major component of the fragmentation of the electorate that did not exist to a relevant degree before 1975 in San Francisco, and which is less significant in Boston. Acknowledged gays account for approximately 17 percent of the total population and roughly 21 percent of the city vote.[80] And, because of their concentration in the Castro and Polk/Van Ness areas and the discriminatory and exclusionary practices that they have encountered, the gay community has become a single-bloc, powerful force in San Francisco city politics. Whereas gays had aligned themselves with liberal groups in the 1950s and 1960s, this coalition began to fall apart in the 1970s as the gay community came politically into its own. In addition, there was no political party or similar mechanism to keep the gay-liberal alliance together. This split constituted a further fragmentation of the electorate and an important one. By virtue of their numbers, their high voter turnout, and their ability to influence liberal sympathizers, the gay community cannot well be ignored by present-day mayors as Alioto did. In fact, the gay vote may have been decisive in the 1979 mayoral election.[81] The gay community was also successful in electing two members to the board of supervisors: Harvey Milk in 1977 and Harry Britt in 1980.

A change in election procedure in 1975 had important consequences for mayoral leadership. Before 1975, mayoral elections were by pluralities. In 1967 and 1975, Alioto received less than 50 percent of the vote.[82] In 1975 the charter was changed to require a runoff election if no candidate received a majority of the vote in the preliminary election. Thus, candidates for mayor were forced to appeal to a wider variety of interests among a more fragmented electorate.

## 1975 Mayoral Election: A Watershed Election

In the same way that the police and fire strike marked a watershed in San Francisco's labor relations, the 1975 mayoral election between George Moscone and John Barbagelata was a watershed in its political relations. The most important characteristics of this election were the decreased role of labor, the politicization of new groups, and the liberal-conservative dichotomy.

Although Moscone had the formal endorsement of the Labor Council and the support of the ILWU, they were not the capstone of his support system as they had been for Alioto. Moscone's constituency consisted of a variety of politicized groups not appealed to by Alioto— neighborhood activists, environmentalists, gays, the more militant segments of the black community, and the younger and more liberal elements of the Chinese community.

A combination of Moscone's supporters, his liberal reputation as a state senator, and Barbagelata's conservative reputation (especially fiscally) helped to paint the entire election as a liberal-conservative battle. Despite San Francisco's image as a very liberal city and Moscone's strong political advantages (strong financial support, abundance of campaign workers, endorsement by every major slate, and good reputation as state senator), Moscone won the election by only a 2 percent margin; he defeated Barbagelata in the run-off by 4,443 votes out of 200,000 cast. The major problem faced by Moscone was the emergence of a large conservative element within the electorate.

The ideological climate of the 1975 election was significant for Moscone's administration and the city's politics in general. First, it indicated the type of groups that were entering the political arena and the increased fragmentation within that arena. Second, it provided an interesting contrast with the political climates in other cities at that time. By 1975 most other cities had already gone through their ideological periods and returned to the status quo ante. In Boston, White had cashed in his progressive ideology and Little City Halls for pragmatism and a machine. In New York City, the charismatic and liberal John Lindsay had been replaced by the bureaucratic Abe Beame. In Detroit, Jerome Cavanaugh's decision not to seek re-election was followed by a new wave of racism. In 1975, San Francisco, the city where new ideas are born, discovered the old idea of liberalism. But although the liberal candidate had won, he would confront a situation full of pitfalls for mayoral leadership.

## POLITICAL CULTURE

California, the state that has everything, doesn't. It doesn't have Massachusetts politics. It doesn't have Boston politics. It doesn't have pols, at least by our standards. It has only "elected officials."

Alas, the state of outrageous lifestyles is the land of somber politics. California's politicians are like its drivers: courteous, thoughtful, measured. They never change lanes without using directional signals. Our politicians are like our drivers: aggressive, outrageous, abrasive, unpredictable, and prone to accidents and the inflated injury claims that follow.[83]

These observations of a *Boston Globe* reporter capture important differences in the political climates of Massachusetts and California and, consequently, in Boston and San Francisco city politics.

The working class character of Boston, the Irish influence on the political system, and the absence of a significant middle class or liberal population to support reform organizations shaped a more traditional political ethos in the Northeast. A personal style of politics, emphasizing individual favor-doing, is preferred over abstract calls to support broad social issues. Behind-the-scenes politicking, as well as outright corruption, may be publicly criticized but is privately tolerated. This view was very well summed up by former school committee candidate Ellison. After receiving a jail sentence for stealing City of Boston funds while on the school committee (1972–1973), Ellison ran for office in 1979. When questioned by a reporter about the reaction of voters to his problems, Ellison replied, "Boston understands those things."[84] Although Ellison lost the election, he finished a strong sixth in the preliminary election and ninth in the final election. It may be said, following Ellison, that Boston politicians understand what Boston understands.

By contrast, San Francisco shows a strong reform ethos. Important features are an emphasis on open government and a consequent distaste for behind-the-scenes politicking, an emphasis on broad participation, and an administrative rather than political approach to government. San Francisco, in short, is a West Coast city rather than a Northeast city. Like other parts of California and the West Coast, San Francisco has attracted a younger, more educated, and more professional population than the older cities of the Northeast. The median age of people moving west between 1976 and 1979 was 25.8, with one in five having a professional job and one in seven having more than four years of college.[85] This difference in the political makeup of the two cities must be considered when analyzing patterns of executive leadership.

### The Mayors: Boston

### John Collins

John Collins was mayor from 1960 to 1968. Before becoming mayor, Collins had served as a Massachusetts state senator for eight years (1946–1954). In 1954 he won the Democratic nomination for state attorney general but then lost to the Republican incumbent. In the following year, Collins was elected to the Boston city council, where he served one term (1955–1957). He then went on to become register of probate for Suffolk County, the county that includes Boston.

When Collins ran for mayor in 1959, he had ambitions of returning to state office, either as a legislator or as governor (neither of which he achieved). Using the mayor's office as a base from which to build statewide support, Collins embarked on a major urban renewal program in order to attract suburban support. Although there was substantial federal money available, the cooperation and support of Boston's business community was crucial. Through the creation of the Vault, a group of seventeen influential businessmen who met frequently with Collins to plan urban renewal strategies, he developed a close relationship with key Boston businessmen and bankers.

Although the Boston Redevelopment Authority (BRA) was set up by Collins's predecessor (John Hynes), it was a relatively weak and unstructured agency when Collins took over the mayor's office. In order to strengthen the BRA for implementing the urban renewal strategies, Collins brought in Ed Logue, who had executed Mayor Lee's urban renewal policies in New Haven. Under Logue's direction, the BRA became a very powerful agency that implemented major urban renewal projects in the West and South End areas of the city.

Collins's emphasis on the central business district and his neglect of city government and city services led to a backlash against urban renewal. Kevin White took advantage of this climate early in his administration to develop and then enhance his support within the neighborhoods.

This study does not analyze John Collins, but I refer to his administration in sketching the context of White's mayorality.[86]

### Kevin White

Kevin White was mayor of Boston from 1968 to 1984, when he decided not to seek re-election. His was the longest mayoral tenure in any major American city.[87]

Before becoming mayor, White was the Massachusetts secretary of state. He began his mayoral career in the fashion of John Lindsay: a charismatic, media-oriented, liberal, progressive mayor with ambitions for higher office. In 1970, he ran for governor of Massachusetts and lost to Republican incumbent Francis Sargent. In 1972, White was considered as the vice presidential running mate by George McGovern but was dropped when Edward Kennedy objected.[88] In 1974, observers speculated that White intended to run for president in 1976 but withdrew his efforts when the busing controversy in Boston grew violent.

Thwarted political ambitions, media attacks in 1975, and a changing public climate led White to shift strategies. Moving from his left-of-center, audience-directed position, White adopted a machine brand of politics. In 1975, he built a political organization modeled after Richard Daley's in Chicago. He directed his appeals toward constituents, relied heavily on material incentives, and employed a strong bricks-and-mortar approach.

## The Mayors: San Francisco

### Joseph Alioto

Joe Alioto was mayor of San Francisco from 1968 to 1976. This was his first elected office, although he had served as chairman of the San Francisco Redevelopment Agency (SFRA) from 1955 to 1958 and was a member of the Board of Education (1948–1954) and its president from 1952 to 1953—all appointed positions. Before becoming mayor, Alioto was a highly successful antitrust lawyer. Like White and Lindsay, Alioto was a very charismatic, media-oriented mayor with ambitions for higher office. In 1974 he unsuccessfully ran for the Democratic nomination for governor of California. Alioto's administration was characterized by strong ties with labor, key business figures in San Francisco, and conservative elements within the black and Hispanic communities. Alioto was a pro-development mayor who advocated building up the downtown financial district, facilitating tourism, and commercializing the waterfront.

### George Moscone

George Moscone was mayor from 1976 to 1978 when he was assassinated by a former member of the board of supervisors. Before becoming mayor, Moscone was a California state senator. Moscone was a left of center candidate with a broad constituency that included labor; liberal and militant segments of the black, Hispanic, and Chinese communities; gays; neighborhood activists; and environmentalists. Moscone emphasized broadening representation within city government, curbing downtown development, and preserving neighborhoods.

## Dianne Feinstein

Dianne Feinstein was president of the board of supervisors when Moscone was assassinated. She took over for him in 1978 and was elected mayor in 1979. While more conservative than Moscone, Feinstein sought to accommodate the same groups that made up Moscone's constituency. In her attempts to govern from the middle, Feinstein continued the trend established by Moscone of broad representation within city government.

This study does not include a close examination of Feinstein, since she was in elected office for only one year when my research was conducted. However, I will use examples from her administration to support broad theoretical points.

# PART ONE

## The Public Arena: Mobilizing Support

# THREE

## The Manipulation of Conflict: Electoral Appeals and Activist Mayors

> Since politics has its origins in strife, political strategy deals with
> the exploitation, use and suppression of conflict.[1]

The manipulation of conflict is indeed one of the most important political tools available to executives. It can be used to set cleavages, mobilize support, and deflect other issues. Political parties in the United
States have a history of substituting one conflict for another. The Republican party emerged out of the conflict over slavery; after the Civil
War, the Populists unsuccessfully attempted to substitute that cleavage
with an economic one. The Democratic and Republican parties pre-
empted the Populist threat by reviving the old sectional cleavage between North and South. With the Great Depression and the subsequent
realignment of 1932, the nationalization of American politics de-
stroyed the sectional cleavage (except for the Solid South) and replaced
it with an economic one.[2]

At the executive level, conflict has been used to mobilize support. In
Philadelphia, Frank Rizzo solidified his white support by making race
the main issue. In Louisiana, Huey Long forged a broad coalition that
crossed racial lines by substituting an economic conflict for the race
conflict.[3] In New York, Ed Koch has effectively used the "people vs.
bureaucracy and unions" conflict to solidify his support among large
segments of the middle class.

The use of conflict to deflect attention from other issues is a strategy
found at all levels of government. V. O. Key's analysis of southern
politics provided numerous examples of state and local executives who
used the race issue to deflect economic issues. And, at the presidential
level, there has been a recent trend toward displacement of domestic
conflicts by foreign policy conflicts in nonelectoral times.[4]

Although a viable tool, conflict strategy in practice is complicated
by the dynamics of conflict. Schattschneider and Key emphasized the
importance of political organization, political participation, and the
scope and arena of issues to the use of conflict strategy.[5] The impact of
these variables on the outcome of the strategy points to the need to

distinguish between electoral coalitions and governing coalitions. Electoral coalitions are often too weak and fragmented to provide the support needed for governing. Moreover, the issues around which they are forged may be too divisive in the governing arena. This was a problem encountered by White and Moscone. In contrast, Alioto's coalition of labor and business was broad enough to deflect divisive issues (see Figure 4).

To make the transition from an electoral to a governing coalition often requires successful conflict substitution. But use of this tool depends on the target of the appeal; external targets are more apt to accept substitutions than are internal targets. White substituted conflicts after the election because the target of his appeals was primarily an audience (external), not a constituency (internal). With his audience more concerned with policy appearance (is it progressive?) than with policy content (what's in it for me?), White could alter his policies and still appeal to his audience as long as the new policies were progressive. By contrast, Moscone's target was an issue-oriented constituency that could not be bought off with symbolic appeals.

Moscone's experience also highlights the relationship between political organization and conflict management in the governing arena. By bringing activist and issue-oriented constituents into his administration, Moscone elevated many issues to a citywide level. Moscone's ad-

FIGURE 4: Arena of Conflict

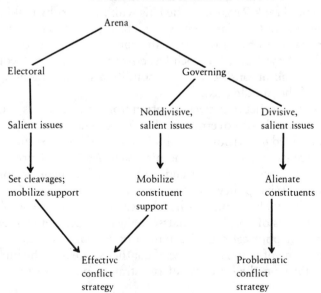

## FIGURE 5: Conflict Strategy in the Governing Arena

| Components of Target | Description | Characteristics | Effectiveness of Strategy |
|---|---|---|---|
| Composition | Internal (constituency) | Limits flexibility | Decrease effectiveness |
| | External (audience) | Provides flexibility | Increase effectiveness |
| Organization | Narrow | Fragmented interests | Decrease effectiveness |
| | Broad | Aggregated interests | Increase effectiveness |
| Orientation | Issue-oriented | Specific demands | Decrease effectiveness |
| | Not issue-oriented | Easily bought off | Increase effectiveness |
| | Broad, ideological | Symbolic concerns | Increase effectiveness |

## FIGURE 6: The Mayors and Conflict Strategy

| Mayors | Components of Target | | Orientation | Outcome |
| | Composition | Organization | | |
|---|---|---|---|---|
| Early White | External | Broad* | Ideological | Problematic, but with substitutability |
| Later White | Internal | Narrow | Not issue-oriented | Highly effective |
| Alioto | Internal | Broad | Not issue-oriented | Effective |
| Moscone | Internal | Narrow | Issue-oriented | Problematic; limited or no substitutability |

*The degree of organization was less significant than for the other three since the target was an observer audience rather than a voting constituency.

ministration, like Lindsay's, took on a "crisis-hopping" appearance that enhanced the "street fighting pattern" in city politics (see Figures 5 and 6).[6]

## ELECTORAL APPEALS

In the absence of political parties to get the vote out, candidates for office have had to rely on other mechanisms to generate electoral support. Increasingly, we have seen this trend in national, state, and local elections where candidates have substituted issue or personality politics for party politics to mobilize support. In nonpartisan Boston and San Francisco, we find a similar reliance on alternative mechanisms in electoral competitions.

Accepting Schattschneider's theory that the choice of conflicts is at the heart of political strategy, I examine the use of conflict to mobilize electoral support.[7] White, Alioto, and Moscone all took advantage of situations in which there was a vacuum of leadership. By identifying with one side of the conflict, they established strong images and leadership positions in these conflicts: White established a pro-minority and pro-civil rights image, Alioto a pro-labor image, and Moscone a pro-neighborhood image. The differences in how the strategies were executed highlights the importance of political organization. Alioto's campaign, which had the support of a strong labor movement, resembled a partisan campaign. Thus, while Alioto and White both had ambitions for higher office and a need to attract statewide support, their strategies differed because of the different political organizations in the two cities.

Political organization as well as target composition also influences the outcomes of strategies. White and Moscone both established images as left of center candidates, which helped to eliminate challenges from the left. But the target of their appeals was different. White appealed primarily to a liberal audience and secondarily to a black constituency. The latter constituted only 16 percent of the population and had poor voter registration rates. These two factors allowed White to satisfy their demands and maintain their support largely through co-optation. By contrast, Moscone appealed to many highly politicized and issue-oriented groups. The number of groups, the nature of their demands, and their high degree of politicization led to escalating demands on the mayor's office. Thus, while both candidates eliminated challenges from the left, the results of their strategies differed significantly, showing the important difference between electoral and governing coalitions.

In contrast to White, Alioto, and Moscone, Feinstein adopted a middle-of-the-road position. Although her approach to dealing with a fragmented electorate differed from Moscone's, her administration was equally problematic. Let us look at their electoral strategies side-by-side to preview the dilemmas faced by executive leadership in a fragmented and weak political system.

## Kevin White: The 1967 Election

Early in his campaign, White centered his appeals largely on the race issue by taking a pro–civil rights stand. Then, to broaden his constituent support, White began to downplay the race issue and to emphasize the fiscal issue.

## The Selection of a Conflict: The Race Issue

White's selection of the race issue as a major electoral appeal was strongly influenced by his personal ambitions for higher office and the controversy surrounding the 1965 Racial Imbalance Act (RIA) ordering racial balance in Boston public schools (see Chapter 2). The first factor created a need to appeal to a wider liberal audience. The second factor enabled White to identify with a salient issue and to fill a leadership vacuum.

When White ran for mayor in 1967, he hoped that the office would serve as a stepping stone to the gubernatorial race in 1970. In his position as secretary of state (1960–1967), however, he had not built a sufficient base of support. Governor Sargent's intention to run again in 1970 meant that White would be challenging an incumbent, thereby making his paucity of support an even greater handicap.

One way to mobilize support would have been to use the Democratic party, but this was not a viable strategy. The Democratic party machinery in Massachusetts was not so strong as it had been, as evidenced by the increase in ticket splitting and the large electoral margin that Sargent, a Republican, had picked up in traditionally Democratic Boston. Further, White's standing with some of the old line Democrats was poor.

By adopting the race issue, White simultaneously appealed to the black community, which was not represented by any of the other candidates, and to liberal suburban voters whose influence in state politics increased as party lines became more tenuous. The pro-minority stance represented a sharp departure for a Boston city politician. This bold move enhanced White's appeal among his two target groups and helped him to sew up their support early on. It was also a key factor in gaining favorable media attention. When White ran for office in 1967, the *Globe* had undergone a change in editors. With the arrival of Tom Winship, the paper took a liberal turn. Attracted by White's liberal positions and his charismatic appeal, the *Globe* reversed its traditional policy of not endorsing candidates in local elections and endorsed White for mayor. The break with the past added to the prestige of the endorsement and helped to silence challenges from the left, since the endorsement was from a liberal and powerful newspaper.

Through his pro-minority stance, White also established himself as a leader in a leaderless situation. The controversy surrounding the RIA represented a "leaderless" situation because of the actors involved and their incentives. The almost symbiotic relationship that evolved between the School Committee officials and the teachers and administrators, each representing a strong part of the opposition to desegregation, created incentives for Boston leaders to challenge, not support, any desegregation plans. Indeed, the RIA gave School Committee officials a salient campaign issue.

Although the black community, with the support of the NAACP and liberal suburbanites—the three groups primarily responsible for the passage of RIA—presented a successful challenge at the state level, they were not successful at the local level. They could not influence the School Committee or the School Department, as each had strong incentives to oppose the act and few incentives to compromise.[8]

This last factor illustrates the different imperatives for conflict management in partisan and nonpartisan cities. Under a strong party system, where the primary need is organizational maintenance, divisive issues are worked out or suppressed for the sake of party unity.[9] In a nonpartisan system, where the candidate is the end of all activity, there are fewer incentives for compromise.

White took advantage of this situation and of the reluctance of other public officials to risk a leadership role. Through his pro-civil rights appeals, White filled this vacuum and established a solid support base among blacks and liberals.

### Broadening the Base of Support: The Fiscal Issue

While White's strategy was skillful in theory, in practice it encountered the audience dilemma faced by many crusader type mayors.[10] Seeking to attract outside support in the absence of a strong political party, these mayors identified with liberal and progressive issues that were popular among their audience but which tended to alienate their less liberal constituents. It was Bostonians who would elect White, not Cambridge academics. Using the race issue in Boston was problematic because of the city's relatively small black population and the absence of a liberal population. In contrast to New York City, which had a sizable and growing black population (21 percent) and a large Jewish population (25 percent) who tended to vote liberal on social issues and to ally with blacks, Boston had a relatively small and stable black population (16 percent), an insignificant Jewish population (5 percent), and a liberal population that lived outside of the city.[11] Where Lindsay could use a similar platform and forge a coalition of blacks and liberal Jews sufficient in number to elect him, White could not in Boston. Thus, for example, while White received considerable support in the three predominantly black wards (84 percent in ward 9, 94.5 percent in ward 12, 53.8 percent in ward 11), these combined figures represented only 9.3 percent of his total vote.[12]

Needing to widen his constituent support, White began to downplay the race issue and to emphasize the fiscal issue. The latter came as a response to Hicks's (White's opponent) fiscal platform that included sizeable pay raises for police and, in general, tended to reveal a certain fiscal irresponsibility.[13] Seizing this opportunity to appeal to the business community, White attacked Hicks's "fiscal folly," refused to agree to the wage increase requested by the police (and that Hicks promised), and proposed structural tax reforms. These positions assumed increased importance as the runoff election came down to a contest between White and Hicks. Alienated by Hicks's fiscal positions, the business community threw its support behind White. Similarly, many homeowners, fearing a rise in property taxes, gave their support to White. Defeating Hicks by a 6.2 percent margin, White assumed the office of mayor in 1968 and held it until 1984 when he decided not to seek re-election. In the 1971, 1975, and 1979 elections, White held the liberal and black vote even though his positions had shifted to the right. Indeed, it was because he had sewed up this support early on that he was able to move to the right and broaden his constituent support.

### Joe Alioto: Labor and the 1967 Election

The contrasting styles of Alioto and White's campaigns point to the important relationship between conflict strategy and political organization. Like White, Alioto had ambitions for higher office—in 1974 he ran for governor of California (unsuccessfully). Thus, we would expect to find Alioto appealing to a wider audience, and his administration does provide examples, but the 1967 campaign was not dominated by such appeals as White's was. Rather, it was closer in style to a partisan campaign. Although Boston and San Francisco are both nonpartisan cities and hence lack the party vehicle for mobilizing support, Alioto had the advantage of support by a strong labor movement that was organized and influential in city politics. The electoral machinery (campaign contributions, workers, endorsements) provided by labor limited the need to rely on alternative mechanisms such as issue politics to generate support. Thus, while White and Alioto both filled leadership vacuums, they employed different means.

Through skillful negotiating, Alioto acquired valuable resources from an existing coalition. The coalition, which consisted of the ILWU and the Labor Council (the two major labor groups in San Francisco; together they had approximately 120,000 registered voters) and key financial figures (Ben Swig, Cyril Magnin, Walter Schorenstein) had recruited state senator Eugene MacAteer to run for mayor. Several months before the election, MacAteer died of a heart attack. The coalition was without a candidate when Alioto announced his intention to run. Through bargaining and negotiations, Alioto took over the electoral machinery that had been set up for MacAteer.

Although his legal career as an anti-trust attorney had made him attractive to labor, Alioto did not win its immediate endorsement. The ILWU and the Labor Council (AFL-CIO) were divided internally between Alioto and Jack Morrison, a supervisor who had union endorsement as a legislator. Both candidates lobbied the ILWU; Alioto won its formal endorsement because it felt that he was the stronger of the two candidates and because he was more liberal in his promises to appoint labor representatives to city government.[14]

The Labor Council did not resolve its internal split between Alioto and Morrison but did provide electoral resources. Labor officers representing more than 100 of the city's unions and more than 100,000 members endorsed Alioto and set up an Action Labor Committee for Alioto.[15]

The key financial figures in the coalition were crucial in raising money for the campaign. Ben Swig, for example, raised $203,500 for Alioto in "exactly 45 minutes."[16]

The coalition also served as an important cue to voters. Labor's endorsement helped Alioto in the minority and liberal communities. The ILWU, a predominantly black union, gave Alioto access to the black community. This was accomplished largely through the efforts of the Baptist Ministers Union (part of ILWU), which was one of the first black organizations to support Alioto.[17] According to a union spokesman, the ILWU was responsible for delivering all of the black precincts to Alioto in the 1967 election.[18] The ILWU's history as a progressive labor union gave Alioto an entrée to the liberal community. This was critical since Morrison was perceived as the liberal candidate. Morrison had the support of the Burtons and Willie Brown who represented the liberal contingent in California state politics and who painted Alioto as a conservative. The ILWU's formal endorsement, however, served as a counterweight.

Through the support of Local 261 of the Laborers' International (AFL-CIO), Alioto gained access to the Hispanic community. The Centro Social Obrero, the Mission-based caucus, was a major neighborhood political force with substantial influence over the Mexican American Political Association (MAPA). With their help, Alioto established a strong base of support among the city's Spanish-speaking population, who constituted 14 percent of the total population, a slightly larger proportion than blacks. Local 261 was important financially as well, giving Alioto a "not insubstantial amount of financial backing."[19]

With the support of this coalition, Alioto won the 1967 election by a 6.3 percent margin and was re-elected in 1971 with a 14 percent margin.

### George Moscone and the Neighborhood Issue: The 1975 Election

Moscone's 1975 election provides further illustration of the relationship between conflict strategy and political organization. While Moscone's strategy was similar to White's and Alioto's, Moscone's was less effective. Organizationally, the key variables were labor's declining influence and the increasing fragmentation of the electorate.

Moscone's election in 1975 paralleled White's in 1967 in several ways. Both men came from outside city politics; Moscone had served as a California state senator for twelve years with a strong pro-labor record. Both men were viewed as the liberal candidates and their opponents as the conservatives; both faced opponents who held elective office at the time of the campaign (Hicks, School Committee official; Barbagelata, supervisor); both elections were surrounded by existing conflicts.

The 1975 election was fought in the wake of a pro-development administration that had generated a lot of opposition. Alioto's emphasis on commercial development had stimulated opposition from many neighborhood and environmental groups. But they had been either too weak or too fragmented to produce a single spokesperson. Through appeals to neighborhood concerns (downzoning, curbing downtown development), Moscone firmed up the cleavage between the neighborhoods and the downtown, establishing himself as a leader of the former. As with White's use of the race issue, Moscone's identification with these groups represented a change from the previous administration. This "relativism"—a perceived difference relative to what had gone before—strengthened Moscone's appeals.

By making the neighborhood cleavage the major one, Moscone also deflected the labor issue, which Barbagelata, his opponent, sought to emphasize. Barbagelata, who had co-authored the anti-union legislation after the police and fire strike, had fashioned a strong fiscal austerity campaign that featured a harsh anti-union position. Although labor's influence in city politics was much less in 1975 than it was in 1967, it was still an important factor. Moscone, having the formal endorsement of the Labor Council and the ILWU, could not take an anti-union position. But taking a pro-union position could have damaged his nonlabor support. By focusing on the neighborhood-downtown conflict, he avoided the labor issue completely.

While Moscone's use of conflict to mobilize support and establish a leadership position was similar to White and Alioto's strategies, his target differed. Where White had secured his liberal support through appeals to a liberal *audience*, Moscone had appealed to a liberal *constituency*. This difference would have significant consequences for Moscone's administration. When the electoral strategies used by White and Moscone proved too divisive to use as governing strategies, White was able to write off his target without damaging his electoral support but Moscone was not able to. In contrast to Alioto, whose target was also a constituency—a coalition of labor—Moscone's target was much more fragmented and issue-oriented. Thus, where Alioto's support system helped to deflect issues, Moscone's was the source of issues. Moreover, his small margin of victory (2 percent) left him vulnerable to his conservative opposition.

### Dianne Feinstein and the Politics of Accommodation: The 1979 Election

Feinstein took over the mayor's office in 1978 when Moscone was assassinated. Thus she ran in 1979 as an incumbent. Her electoral strategy departed sharply from the other three mayors in its lack of conflict strategy. The neighborhood-downtown cleavage still existed, but Feinstein did not take a leadership position even though she had often supported neighborhood issues as a supervisor. Rather, she adopted a middle of the road position in an attempt to attract a wide variety of interests. Although she won with the support of a broad constituency—

gays, neighborhood groups, downtown interests—she came out of the election with a constituency that was a "mile wide and an inch deep."[20] Consequently, Feinstein was in a very tentative position for governing. In trying not to upset her delicate and uncertain constituency, Feinstein was often slow in taking actions, since gestures to one part of the constituency would be opposed by other parts.

## ACTIVIST MAYORS: OPPORTUNITIES AND DILEMMAS

### The Visible Mayor

Mayoral visibility is a viable mechanism for sustaining a conflict. Through community presence, media coverage, policies, and programs, mayors set a tone for their administration. Robert Salisbury referred to this as the ability to "command and structure public attention." Sayre and Kaufman referred to the "ceremonial hat" of the chief of state as "one of the most important ways by which the mayor establishes the popular image of himself and his office."[21] In the 1960s and early 1970s, mayors established popular images that reflected their positions on a variety of issues (such as decentralization, minority rights, unionism). Thus, their mayoral images, like their electoral strategies, helped to set cleavages within the electorate.

These cleavages and the tone established took on increased importance in urban politics as political parties declined at the local level and as the media became the principal means of communicating with the public. The tone set or image created by the mayor often influenced the political behavior in the city. Douglas Yates suggested that the "crisis-hopping" of the Lindsay administration taught interest groups that symbolic politics was the way to obtain concessions from city hall, thus exacerbating the "street fighting pattern in city politics."[22] Lindsay set the tone, the media emphasized it, and organized groups responded accordingly.

Such interlocking relationships are why it is difficult to use conflict strategy. As we have seen, issues that mobilize electoral support often are too divisive to use as governing strategies. This can occur when the target of appeals is highly fragmented and issue-oriented or when it is an audience that is more liberal than the constituency. Moscone encountered the first situation in his attempts to use his electoral coalition as a governing coalition. White met the second.

By contrast, noncontroversial issues can often be used to mobilize public and media support, which, in turn, can eliminate potential opposition. This characterizes many of Alioto and White's community activities. Again, relativism influences the effectiveness of this strategy.

Alioto and White followed administrations that were not known for a 1960s sense of community and minority involvement. In many ways their experiences resembled John F. Kennedy's. Following the sleepy years of Eisenhower, Kennedy faced a public that was ready for a vigorous and innovative presidency. Similarly, Lindsay and Koch's activities in New York City benefited from the contrast with those of previous noncharismatic administrations. But relativism can also be a negative influence. Following Alioto's highly visible administration, Moscone was criticized by the media for his low profile in certain situations. Thus, while the use of conflict strategy is difficult, nonparticipation in a conflict can also cause problems. Since executives do not always have the choice of which conflict to emphasize, it is crucial that they be skilled in the art of conflict management. This involves the selection *and* deflection of conflicts, the choice of targets, and the definition of issues.

## Mayors Take to the Streets

### The Streets of San Francisco

Alioto's administration was characterized by a high degree of mayoral visibility. Alioto was skilled in reading an audience, in using noncontroversial events to create the image of an activist mayor, in using the media to further administration priorities, and in negotiating with other powers in the civic arena.

Despite its cosmopolitan reputation, San Francisco retains a strong provincialism. Alioto appealed to this provincialism by putting his personal touch on the mayor's office. It was not uncommon for Alioto to walk into a local restaurant and play his violin while people dined. On several occasions he led the San Francisco Symphony Orchestra before a full house. On one occasion, he held an earthquake party, open to all, commemorating the famous quake of 1906. A former student at Hastings Law School remembers that Alioto often went to the school, which is around the corner from city hall, and debated the students on various issues. She observed that whether you supported or opposed Alioto, one thing was certain: "You were always aware of his presence."[23]

Alioto made extensive use of the media to enhance his presence and to stifle potential opposition. When he entered office in 1968, both of the major dailies were on strike. Alioto saw a vacuum and quickly filled it. He became the media. Like LaGuardia, he read the comics over the radio. And, like LaGuardia, he received a warm reception from the public. Simultaneously with the strike, Channel 9, the public broadcasting station, began a news program, part of which Alioto helped to shape. He used the Channel 9 program as a link to the communities by persuading the station to accept calls from the public.[24]

When the strike was settled, a settlement which the mayor mediated, Alioto was in business. The press often sought his opinions on general issues and policies as well as his statements on the life of the city. And the coverage did not stop at the city limits. Alioto was the first San Francisco mayor to be interviewed by the *New York Times* editorial board.[25] Like Kevin White, Joe Alioto possessed that gift of charisma, which journalists found hard to resist.

Alioto's command of the spotlight often inhibited those with opposing viewpoints. In the words of one reporter, Alioto used the media to "overwhelm the board with public pressure."[26] In contrast to White, however, Alioto did not eliminate challenges from the left and so constantly had to suppress them, a process which usually cost him political capital. During his entire administration, he fought a running battle with Herb Caen, a prominent columnist for the *Chronicle*, who criticized his pro-development policies. Many neighborhood groups opposed these policies as well. Nevertheless, much potential opposition was suppressed by Alioto's quick and forceful preemption of the media world.

Alioto also used the media to mobilize support for controversial policies. In the Market Street Beautification Project, a major renovation of one of San Francisco's major streets, Alioto successfully played the role of Banfield's "publicist," in which the executive vigorously supports an issue in order to persuade the public to approve it.[27]

In 1967, the Market Street Redevelopment Corporation, a private, nonprofit corporation set up to monitor the development of BART, submitted plans to the CAO to renovate Market Street and to issue $25 million worth of bonds to pay for it. The CAO and SPUR, an influential citizens' organization, endorsed the plan but felt that the public would not approve the bonds.[28] The Chamber of Commerce and many downtown merchants opposed the construction as well because of the temporary loss of business that would result.

Despite the opposition, Alioto endorsed the plan and began a vigorous campaign that included talks and speeches in various communities. His community lobbying mobilized support for the bond, but the keystone of the campaign was Channel 4's documentary program on the project. Accounts of the telecast described Alioto "waving his arms" and likening San Francisco to Italy and the proposed development to one of Italy's piazzas.[29]

The entire presentation was strongly colored by romanticism.

Through the media, Alioto put the full force of his personality and gift for elocution behind the proposal. When the vote was taken, the bond issue passed.

The positive contribution that the executive can make in the role of publicist is evidenced by examples from other administrations. In New Haven, Mayor Lee's initial public relations activities were instrumental in the success of an urban renewal campaign. Similarly, Mayor Houlihan's public endorsement of the BARTD bond issue was crucial in Oakland's close but favorable public vote.[30]

In addition to manipulating the media and social events, Alioto made strong appeals to labor, whose organization limited the demands on the mayor's office. Labor's primary demand was wages, which Alioto satisfied through skillful negotiations. Moreover, the abundance of labor disputes in San Francisco provided Alioto opportunities to maintain constant visibility, strengthen his ties with labor, and increase its power through favorable wage settlements (See Tables 7 and 8).

Throughout his administration, Alioto mediated many public and private labor disputes—including the symphony strike, the cemetery strike, and municipal strikes—creating for his administration strong identification with labor and establishing himself as a leader in labor negotiations. While there were many strikes in San Francisco, the majority lasted only a few days. In fact, it is quite possible that Alioto could have prevented some of them but did not in order to have the opportunity to negotiate them and enhance his record. The record he established was an enviable one. Labor considered Alioto the best mayor they had seen in recent times. This was especially true for Local 400 of SEIU (the city workers) who, under Alioto, gained wage settlements that put them on par with their private sector counterparts.

By the public, Alioto was perceived as keeping labor peace at a time when other cities were undergoing severe labor problems.[31] In New York City, Lindsay faced a long transit workers strike, several long teachers strikes (one of which lasted fifty-five days), sanitation workers strikes, and police and fire slowdowns. In Memphis, there was a bitter sanitation workers strike in 1968. In Detroit, public school teachers struck for thirteen days in 1967. In the following year, public school teachers in Florida state struck for nineteen days.[32]

Alioto reinforced his leadership role with organized labor through symbolic gestures as well. When the dockworkers struck, Alioto went to the waterfront with sandwiches and beer. In a more sensitive incident in Marin County, a management change at the *Independent Journal* (a union journal) had led to a bitter strike and the arrest of four union officials. Alioto gave the officials a send-off, delivering a short speech in which he expressed outrage at the use of injunctions against labor in the twentieth century and deplored it as a violation of civil liberties.[33]

These actions contrasted sharply with Lindsay's approach to organized labor. Rather than currying favor, Lindsay's symbolic gestures were part of a politics of attack that alienated organized labor, a powerful factor in New York City politics. This encouraged strikes, slowdowns, and heated controversies that helped to defeat some of Lindsay's policies and weakened his support.

In contrast to Alioto and Lindsay, Moscone maintained a low profile in relation to labor. Following Alioto's lively performances, Moscone was hurt by seeming less effective, particularly in his handling of the craftworkers strike shortly after he took office.

The city's craftworkers struck when the board of supervisors denied their request for a wage increase. They were soon joined by the city bus drivers. The strike was a politically sensitive issue because it came on the heels of the unpopular police and fire settlement that represented a turning point in labor's position in city politics (Chapter 2). This settlement inspired legislative changes that eliminated the mayor's authority to invoke emergency power unilaterally and gave responsibility for labor negotiations to the Board of Supervisors. A combination of anti-union sentiment in the public, negative press on the unions, and supervisors' appeals to anti-union feelings created strong incentives for the board to take a hard line against the strikers. Unable to persuade the board to negotiate, Moscone cited the recent amendments as his formal justification for not getting involved.

Although labor's influence had declined, the unions were, and still are, an important force in San Francisco's politics. Their campaign contributions, endorsements, and electioneering can make a difference in an election. Moscone had had the Labor Council's endorsement and had received money from them for his mayoral campaign.[34] Adopting a stance against the strikers could have damaged his relations with labor. But supporting a favorable settlement for the strikers would have been viewed as a giveaway by the public and criticized by the press, hurting his support in nonlabor arenas. Caught on the horns of a dilemma, Moscone took the middle position.

Publicly reiterating his formal position that he had no authority, Moscone and his aides adopted the roles of overseers and troubleshooters. They remained in City Hall around the clock, where they answered phones and tried to help with problems. Although the public had voted two to one for Proposition N, the amendment that removed the mayor's authority in strike situations, they were dissatisfied with Moscone's performance.[35] This illustrates one of the major dilemmas of executive leadership: the public does not want to give executives power but does want them to solve all problems that arise. In the hyperpluralistic and strong reform ethos of San Francisco city politics, every exercise of executive power seems to be followed by a proposal to remove that power. In many cities mayors must be careful not to give the impression that they are grabbing power. In San Francisco, mayors must avoid giving the impression that they are using power.

The Catch 22 of mayoral leadership finally exploded in the strike case when the newspaper printed photographs of Moscone and his aides playing cards in the mayor's office at four in the morning. With the negative press coverage and the increased demands from the public, Moscone switched strategies. He persuaded the board to set up a grievance committee in exchange for the strikers' return to work. Establishment of the committee carried no promise to grant any of the workers' demands, and so the supervisors were able to maintain their original position. In fact, accepting the committee appears largely to have been a face-saving device for the unions. The strike had lasted thirty-four days with no increase in the union's chances of winning its demands. The committee was set up, the workers went back, and the unions did not realize any of their demands.

The city probably fared better in this way than if the board had negotiated in the beginning; it is probable that early negotiations would have resulted in at least some concessions to the unions. As it turned out, no demands were granted and the city saved thirty-four days worth of pay. Nevertheless, Moscone's inability to persuade the board to take early action and his subsequent nonnegotiating stance created pressure and, ultimately, negative publicity for the mayor's office.

### Kevin White and the Heating Crisis

Like Alioto, White made himself highly visible in the neighborhoods to create an image of constant activity and involvement. White's departure from the previous administration's emphasis on the downtown was attractive to the media, which built him up as the energetic young mayor who would give a facelift to the city. Their continued attention strengthened White's image as a left of center politician.

White was aided early on by a crisis that he turned into a success for his administration. Like Alioto's participation in social events, this was an opportunity to be visible in a noncontroversial setting. Shortly after White took office in 1968, there was a heating crisis in Boston. Through the planning efforts of a top staff member, City Hall was kept open twenty-four hours a day. White and his aides answered more than

10,000 calls and provided assistance (food, fuel, or home repairs) to 3,500 people and temporary rehousing for 700 people. As a new mayor, White scored very high points for his effective handling of a crisis. In the words of one reporter, "largely because of Finn's pre-planning, a potential crisis became a cozy triumph for White."[36]

The concept of a twenty-four hour City Hall was continued with the establishment of the Little City Halls (discussed below) and through the dedication of energetic aides like Barney Frank who insisted that people call him any time of the day or night. This orientation was a sharp departure from the practice of the previous administration. Although the Collins administration was actively involved in urban renewal policies, the *type* of activity differed from that of the White administration. While Collins might be imagined rushing from meeting to meeting with bankers and developers, he could hardly be pictured walking through the streets of Roxbury (the city's black area) with his jacket slung over his shoulder. The White administration's early activities were fresh and created an image of involvement and municipal responsiveness that Boston residents were not accustomed to and that the press fell upon like a free meal. Using this visibility in conjunction with other strategies (such as appointments, use of conflict, and the like), White was able largely to eliminate challenges from the left.

### The Dilemmas of Liberal Appeals

Salient issues that mobilize electoral support are often too divisive to use in governing, as we have noted repeatedly. This dilemma was faced by many audience-seeking mayors in the 1960s.[37] When the mayors' liberal policies made demands on the more conservative segments of the electorate, these constituents tended to be alienated. This was the pattern in the early part of White's administration and throughout Moscone's administration.

### Kevin White and the Race Issue

Although White shifted his emphasis from school racial balance to the fiscal issue during the campaign, the race issue survived and became part of his early administrative agenda. The divisiveness of the issue and the larger problem of audience dilemmas undermined White's efforts in the Infill Housing program and his attempt to reform the Boston Housing Authority (BHA). Both were attempts to appeal to an audience by focusing on minority concerns.

The Infill Housing program was similar to Lindsay's scattersite housing program in New York City. The objective was to construct a thousand low-income housing units on vacant city-owned land.[38] By scattering this housing throughout the city, the program hoped to achieve a racially and economically integrated housing mix on a small scale. This marked a departure from the traditional large scale public housing project.

Like Lindsay's scattersite housing, White's proposal was an innovative program geared primarily for blacks. And, like Lindsay's plan, the Infill Housing program was defeated. Neighborhood objections to integration, both racial and economical, dealt a serious blow to the proposal. To date, more than ten years later, only six housing units in Boston have come out of the Infill Housing program.[39]

White's move to restructure the BHA to make it more responsive to tenants (the majority of whom were minorities) was another attempt to further his identification with minorities. To implement his policy, White appointed tenants to the board. This was an innovative move at the time because the state statute, which had just been changed, had always prohibited tenants from serving on the board. It also departed from the traditional practice of using BHA appointments as patronage. The appointments made by White were more symbolic than political. One result was that White could not control his appointees. One of the board's first actions was to fire the director that White appointed. Following an unsuccessful series of hearings and court cases to remove one of the board members (Doris Bunte), White abandoned his BHA reform policy—after expending resources and extracting no gains.

Contrasting with these unsuccessful attempts were White's creation of the Office of Human Rights (OHR), the establishment of the Summerthing program of events in the communities, and the appointment of blacks. The creation of OHR and Summerthing gave the black community and White's liberal audience tangible expressions of his commitment to the race issue and created administrative positions for blacks as well. Unlike the attempted BHA reorganization, these innovations were new programs in new agencies and so encountered no resistance from entrenched interests or internal conflict over policy matters between new recruits and established managers.[40] In addition, White maintained more control over these programs than he had over the BHA. Implementing the programs through his own office, White had the authority to remove appointees at any time, a power that he lacked with the BHA. Finally, and perhaps most importantly, the programs did not upset his constituency because, unlike the Infill Housing program, they made no demands on the white community.

This last factor recalls the difference between Lindsay's success with the Community Action Program (CAP) and his failure with the scatter-site housing program. The CAP was limited to the minority communities and was a distributive program at the local level. The scattersite housing program extended beyond the minority communities and aroused opposition from the white communities selected as sites.

Another mayoral strategy that made no demands on the white community was the appointment of blacks. By appointing blacks to key positions in city government, White used his formal authority to appeal to his liberal audience and to co-opt potential opposition from the black community. Several of his appointees were very active in the black community and some—Eaves and Parks—had risen to leadership during the Racial Imbalance Act controversy. The departure that these appointments represented for Boston city politics, combined with the generally weak political position of Boston's black community, enhanced his ability to solidify his liberal and black support.[41]

Despite White's success in these instances, using the race issue as a governing strategy could only create problems in Boston. With blacks making up only 16 percent of the population and no meaningful liberal constituency with which to forge an alliance, White could not hope to attract constituent support with racial issues. The divisiveness of the issue alienated the more conservative areas in the city. Part of the reason for White's poor showing in the Irish working class neighborhoods was his pro-minority stance.[42] While the name "Mayor Black" might have been an electoral asset to a mayor of Detroit or to Lindsay, it was not a sign of affection as applied to Kevin White in many conservative areas of Boston. The narrowness of his support was probably best epitomized when he lost Boston in the 1970 governor's race to Republican Francis Sargent.[43] The solid support that he developed in the black and liberal communities, however, did enable him to abandon the divisive race issue.

### George Moscone and the Neighborhood Cause

Like White, Moscone found that liberal appeals, as expressed in his identification with minorities and neighborhood activists and the appointment of many of these to city government, posed difficulties for him as mayor. The coalition that had elected him was too fragmented, and their concerns too divisive, to serve as a governing coalition. In contrast to Alioto's highly organized target (labor), which helped to deflect issues, Moscone's fragmented target generated issues that strained his political resources and his ability to resolve the conflicts. Like Lindsay's administration, Moscone's took on a crisis-hopping appearance. Issues that had remained private under Alioto became public under Moscone and often assumed symbolic proportions. Since these issues pitted constituent against constituent, Moscone's identification with one side would alienate the other side.

THE INTERNATIONAL HOTEL   A major issue in San Francisco's neighborhood-downtown conflict was the loss of housing caused by commercial expansion. The controversy over the International Hotel revolved around this issue. Its development shows the important relationship between the composition of city government and the scope and arena of issues.

The International Hotel was an old residential hotel near Chinatown. The hotel—owned by Milton Meyer, Inc., the largest real estate agency in San Francisco, all of whose shares were owned by Walter Schorenstein—was occupied by 130 people in 1969, 90 percent of them Asian. Because of the critical housing shortage in Chinatown, the hotel was important to the community.[44]

Although the owner first attempted to evict the residents in 1969, the hotel did not become a citywide issue until the Moscone administration. Under Alioto, the battles largely had been between the tenant association and the owners. Alioto's appointments and statements had set a pro-development and pro-labor tone for the city that did not offer much scope to neighborhood groups. In addition, Schorenstein was a major contributor to Alioto's campaigns.

With the changing of the guard under Moscone's administration, the tenant association gained access to city government. They brought the city into the battle as an active participant, which raised the conflict to a citywide level. Other neighborhood groups joined in and the I-Hotel soon became a symbol of the struggle between the neighborhoods and the downtown.

The building inspector's office issued a stop-work order, while Moscone, attorneys for the residents, and the Housing Authority worked through the courts to save the hotel. Moscone allocated $1.2 million in community development money, proposing that the Housing Authority take over the hotel through eminent domain and manage it as a low income housing project. Although Moscone won approval from the Board of Supervisors, the voters overwhelmingly rejected the plan in their defeat of Proposition U.[45] Moreover, the court ruled that the Housing Authority did not have the power to take over the hotel and run it as a housing project. On August 5, 1977, 60 sheriff's deputies and 250 police officers evicted the remaining tenants. The issue was dead.

Although the cause was lost, the protestors succeeded in making and sustaining the I-Hotel as a heated public issue for eighteen months through their access to city government. In fact, the I-Hotel had become the *cause célèbre* of the left, which, after its long exclusion, now reveled in its access to and influence with city government. Many of Moscone's appointments had strong support among this segment of the electorate and acted in ways that appealed to their supporters. It was Moscone's community development director who persuaded Supervisor Feinstein not to rescind the board's resolution on municipal purchase of the hotel until the court had ruled on its legality. And, during the controversy, Sheriff Richard Hungisto was arrested for not complying with the original eviction notice. His was an elected, not appointed, position, but as part of the government, Hungisto helped to influence the environment of conflict and protest that pervaded city politics.

Thus, the composition of Moscone's administration influenced the selection of issues that entered the public arena. The controversy also illustrates the relationship between political organization and conflict management. Had this incident occurred in Chicago, for example, it is highly probable that the ward leader would have taken care of the residents individually either by finding them other housing or by giving them carry-over money. In San Francisco there were no ward leaders or functional equivalents to provide the brokering service that could have localized the issue.

In addition, the fragmentation of Moscone's constituency was an impediment to conflict management, where Alioto's labor coalition had been sufficiently unified to deflect issues.[46] As in the Lindsay administration, media emphasis on City Hall crisis-hopping only exacerbated conflict and sharpened the cleavages within the constituency. By depicting Moscone as the champion of the neighborhoods, the media helped to alienate some of the more conservative parts of the electorate and portions of the business and financial communities.

POLICE REFORM    Police reform in San Francisco offered another example of the difficulties of appealing to a highly fragmented and issue-oriented target. Police harassment was a major issue in San Francisco's gay community, an important segment of Moscone's constituency.[47] When Moscone took office, he implemented a police reform policy designed in part to alleviate this concern. His progressive policy achieved its objective but alienated more conservative elements of the electorate and angered some of Moscone's constituents.

As in Chicago and Oakland, a professional, Charlie Gain, was brought in from outside to reform an old style police department. In fact, Gain came from the Oakland police department, which had become a model of reform. Through reorganizations centered on promotions and demotions, Gain broke up the old-boy network in the department. The implementation of new administrative policies helped to increase control at the top and to improve departmental record keeping and information flow. Gain improved conditions between police and the gay community through promotions and demotions intended to end harassment and through frequent trips to the gay community. He also asked gay members of the force to come out of the closet.[48]

While Gain was well received within the gay community, he was not well received by the public at large and by some segments of the black community. Many of Gain's actions, most notably his close identification with the gay community, alienated the public who, in concert with the media, blamed Gain for the low morale of the police.[49] Gain's dismantling of community relations units, set up before his appointment to facilitate relations between the police and the community, angered some black leaders.[50]

Thus Moscone had a police chief who was favored by an important component of his constituency, disliked by other parts, and not well received by the public and media. Removing Gain would have angered Moscone's gay supporters but keeping him angered some black leaders. Moscone did retain Gain, but it was a costly appointment, leading to public opposition, dissatisfaction among some constituents, and negative press. This last factor tended to overshadow the achievements of the reform policy—improvements in police department organization and increased policy sensitivity toward a major element of the community—and the potential support or credit that Moscone could have obtained from it.

## Liberal Appeals and Practical Politics

As we have seen, White's liberal appeals targeted primarily an audience, whereas Moscone's addressed a constituency. Having an external target (audience) rather than an internal target (constituency), White was able to use nondivisive symbolic appeals to maintain his audience support. This distinction between external and internal targets recalls Raymond Wolfinger's distinction between extrinsic and intrinsic support. The first is for the politician; the second is for the particular policy. Intrinsic supporters expect "commensurate policy commitments."[51] The tenant association in the I-Hotel case was seeking to retain the structure for housing. Since their perceived benefit was a particular good, Moscone could not buy them off with liberal or symbolic appeals. By contrast, White's audience could be bought off with such appeals: policy content was less important than policy appearance (i.e., is it a progressive policy?).

This distinction adds an important dimension to the literature on audience-seeking mayors.[52] Like his 1960s counterparts, White sought support from a wider liberal audience. In doing so, he encountered the tensions between audience appeal and constituency demand. But in contrast to predictions in the literature, based on the experiences of many 1960s mayors, this was not a permanent bind for White. Through his political skills, he took advantage of the policy flexibility provided by his target to ease those tensions. The key factor was that White's target consisted almost completely of an audience. By contrast, Lindsay's audience appeals had a significant constituency as part of the target; constituency demands on his office decreased his policy flexibility. White could shift gears without losing constituency support; Lindsay could not.

White's pro-civil rights stand and the policies he forged around it appealed to his audience but were not well received by the electorate. Early in his administration, White substituted the neighborhood issue for the race issue. His solid support in the black and liberal communities enabled him to make the shift without losing electoral support. Emphasizing the need to make government more responsive to the people, White broadened his constituent support while, simultaneously, the progressive orientation of the issue appealed to his audience. The appeal was equally attractive to the media, who praised White's innovative efforts in the neighborhoods. And, unlike the race issue, the neighborhood issue in Boston was not divisive.

### Kevin White and the Neighborhoods

Focusing on the neighborhoods was a more effective strategy in Boston in the 1960s and early 1970s than it was in San Francisco when Moscone applied it. The difference in outcomes is directly related to the political orientation of the targets. San Francisco neighborhoods and groups were highly politicized and issue oriented. By contrast, Boston neighborhoods were not ideological and many had no effective organizations. Boston's demographics—working class, strong ethnic cleavages, sociological separation—combined with the physical separation of its neighborhoods helped to shape an alienated electorate.[53] The absence of a party or similar device to integrate the individual into the political system deprived Boston of a mechanism for preventing that alienation. And the concentration on downtown and neglect of city services under John Collins's administration (1960–1967) increased that alienation. Thus White was dealing with a politically weak target that he could satisfy through the nondivisive means of basic services and jobs.

LITTLE CITY HALLS    The major symbol of White's neighborhood focus was the Little City Hall (LCH) program, a citywide system of administrative adjuncts to City Hall designed to decentralize city government. Beginning in two neighborhoods and expanding to fourteen, the LCHs helped to formalize White's ties with the neighborhoods by giving structure to the administrative presence in the neighborhoods. In addition, they provided White with mechanisms through which to disaggregate benefits: LCH staff handled complaints, helped individuals fill out tax forms or find jobs, and the like.

An important LCH policy was that managers be from outside the neighborhood. This helped to create an administrative rather than political image for the LCHs, a feature well received by White's audience and the media. Moreover, it served a real political function. Headed by people from outside the neighborhoods, LCHs could not be used by neighborhood politicians as advocacy groups to advance their own political power. In his study of the LCHs, Eric Nordlinger suggested that the managers' roles as administration representatives were often constraints to acting as advocates for issues.[54] By contrast, Moscone recruited neighborhood activists who had constituencies of their own. They saw themselves as representing the neighborhood to the city government, not as representatives of the city to the neighborhood.

White's approach to the neighborhoods, as expressed in the LCHs, also contrasted to Lindsay's experience in New York. Both mayors focused on the neighborhoods, but where Lindsay took concrete steps toward actual decentralization (such as substantive participation in CAP by minorities), White mostly paid lip service to decentralization, extracting political mileage from the rhetoric and avoiding the political costs of the reality. While the LCHs decentralized city services, *they did not decentralize power* to the neighborhood level as Lindsay's CAP program did.[55]

In addition, White's neighborhood policies and positions did not alienate important actors as Moscone's activities did (the I-Hotel battle alienated the financial and business community) or pose major threats to important forces as Lindsay's did (his school decentralization stand angered the teacher's union). While the LCH program drew initial hostility from some bureaucrats, it did not create hostility in their formal organization, the union.[56] White's neighborhood orientation included increased city services which meant more hirings and more money, both of which were in the interests of union leadership.

POLICE REFORM   Contrasting White's police reform policy with Moscone's gives further evidence for the importance of target in the use of conflict strategy. Both policies were progressive, both were directed towards the neighborhoods, and both encountered opposition. But White's neighborhood targets did not represent conflicting needs and demands to the extent that Moscone's did. The strong consensus that developed around the policy in Boston helped to defeat the opposition and strengthen White's constituent and audience support. He also enjoyed media endorsement.

In 1972 White recruited Robert DeGrazia, a professional from St. Louis, to reform the Boston police department. The police union objected but their opposition was diluted by several factors. First, most police lived outside the city and so White was not sacrificing much in the way of votes. Second, the police department had a history of corruption, which weakened its position. Opposition to reform translated, at least partially, into approval of corruption. Third, the public overwhelmingly supported the policy. White's single target—the neighborhoods—was much less fragmented than Moscone's multiple one— gays, neighborhoods, minorities—and thus did not divide the public into supporters and opponents. Rather, the cleavage was drawn between the public and an old time, inefficient, and somewhat corrupt police department. Finally, DeGrazia was very popular in the neighborhoods and with the media.

As Daley had done with Orlando Wilson, the police chief he brought in to reform the department, White gave DeGrazia complete control over internal matters. This was a major contribution to Wilson's success in Chicago and to DeGrazia's success in Boston. Through administrative reorganization and personnel reforms, DeGrazia increased responsiveness and accountability to the commissioner, increased responsiveness to and contact with the public, and improved internal efficiency. While these policy outcomes were similar to the ones in San Francisco, the results for the mayors differed. This latter point underscores the important relationship between a policy and its setting or, to use the terminology of this chapter, between conflict strategy and target. Most important, it highlights the complexity and difficulties of mayoral leadership.

LOGAN AIRPORT   White's position in the Logan Airport controversy represents another example of audience appeals and broadening constituency support. Contrasting it with Moscone's position in the I-Hotel controversy, which pitted constituent against constituent, illustrates the importance of target in conflict strategy. White's action in the airport case was represented as an attack on an outsider—the state.

When plans for the expansion of Logan Airport in East Boston sur-faced, the residents rose up in opposition. White publicly sided with the residents and committed the city's legal resources to help them. The proposal was challenged in the courts and the court ruled in favor of the residents. The airport expansion plans were finally shelved and White emerged a hero in East Boston. In the 1967 election, White had lost East Boston by 300 votes. In 1971, running again against Hicks, White won East Boston by 3,300 votes. In addition, East Boston was one of the seven wards that White carried in the 1970 governor's race.[57]

### Protect Appeals, Redefine the Issue: Kevin White and Busing

A major component of conflict strategy involves defining the issue. Schattschneider suggested that there is a positive correlation between the scope of an issue and the scope of the conflict. In a debate, narrowly defined issues will tend to attract fewer participants than will broader issues. Schattschneider empirically documented this theory by demon-strating the difference in participation rates between the pressure system and the party system. The pressure group system is narrower in its focus than the party system and consequently has a smaller membership.[58]

Banfield further demonstrated the operation of this theory when he examined issue definition as a political strategy in Chicago. Banfield suggested that the five civic controversies that he studied were all stimu-lated by the private organizational maintenance needs of the partici-pants. In order to attract support, however, they couched their objec-tives in the broader term of the public interest.[59]

White's handling of the busing controversy represents a somewhat different use of this conflict strategy. White, in pursuing his ambitions for higher office, had substituted the neighborhood issue for the race issue. When the school desegregation order was issued in 1974, White again encountered tensions between audience appeal and constituency demand on a racial matter. White resolved this tension by redefining the issue, a testimony to his political skill.

The conflict surrounding the Racial Imbalance Act came to a head in July 1974 when Federal District Court Judge Arthur Garrity ordered the Boston public school system to implement the state's desegregation plan, which had been devised earlier that year. The school committee remained opposed to desegregation and adopted a position of noncom-pliance. The school department, six weeks before the start of the school year, had made no preparations for implementing the plan. Facing a suspension of federal funds if the order was not obeyed and the poten-tial for racial violence in the schools if the plan was implemented, the mayor's office had to take some action. The problem was to protect White's liberal image with his wider audience while not alienating his Boston constituency, the majority of which vehemently opposed the order. Indeed, many elected officials had built prominent careers in Boston city politics on their opposition to desegregation.

Satisfying the audience required a pro-busing stance. Satisfying the constituency required an anti-busing stance. White drove between the poles and manipulated the conflict so as to minimize his losses. He took no stand on busing: rather, he declared his support for "public safety." Thus he substituted a consensus-generating issue for a divisive one and avoided identification with either side of the real issue. All activities, policies, and directives that came from the mayor's office were placed under this broad heading of public safety. Thus, while the mayor's office coordinated all desegregation activities—sending out school assignments, scheduling bus routes, and setting up meetings with police, community leaders, and parents—White defined these as public safety measures, not desegregation activities.

By skillfully manipulating this conflict, White minimized his losses. While South Boston and parts of the black community were not satisfied with his handling of the busing controversy, their unhappiness did not constitute serious political setbacks for him. South Boston had not supported White in the 1967 or 1971 elections. And for the black community as well as for White's liberal audience, there was no alternative to Kevin White. Many observers of Boston city politics argued that a successful challenger to White would have to look very much like White himself.

The importance of issue redefinition in a conflict situation and White's skillful use of it is illuminated by Lindsay's opposite approach in New York. Caught, like White, in a tension between audience appeal and constituency demand, Lindsay chose to go all the way with his audience. He used the school issue as an extension of his conflict strategy, which centered on the race issue. Lindsay unfortunately miscalculated the extent of his support from the liberal Jewish and black alliance as well as the strength of the UFT. His push for decentralized school boards threatened the recently acquired policymaking powers of the UFT. The conflict was raised to a symbolic level when charges of racism and anti-Semitism were exchanged between the local school board in Ocean-Hill Brownsville and the UFT, which had a large Jewish membership. The racial and anti-Semitic overtones broke up the black-Jewish coalition that pre-dated Lindsay's administration.

Thus, Lindsay's handling of the school controversy, which attempted to use the underlying issue of race, resulted in an irreparable rupture of his support system. By contrast, White's redefinition of the issue deflected the divisiveness of the race issue and resulted, at worst, in a marginal loss of support.

White's strategy also contrasted with Moscone's actions in the craftworkers' strike. Moscone's strategy involved not acting, in line with the public's voting earlier to take power away from the mayor. Further, in the end, the city was not the victim of a large wage settlement. Despite these two factors, Moscone was criticized by the press and the public in large part because he had failed to convince the public that he was doing what they wanted. In Boston, most residents were strongly opposed to busing, a stand that White did not challenge. But White was not busing children; rather, he was "protecting their safety." When Alioto was giving high wages to workers, he was "keeping labor peace." Moscone's failure to redefine the issue denied him credit for a strike settlement that was costless to the taxpayer. In the era of Proposition 13, this might have garnered substantial political mileage. But it remained an unclaimed opportunity. As a component of conflict strategy, redefining issues is an important political skill that can be used to acquire power and minimize losses.

PART TWO

# The Formal Arena: Taking Charge

# FOUR

## Building an Infrastructure: Personnel Policies

> Infrastructure contributes to the increased mobility of resources in much the same way that transport systems contribute to greater efficiency of economic production.[1]

The type of infrastructure that an executive builds affects his or her ability to acquire resources, manage conflict, and implement policies. Hence, it is a key factor in establishing a climate for effective leadership. A more centralized infrastructure facilitates the executive's ability to pyramid resources, to minimize conflict, and to enforce administrative priorities.[2] Moreover, it reduces the costs to the executive of achieving these outcomes because achieving them becomes more certain:

> When benefits, sanctions, norms, or simply expectations are established with respect to a given pattern of political competition or exercise of authority, compliance may be achieved with the expenditure of fewer resources because political activity and attitudes can be more reliably predicted.[3]

Personnel policies are a major component in building an infrastructure. This chapter explores two different approaches to that process: one using centralized control, and the other using consolidated influence. In the first model, favored by White, the executive centralizes control over city government and then uses those resources to extend control to nongovernmental arenas. In the second model, followed by the San Francisco mayors, the executive attempts to pull power from the sides to the center. Powerful individuals are brought into the administration who then use their resources to pressure governmental actors. As Figure 7 indicates, the first model tends to be a more effective way of accumulating power. Having direct control over governmental resources, the executive approaches others from a relatively strong bargaining position. In the second model, however, the executive approaches others from a relatively weak position, which requires making concessions to gain cooperation. Furthermore, the process is continuous as the executive must still bargain with these other actors even after they are brought into the administration. This reciprocal influence is an impediment to centralizing control.

## FIGURE 7: Resource Acquisition Models

### 1. *Centralized control model*

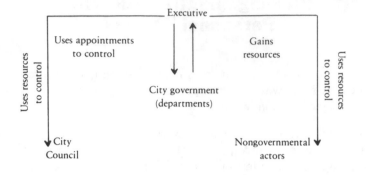

### 2. *Consolidated influence model*

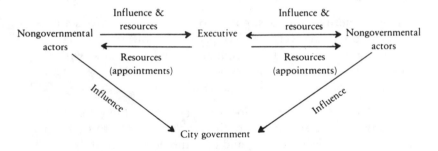

The consolidated influence model yields even more problems when the sides are fragmented (see Figure 8). The executive must then bargain with more groups, most of whom are weak, narrow in focus, and often in conflict with other groups. This situation hampered Moscone and Feinstein's use of the consolidated influence approach. By contrast, Alioto used the strategy when labor and business were strong enough to provide the basis for a coalitional politics. Of the San Francisco mayors, Alioto was the most successful in acquiring resources, implementing policy priorities, and managing conflict.

### KEVIN WHITE

In his administration, White used two different appointment strategies. In the early period, his emphasis was on audience and media politics.

FIGURE 8: Consolidated Influence Models

*1. Consolidated influence model (Alioto)*

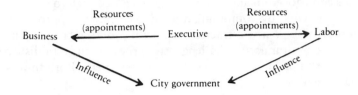

*2. Consolidated influence model (Moscone and Feinstein)*

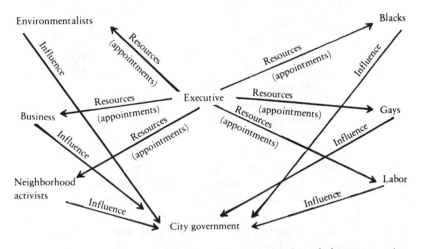

Many of his appointments during this time furthered the progressive, good government image that White successfully created for his entire administration. In the mid-1970s, White shifted his focus to constituency and organization politics. He then abandoned the good government appointment strategy and took a more political approach. A consistent and important theme throughout his administration, however, was centralizing control of key resources within city government.

## Audience and Media Politics: The "Good Government Wrapping"

Although most observers of the White administration refer to White in his early years as a "good government," progressive mayor, Alan Lupo was probably more accurate when he described White as a man who "walked a line between the charisma and goo-gooism of a Lindsay and

83

the dictatorship of a Daley."[4] White's early appointment strategy reveals the skill with which he walked that line. The appointments he made were a mixture of progressive and political types, but the administration's good government wrapping was bright enough to conceal the political contents. By combining a good government approach with political activity, White attracted the liberal endorsement, which was instrumental in eliminating challenges from the left, and established his control over important resources in city government. Both moves increased his power.

This dual approach was similar to the strategies employed by Daley in Chicago and Thomas D'Alesandro, Jr., in Baltimore. While both mayors governed with traditional partisan machines, they sought input from the business community, not only to appeal to business but also to create a good government image for their administrations. By contrast, Lindsay's almost complete reliance on reform strategies and liberal appeals often hindered his acquiring resources and was a weakness.

White's top aide in his first term and the man who came to symbolize the liberal and good government qualities of the administration was Barney Frank. Frank was working on his Ph.D. dissertation at Harvard when he was recruited to work for White's electoral campaign. Impressed by Frank's performance and his knowledge of people and politics, White appointed him his executive assistant when the campaign was over. Oral and written accounts—which described Frank as "a dynamo," "innovative," and "energetic"—identified him more than any other aide with the early administration.[5] Although Frank had a political background—he worked in other campaigns and his father was active in New Jersey machine politics—his activities in the White administration were instrumental in creating an image of a progressive and responsive mayorality.

Although Frank stood out in the list of early aides, he was not the only member of the White team to project the good government image. White's first BRA director, Hale Champion, was a Harvard academic with highly respected professional credentials and a former financial director for the state of California. Like Frank, Champion had political experience; he had worked for former California Governor Pat Brown. Robert Weinberg, who replaced Frank in the third year of White's first term, held an M.B.A. and J.D. from Harvard. Paul Parks, a black engineer and very active member of the NAACP, was appointed administrator of the Model Cities program. Reginald Eaves, also active in the black community and civil rights movement, was appointed executive director of the newly created Office of Human Rights in 1969. Richard Wall, White's first deputy mayor for fiscal affairs, was recruited from

Philadelphia where he had instituted PPBS, a budgetary system that received much favorable attention in the 1960s, especially from reformers applauding the application of modern management techniques to government. Another member of White's budget team, Jim Young, recruited in 1973, held an M.B.A. from Harvard and was described by respondents as "hard-working," "exceptionally bright," "dedicated," and "very professional."

Other top aides included Robert Kiley, who held a Ph.D. from Harvard in public administration. Kiley came to the White administration from Washington, D.C., where he had served as executive assistant to the CIA director, Richard Helms, and as associate director of the Police Foundation. Ira Jackson, White's administrative assistant from 1972 to 1975 and one of his speechwriters, was formerly Mayor Gibson's chief of state in Newark. Through a national search headed by Kiley, the administration brought in Robert DeGrazia as police commissioner to reform the police department. As we have seen, DeGrazia had served as police commissioner in St. Louis County and had achieved a national reputation as a professional and reformer.

Appointment of progressive, good government personnel was not limited to White's top aides. Several of his Little City Hall managers had academic backgrounds as well. Fred Salvucci in East Boston had an M.A. in transportation planning from MIT and Claudia Delmonico in the North End had a degree in government.

While recruiting good government types for the highly visible positions, White appointed non–good government types in less visible areas. In contrast to Lindsay's unsuccessful attempt to shake up bureaucracy with management experts, White relied on the old-boy network, bringing with him political reliables from the secretary of state's office to important positions in city government. Theodore Anzalone, assessing commissioner and important fundraiser; Joe Fallon, assistant assessing commissioner; Joe Twiss, special assistant to the mayor; and Ed Sullivan, deputy mayor, came from inside the system and had political rather than academic credentials.[6] Another important political appointment was Jimmy Kelly, who rose through the ranks to head White's political organization.

Anzalone, Sullivan, and Kelly remained for the entire administration. Anzalone was removed as assessing commissioner after a scandal in 1975 and given a job with the city-owned Hynes Auditorium. He remained crucial to White's political operation and his most important fundraiser. Ed Sullivan remained as White's deputy mayor, and Kelly became head of White's political organization.

The long tenures of Kelly, Sullivan, and Anzalone contrast with the much shorter tenures of the good government appointments. Jim Young, who remained with White from 1973 to 1980, was an exception to that group. The mode and mean duration for the earlier appointments was approximately three years.[7] In addition, most of these appointments were gone by 1975–1976 when White shifted from media and audience politics to organization and constituent politics.

White's more political appointments tended to be overshadowed by media attention given to the good government types. The following excerpts illustrate the nature of the media's coverage.

. . . the breadth of talent represented in White's Cabinet is unprecedented in Boston government and the meetings are a sign of fundamental change in the management of city business.[8]

After a long period of searching and interviewing, Mayor White has taken aboard a group of bright, young assistants to specialize in various fields of municipal concern.[9]

Even when journalists took cynical stabs at White, they still dwelt on those same administrative qualities. In his article, "Title, Title, Whose Got the Title . . . It's the Latest Thing," Robert Hanaan wrote:

Boston Mayor Kevin H. White has put together his new brain trust of bright young thirty-ish staff assistants. They are to help him chart an innovative course in municipal operations.[10]

While the media emphasized White's good government image, helping him to sew up liberal support, White was using his less visible political appointments to gain control over important resources in city government and increase his power. With Anzalone as the assessing commissioner, White had access to abatements and assessments which he used as rewards and sanctions to win votes, attract campaign contributions, and bargain with city councillors. When the Assessing Department increased the valuation for industrial and commercial properties (1973–1975), White maintained expenditure levels without raising the tax rate.[11] The latter was an important factor in attracting votes and, according to a former aide, was White's "biggest campaign asset."[12] Similarly, abatements were issued to important Boston property owners in exchange for substantial campaign contributions.

White's relationship with Councillor Fred Langone illustrates his use of the Assessing Department to deal with city councillors. The funeral parlor owned by Langone's brother was underassessed by the administration for several years. During this time White enjoyed a cordial relationship with Langone, who voted for his proposals in the city council and who mobilized electoral support for White in the Italian community. When the relationship deteriorated, Langone publicly attacked White and, in 1980, requested an investigation into expenditures at the Parkman House, used by the mayor for functions, dinners, meetings, and the like. Although the investigation came to naught, White retaliated by increasing the assessment and rent on the funeral parlor. (White could raise the rent because the property was owned by the BRA.)

Another component of White's political approach was the use of holdover appointments: not filling vacancies but keeping the old appointees on to serve at his pleasure. Although this tactic became more prominent in the later part of his administration, White used it as early as 1970 with the Board of Examiners.[13] By 1971, those boards that contained the greatest potential for extending the mayor's influence had holdovers; Boards of Examiners, Zoning, Real Property, and Redevelopment. Having appointments that serve at the pleasure of the mayor is a characteristic associated with the political boss or machine politicians, not the crusader or good government mayors. Nevertheless, White used this approach in important but less visible areas of city government.

Thus White displayed his good government side for the media and his liberal supporters, but he took a more political approach to take control of important resources within city government. His progressive stance was popular and helped divert attention from the more political side of his leadership.

## Professionals and Politics

Despite the success of the good government appointments in fostering the image of a progressive mayor, some appointments were problematic. The difficulties, however, were not insurmountable and, in retrospect, appear to have been outweighed by the gains.

In his analysis of national policymaking, Hugh Heclo suggested that the divergent incentives and constituencies of professionals and politicians (or elected officials) often lead to policy conflict and stalemate and a weakening of executive control.[14] These problems can arise at the local level as well when an administration is dominated by professionals who are not easily bought off (if bought off at all) by material incentives. We see this early in White's administration. By selecting people like DeGrazia, Kiley, and Weinberg from outside the city and state, White had no way to insure their loyalty. And, as professionals, these appointees had their own constituencies—other professionals in their field—which differed from White's. Finally, the reputations and high quality of many of White's early appointments made them independent of him in a way that a less qualified or more political appointee would not have been.

Many of White's early appointees were motivated by the sense of purpose associated with their reputations in their fields, with professionalism, and with the chance to experiment. One former aide commented, "The inducements to work for White in the early years included an exciting city and a dynamic mayor." Another former aide said, "You felt that you were part of an experiment that would make cities better, would help the poor."[15]

How does this incentive structure, which is more responsive to purposive rewards than to material ones, effect the executive's relationship with appointees? Heclo suggested that it results in policy conflict. White's experience with several BRA directors supports that assertion. His first director, Hale Champion, resigned after one year because of conflict over the Infill Housing program, favored by White and criticized by Champion.

White's relationship with Robert Kenney, two appointments later, was also stormy. Aside from personality differences, the two clashed on the Park Plaza project and its developer, Mortimer Zuckerman, who later became an important fundraiser for White. Kenney had design and architectural objections to the project and he did not get along with Zuckerman (see Chapter 8).[16] Zuckerman had complained to White about Kenney and recommended a replacement, Stewart Forbes. White appointed Forbes as Park Plaza project director and worked closely with him but their relationship soon deteriorated. Forbes perceived his role as supplying market and financial information to the mayor, which would then be combined with political considerations. According to Forbes, however, political considerations dominated the entire process.[17] Valuing his professional independence and concerned about his career, Forbes, like Champion, finally left.

Apolitical recruitment can also lead to competition and rivalry between the appointee and the executive—another obstacle to the executive's control. This characterized White's relationship with Police Commissioner DeGrazia. DeGrazia's reputation and his popularity in Boston, while important to the success of the reform policy, led to difficulties between himself and the mayor. As a professional with a national reputation, DeGrazia responded to an audience of his peers and was reluctant to take orders. Nor did he have to: White had given him absolute control over internal matters, which was necessary to implement the policy. The charismatic and independent DeGrazia projected a personality that was very attractive to the media. Their extensive coverage of him, including speculations that he would run for mayor, severely strained his relationship with White.

The difficulties between White and DeGrazia increased with time, but Kiley acted as an intermediary to cool things off. When Kiley left for Washington, White and DeGrazia's direct dealings became more frequent and their relations again deteriorated.

Toward the end of his first appointed term, DeGrazia asked White for a salary increase. With a divorce approaching, he needed the money. When White did not respond, DeGrazia began looking elsewhere for a higher salaried position and soon left for Maryland. As in BRA appointments after Walsh, DeGrazia was replaced with a less professional, more subservient figure who had come up through the ranks (Joe Jordan). This is similar to events in Chicago where a professional, recruited from outside the state, was given total control to reorganize the department, and was then replaced with a commissioner whom Daley could control.

Although these incidents support Heclo's observations about difficulties between professionals and politicians, they are not the whole story. The overall outcome of White's appointment strategy is marked by more benefits than difficulties. While DeGrazia caused problems for White, police reform efforts in Oakland, Chicago, Syracuse, and Highland Park—coupled with James Q. Wilson's conclusions on police behavior in general—strongly suggest that effective changes, especially in "watchman" style departments, require the recruitment of a professional from outside the system.[18] Thus, the type of appointment that White made was necessary to implement his policy. And this policy was well received by the public. The difficulties created by the BRA appointments were not insurmountable nor did they result in any policy alterations. The Infill Housing program foundered on public opposition, not Champion's criticism (see Chapter 3). Similarly, the Park Plaza project was not implemented at the time, but this was due to many factors, including the developer's eventual withdrawal (details in Chapter 8). Kenney was not one of the fatal problems. Thus, on balance, we can conclude that these particular appointments did not impede White's specific objectives and, in the case of police reform, the appointment was probably necessary to implement the policy. Moreover, they contributed to the good government image important to White's standing with opinion makers.

## Constituent and Organization Politics

By 1975 the liberal and good government approach was losing its political appeal. This phenomenon was part of a larger trend to the right in American politics. As cities began to experience fiscal difficulties, public approval of social welfare programs was replaced by a fiscal conservatism. In New York City, voters replaced the liberal, progressive, and costly Lindsay administration with the conservative and management-oriented Beame administration. The public's attitude on social issues was also moving to the right. The busing crisis in Boston, which was still going on intensely, drew a sharp cleavage between White's liberal audience and his conservative constituency. During this crisis, President Ford publicly announced his opposition to forced busing.

National attention to the Watergate crisis stimulated intensive investigative journalism at the urban level as well. In Boston in 1975, White's administration came under attack by the media. The charges concerned campaign contributions received by White in his 1970 gubernatorial race and the Assessing Department's alleged role in obtaining campaign contributions. These attacks helped to cut White's electoral margin, which was his smallest in all of his elections. Finally, and perhaps most important, White's liberal appeals failed to gain him the higher office that he sought.[19]

In response to these national and local currents, White switched strategies. The emphasis on audience and media politics was replaced by an emphasis on constituent and organization politics as White centralized his control over city government. This centralization gave White more control over policymaking, decreased the access of others to city government, increased his supply of patronage, and extended his influence in nongovernmental arenas. In short, as other audience-oriented mayors were unable to do, White built a political organization.

Earlier mayors like Lindsay in New York City and Cavanaugh in Detroit had failed to transcend the 1960s pattern of leadership and were overwhelmed by the obstacles inherent in it.[20] White's ability to adopt a new pattern is a testimony to his political acumen and was one of the major reasons for his survival and continued acquisition of power. Furthermore, White's success in light of others' failures suggests that his accomplishments were not easily attained.

## Appointments

White's appointment strategy played an integral part in his success. He decreased his emphasis on professionalism and outside recruitment and increased emphasis on political loyalty and control. Motivations changed from a sense of purpose to material rewards. The replacement of DeGrazia with a police commissioner who had come up through the ranks and whom White could control was repeated in many key areas of the administration. While White probably could not have used an up-through-the-ranks approach as a new mayor, he did not have to employ that approach when he had become an established mayor. Doing so was a political decision.

In addition to the different procedure, the individuals selected differed from the earlier appointments. Most did not have advanced academic degrees or professional reputations outside or even inside the city. White's appointment strategy was showing few good government characteristics. The media no longer referred to White's appointments as progressive or innovative. Other observers of the White administration—including city councillors, state representatives, and former aides—also felt that political considerations dominated the appointment process and that concerns for progressive government had been abandoned.

White also increased his use of holdover appointments. By not reappointing commissioners when their terms were up but keeping them on to serve at his pleasure, White acquired the power to release them at any time. This relationship gave White more control over his commissioners and department heads. By 1978, almost half of the 176 mayoral appointments were on holdover status.[21] And holdovers were most prominent on boards and commissions with the greatest potential for extending the mayor's influence: the Redevelopment Authority, the Building Department's Board of Appeals, the Board of Examiners, the Zoning Commission, the Industrial Development Commission. Thus, those people responsible for making decisions in areas that included or effected contracts, tax agreements, zoning regulations, permits, and jobs served "at the pleasure of the mayor."

By increasing the number of holdover appointments and shifting incentives from purposive to material rewards, White acquired more leverage over his appointments, which he used to broaden his control over the political resources of city government. Consequently, others had less access to these resources. City councillors, for example, could not go directly to department heads for patronage as they had done in the past. Rather, they were forced to go through the mayor's office, a process which was not without a price.

Through his control over department heads and other appointed officials, White was able to affect personnel practices within city government. The control he was able to exercise over job hirings and promotions, two things requiring the cooperation of department heads, gave White a supply of patronage that he used to build a political organization composed of city workers. Thus, his appointment strategy facilitated his shift from media and audience politics to organization and constituent politics.

## Building an Organization

White's political organization perhaps best illustrates his shift from media and audience politics to constituent and organization politics. In contrast to the Little City Halls, which reflected the good government strategy and liberal philosophy of the 1960s, White's organization was more political, more centralized, and more influential and powerful in the neighborhoods. These differences help to explain why White was more successful in acquiring resources than were his counterparts in other cities. The degree of control acquired by White through his organization was not matched by the vehicles used by the 1960s mayors, of which the Little City Halls were a good example.

According to former mayoral aides, White emerged from the 1975 election with the objective of combining his electoral and governing organizations.[22] He started making references to Daley and began reading, with extreme concentration, Frank Kent's book on ward organizations.[23] The mayor who once called the Kerner Report on the causes of violence in cities "required reading for every conscientious thoughtful citizen" was undergoing a transition—and not merely in his literary preferences.[24] Rather, White began rethinking his entire strategy. The following statement, taken from a 1979 interview with the mayor, points to the change that was occurring.

> The rule used to be that he who won had the right to govern. But since 1970, there's been an unstructured assault on the political profession's right to govern, to lead. Until we recapture a very diffuse political process, nobody can do anything! . . . When I'm faced with this kind of situation, you bet your life I'm going to pull together all the scraps of power I can assemble.[25]

White's activities in 1975 represent a major and, more important, a successful attempt to "pull together all the scraps of power" that he could assemble. Operating in a nonpartisan system, White began building a political organization as an alternative to the traditional mechanism for centralizing authority—the political party. The organization was instrumental in resolving citizen complaints, collecting information, and extending mayoral control in the neighborhoods. The experience and influence that the organization acquired made it an effective device for mobilizing electoral and nonelectoral support.

After the 1975 election White set up a committee of five aides to devise ways to maintain the electoral machinery in nonelectoral times. In conjunction with the ward coordinators for the 1975 mayoral election, the committee evaluated the performance of all campaign workers and asked those who received high ratings to become precinct captains and organization workers.[26] As incentives, they were offered jobs and promotions, a chance to further the administration's political security and so their own, and community status—the prestige of being a precinct captain.

One of the functions of the organization was to identify and respond to complaints in the neighborhoods, as did the earlier LCH program. A major difference, however, was that the organization was composed of neighborhood residents. The earlier attempt to give the LCHs an administrative image by recruiting managers from outside the neighborhoods was not repeated. The organization now was expressly political. Each precinct worker was responsible for a designated thirty-five voters in the neighborhood. During elections this meant getting out the vote and, in nonelectoral times, resolving complaints.

Precinct workers also polled voters on their attitudes toward the administration, city services, and policies. Their efforts were supplemented by in-depth research. All this was recorded in computer printouts of voter preferences, attitudes, and complaints, along with information on organization workers' performance. This degree of organization contrasts sharply with the LCHs, which were primarily crisis management operations: most complaints came in and were handled on an ad hoc basis.[27] Many LCH managers had difficulty breaking through the barriers of bureaucracy, a problem not reported by any of the precinct captains or ward coordinators.[28]

The attempt to introduce more stability extended to the holding of weekly precinct meetings, which had not been conducted under the LCH program. The weekly meetings also increased the organization's power in the neighborhoods. In various parts of the city, White's political organization even took over civic associations and community groups that opposed the administration. When the Brighton Civic As-

93

sociation held board elections in 1980, approximately 300 city workers flooded the meeting and elected people who represented the administration. Similar events occured in East Boston, Hyde Park, and Charlestown.[29]

Recruitment of that many people was never attempted under the LCH program. Such recruitment was possible, however, because the organization was composed of city workers who were very responsive to material rewards. The use of promotions by department supervisors was a successful recruiting strategy. Although no one knew how many promotions were actually granted, city workers had a very strong perception of the possibility. This was perhaps one of the most important results of White's political organization; the ability to influence the behavior of people in a given arena by structuring their perceptions.

In his analysis of mayoral leadership, Charles Levine presented a similar theme—the relationship between a mayor's capacity to structure the "expectations and predisposition for compliance and cooperation" of other persons and the ability to generate support for, and secure implementation of, future projects.[30] The following example illustrates White's skills in enforcing administrative priorities and decreasing the impact of opposition. When B'Nai Brith wanted to construct a housing development for the elderly in Brighton, community residents opposed it because they felt the area was already overburdened with elderly housing. The opposition was overruled, however, when the ward coordinator got his organization to vote in favor of the project, which was built. Although the people in the organization were members of the administration, they were also residents of the area. The mayor could always claim, with perfect accuracy, that the "residents" voted for the project.

The organization was also important as a campaign vehicle, which White used to protect his resources in nonelectoral issues. When in 1974 the court ordered all property in Massachusetts to be revaluated at 100 percent of full market value, a state referendum was scheduled. Included on the referendum was a classification amendment that would establish different assessing rates for commercial and residential properties. Passage of this amendment was critical to White because discretionary assessment practices were a valuable resource. The White administration put on an intensive organizing drive within city government. Department heads spent several hours each day identifying city workers who would be the most effective in neighborhood campaigns.[31] Approximately a thousand city workers were recruited and the campaign was very successful; the referendum passed, with the Boston vote higher than the statewide vote.

The campaign also helped to identify Kevin White supporters, an important factor in preparing for the 1979 mayoral election. In fact, it was widely suggested that the classification campaign was a dry run for the upcoming election. Organization heads evaluated the performances of the campaign workers to decide who would work in the mayoral campaign and in what capacity.[32]

The organizational component of the 1979 Boston campaign resembled, in many ways, elections in Chicago under Daley. Precinct workers identified White supporters and got them to the polls. They also identified neutral voters and those opposed to White and won their favor with services like fixing potholes or cutting down trees.[33]

The municipal presence was especially evident in South Boston where the administration repaired buildings, planted trees, and handled individual problems. The patronage dispensed by organization workers helped to co-opt and neutralize opposition. The result was White's first South Boston electoral victory.

While the 1979 campaign was similar to ones under Daley, there was an important distinction. Daley's was a party organization and White's was a personal organization. One of the most serious limitations of the Boston organization was that it was nontransferable. White's people were personally loyal to White. When White tried to transfer this support to other candidates, he was not successful. The organization failed to re-elect incumbents or to elect their own candidates to the state legislature or city council.

White's experience coincides with James MacGregor Burns's analysis of leaders such as Vargas in Brazil, Peron in Argentina, and Martin Luther King: inability to transfer loyalties may be a dilemma of personal organizations in general.[34] While this is an important limitation, White was nevertheless successful in creating an alternative to a political machine in a nonpartisan city. His shift from media and audience politics to organization and constituent politics and introduction of material incentives enabled him to solidify his informal influence into a quasi-institutional structure. The strategy of organization politics was a sharp departure from the 1960s pattern of mayoral leadership, which shunned politics and took an administrative or apolitical approach. White's success in shifting arenas and strategies explains why Boston's crusading mayor of the 1960s was still mayor in 1983 when his counterparts from the 1960s were not.

## SAN FRANCISCO

The importance of manipulative skills in politics becomes even more apparent when we look at the experience of the San Francisco mayors, whose appointment strategies and results both differed from White's. On Levine's index of manipulative capability, the San Francisco mayors score much lower on the key variables: mobilization, integration and centralization of resources, and decision-making power.[35] Consequently, their personnel policies did not establish the conditions necessary for building a viable structure of power. Thus, they had to expend more resources than did White to maintain support and some measure of influence.

Comparing the different mayoral strategies highlights the interplay between structural and cultural variables and the executive's ability to exercise effective leadership. San Francisco's political structure is more fragmented and parts of it more independent than Boston's. The city assessor, a critical appointment for White, was an elected official in San Francisco. The San Francisco controller, who prepares the budget, had lifetime tenure. The CAO, who controlled approximately a third of the city's work force and budget including the important Public Works Department, had a lifetime appointment before 1975 and a ten-year term after. Finally, commissioners could be removed only with great difficulty, resulting in a relatively autonomous commission system. The dominant-subordinate relationship between White and his appointees was not found in San Francisco. The political system there featured potential centers of power that offered obstacles to mayoral leadership. These aspects of the political structure were reinforced by the political culture. San Francisco's strong reform ethos held that government should be a product of administration, not politics.[36] The behind-the-scenes politicking of Mayor White, which was tolerated in Boston because of the more traditional political orientation of the electorate, was not tolerated in the reform culture of San Francisco.

All this meant that a mayor seeking power in San Francisco needed to find alternative mechanisms. Mayors there can and have exerted influence over city government, but it has been through more indirect means of bargaining, persuasion, and lobbying. Nevertheless, several useful comparisons can be made between the appointment strategies in the two cities.

First, the strategies employed by the San Francisco mayors required a larger expenditure of resources than White made. Second, the expenditures did not buy as much power as White acquired. Third, all of the San Francisco mayors attempted to pull power from the sides to the center; Alioto worked through coalitional politics, Moscone through liberal and constituent politics, Feinstein through a politics of accommodation. Of the San Francisco mayors, Alioto was the most successful with this strategy. Analyzing his relative success will highlight the important changes in San Francisco city politics that influence the potential for mayoral leadership there.

## JOE ALIOTO: COALITION POLITICS

Alioto's appointment strategy, like his electoral strategy, was based on a coalition of labor, key financial figures, and minorities—especially blacks and Hispanics. Alioto used his formal appointment powers to bring this coalition into city government, thereby shaping the access to decisionmakers and establishing an informal lobbying force within city government. This was important in San Francisco's highly fragmented political system, since mayors often had to lobby their own commissioners. Drawing his minority appointments from the more conservative segments of their communities, Alioto was able to manipulate the leadership there and deflect opposition. In contrast to White, Alioto did not achieve a high degree of centralization; rather, he acquired influence. His attempt to bring informal pressure from the sides to the center was successful to the extent that labor and business, two of the most powerful groups in San Francisco city politics at the time, were able to influence other civic actors and decision makers. But their power and Alioto's dependence on them made this a more costly strategy than White's. Not having centralized his control over the decision-making points within city government as White did, Alioto continually had to expend resources by means of appointments, wages, contracts, lobbying efforts, and the like to sustain the power of his coalition from which he drew his influence. Alioto relied heavily, for example, on favorable wage contracts to labor to increase their power. When public sentiment and the media turned against labor, these contracts were severely criticized. In the end, this expenditure of resources blew Alioto's support system wide open.

### Labor and Business

Alioto gave labor disproportionate representation in city government, supplementing their private power with public authority. By pyramiding labor's power, Alioto strengthened that component of his coalition and, hence, his own influence. Harry Bridges, the influential ILWU leader, was appointed to the Port Commission; Joe Mazola, head of the Plumbers Union, was appointed to the Airport Commission; Bob Costello from the Plumbers Union was appointed to the Civil Service

Commission; Hector Raueda, business manager for the Elevator Construction Union, was appointed to the Planning Commission; labor representatives were appointed to the housing and redevelopment agencies and the Fire Commission. In addition, David Jenkins, Bridges's political representative in the ILWU and an influential member of the labor community in San Francisco, was awarded a contract as a consultant to the SFRA.

A smaller but equally important number of Alioto's appointments went to key financial interests in the city. Walter Newman, who married into the wealthy and established Magnin family, was appointed to the Planning Commission.[37] William Coblentz, a prominent attorney who had connections with key financial figures, was appointed to the Airport Commission. John Ritchie, owner of a real estate company, was appointed to the Planning Commission.

This component of Alioto's appointment strategy indicates the economic, structural, and cultural differences between the two cities: White's early focus was on neighborhoods, not business. Historically, business played a stronger, better organized, and more influential role in San Francisco city politics than in Boston (see Chapter 2). As we have seen, nonpartisan political systems heighten business importance because of the expense involved in conducting campaigns. Boston politicians value business contributions as well, but San Francisco had the added factor of a strong reform ethos that inflated the influence of business people because of the legitimacy they enjoyed as "civic leaders." This prestige is found in private-regarding political cultures as well but, as we have noted before, it assumes greater importance in more reformed cities.[38] Businessmen were overrepresented on the boards and commissions before Alioto, for example.[39] Finally, Alioto was a pro-development mayor who advocated building up the downtown financial area and furthering commercial interests and tourist industries. By appointing people with key financial interests in the city, Alioto placed individuals on boards and commissions who shared his policy orientation.

The importance of guarding the access points to city government by appointing powerful civic actors with similar policy preferences can be seen in the case of the airport expansion, a controversial issue before, during, and after Alioto's administration. Having labor representatives and business people on the Airport Commission created support for the proposal; adoption of the policy was in the interests of labor and business. Had the composition of the commission been different, it might have rejected the proposal. Moscone's Airport Commission, for example, contained mostly Alioto appointments. When Moscone attempted to stop the expansion, the commissioners resisted his efforts and maintained their original position. By contrast, White's priorities were usually carried out by his appointments because of the control he exercised over them. The San Francisco mayors had little political control over others in city government; therefore, it was important that they appoint people who shared their policy orientation.

The airport expansion case also shows how the composition of the commission determined who would have access to city government. According to opponents of the proposal, groups like San Franciscans for Reasonable Growth that were against the expansion had no influence with the commissioners.[40]

Representing organized interests with money and numbers, the commissioners were also a resource for influencing others. In this case, they lobbied the Board of Supervisors and aided substantially in the bond issue campaign. Both efforts were successful, with the board voting favorably and the voters passing the bond.

The existence of a lobbying force enabled Alioto to influence nongovernmental forces as well. With the support of the Airport Commission, which controlled things like permits, Alioto and his aides persuaded United Airlines and Pan American to institute affirmative action programs at the airport.[41]

### Minorities

By appointing members of minority groups, Alioto gained favorable media attention, which furthered his ambitions for higher office, satisfied labor's requests for minority representation, and helped to co-opt and defeat opposition in the minority communities.

Opening city government to minorities enhanced Alioto's image as an activist and innovative mayor. Like White, Alioto was aided by relativism: he represented an attractive change from the previous regime. San Francisco's commission system had been dominated by business interests. Alioto broke with this trend by appointing the first black to the police commission and the first black to a cabinet position—the deputy for social programs. He also appointed blacks to BART, the Airport Commission, and the Fire Commission.

The ILWU, primarily black, and Local 261, primarily Hispanic, pressured Alioto to hire minorities.[42] Several of Alioto's minority appointments, in fact, came from these unions: the president of Local 261 was appointed to the Housing Authority, ILWU members were appointed to the Redevelopment Agency (SFRA), and the first two Hispanics ever to be appointed to the Board of Supervisors and the Board of

Education were both from MAPA, the Hispanic political organization closely affiliated with Local 261.

Through his recruitment practices, Alioto co-opted the more conservative leadership in minority communities. By strengthening this leadership, Alioto deflected some of the more militant opposition, a strategy similar to Daley's in Chicago. Both mayors used their resources to handpick and reinforce the leadership in the black community so that it could buffer any opposition there.[43]

The effective application of this strategy can be seen in the Western Addition II project, an urban renewal program in a black neighborhood that was stalled by opposition when Alioto entered office. The earlier Western Addition I project, in an adjacent area, had resulted in severe housing and population losses. Seeking to avoid a repetition, residents in the Project II area staged demonstrations. They were joined in their opposition by sympathetic students from Berkeley and white liberals.

The project also generated objections to the Redevelopment Agency. The SFRA resembled a blue ribbon panel, with its composition weighted heavily in favor of San Francisco's elite. Alioto himself, a member of an established San Francisco family and a multimillionaire attorney, had served as agency chairman from 1955 to 1958.

Through the ILWU, Alioto introduced symbolic reforms which met much of the residents' opposition without substantially altering the projects. The ILWU sponsored a housing project in the area and so had an interest there. As a predominantly black union, it had more credibility in the black community than the SFRA, which had an elitist reputation. Alioto used the ILWU's connection with the black community, especially the churches, to mobilize support within the community. In addition, Alioto began to change the SFRA by appointing blacks affiliated with the ILWU and by hiring blacks within the agency. Before he was through, the agency that had had almost no blacks was 60 percent black and had changed its image from an exclusionary body to a representative one.[44] Through the efforts of the ILWU and Alioto's minority recruitments, most of the opposition within the area was silenced. The pickets that had surrounded the Martin Luther King Square in the Western Addition when Alioto entered office were no longer there. The SFRA, after a brief interruption, resumed operation on Project II according to the original plans.

The role played by the ILWU in endorsing and working with the SFRA was crucial. As a black union, they were the best equipped to allay the fears of the black community. They also were helpful in silencing the external opposition from liberal sympathizers. With a black union defending the merits of a program in a black community, it was difficult for nonblacks to argue that the program was not in the interests of the residents. The ILWU's support helped to discredit objectors, who were dismissed as "radicals" or "obstructionists." The fact that the program was still displacing people was also obscured by the ILWU. With their members moving into its housing project in the area, it did not appear that "blacks" were moving out. Of course it was never mentioned that ILWU members were in the top one-half of 1 percent of their racial category in earnings.[45] Thus, poorer blacks were still being displaced. The St. Francis Square project sponsored by the ILWU, for example, consisted of 299 moderately priced cooperative units, not low income. And, in the entire Western Addition I project, 1,199 units out of 1,853 were regular market private units. Thus, only 35 percent of the total were federally subsidized. As in other cities, urban renewal altered the commercial/residential balance. In the Western Addition I project, there was a 33 percent decrease in residential property. As a consequence, population in the area declined from 6,112 residents to 4,200.[46]

Through the support of the ILWU, the addition of blacks to the SFRA, and the endorsement of the program by the black community leaders (especially ministers), Alioto was able to deflect objections and continue the project. The coalitional strategy used by Alioto with the Board of Supervisors and other forces within and outside of city government was effective in overcoming opposition in the minority communities. But sustaining the coalition required expenditures of resources, one of which was very costly.

## Problems in the Strategy: The Price of Labor

In addition to appointments, Alioto strengthened his ties with labor through favorable wage settlements. For most of his administration, this was an effective strategy. But during his second term, public discontent toward city workers and their wages began to increase. This dissatisfaction was not unique to San Francisco. In many cities, the public, encouraged by the media, blamed fiscal difficulties on the wages and benefits of public sector employees. In San Francisco, discontent was probably exacerbated by the number of strikes, which served as constant reminders to the public. In addition, the media was going on about the "large salaries" of city workers. Like White in his second term, Alioto was faced with a shifting public mood. But Alioto had less flexibility than White. The control that White had acquired in the formal arena of city government did not hinge on his public positions or image. In fact, his change of appeal from audience to constituency enabled him to acquire more power. By contrast, Alioto had acquired influence rather than control. Maintaining his influence largely depended on keeping the favor of labor, which he did in large part by supporting good wages. Thus, maintaining his coalition required him to take actions that lost him public support and decreased labor's influence in the city. His strategy culminated in a confrontation with the police and fire fighters that brought an end to labor's special position in city politics.

Toward the end of Alioto's second term in office, the contracts of city clerks and professionals, craftworkers, and police and fire fighters were up for renewal. Going according to the formulas, which were based on average wages for comparable job categories in public settings, the Board of Supervisors granted the first two groups the percentage of increase suggested by the formula. These agreements were reached in March and July and received considerable flack from the media and the public for what were perceived to be high raises. Responding to public pressure—it was an election year—the supervisors took a firm stand with the police and firefighters when their contracts expired in August. They ignored the increase called for in the formula (13 percent) and offered the unions half. The unions rejected this offer and went out on strike. After several days of unsuccessfully lobbying the board to change its position, Alioto assumed emergency power and unilaterally granted the two unions the 13 percent, thereby ending the strike. The public was outraged and gave overwhelming support to Proposition N, which sharply limited the mayor's use of emergency powers, splitting jurisdiction between the mayor and the board.[47] Anti-union legislation followed that provided for firing striking workers, which was also passed by the public. Thus Alioto's attempt to pursue his same strategy and appease labor in the short run dealt a serious blow to labor in the long run.

It is difficult to draw complete conclusions from the event as Alioto was not permitted by law to seek re-election. It could be argued that, if he could have run again, he would have handled the strike differently. This is plausible but it does make his strategy less weak. Not having centralized his control, Alioto had to constantly expend resources to maintain his coalition, his substitute for centralized power. The change in the public's mood, to which Alioto contributed by giving out high wage settlements, strained those resources. Furthermore, it damaged the influence of his coalition. Given these two factors, it is difficult to imagine that Alioto would have maintained his former influence in a third term. His strategy of pulling power from the sides to the center could only work if the sides were sufficiently powerful. By 1974, the sides were breaking down.

## Pressure Politics Is Not Party Politics

Alioto's experience is particularly significant because it highlights a central dilemma in American politics in general; the inadequacies of pressure politics as a substitute for party politics. Schattschneider has suggested that the "pressure system makes sense only as the political instrument of a segment of the community. It gets results by being selective and biased."[48] Alioto and his labor companions were well aware of the latter point, but their behavior suggests that they ignored the former. By granting labor disproportionate influence, Alioto protected this segment, but only temporarily.

In contrast to a party, which has an institutional base and organizational interests broader than those of any of its members, Alioto's coalition did not have an institutional base and its interests were identical with those of its members. When the membership declined and public tolerance for labor gains plummeted, the coalition could not sustain itself; it had no broader concerns to appeal to. In serving the interests of its members, Alioto's coalition remained a special interest group, failing to enlist a wider membership that could have buttressed the effect of a weakening of one of its members.

The lack of an institutional base also made Alioto more vulnerable to the demands of powerful members of the coalition. His settlement of the police and firefighters strike was largely a response to pressure from key figures in the hotel industry and labor movement. Thus, even though public sentiment had already turned against labor, Alioto moved to protect the short term interests of labor and of the hotel interests. Had there been a party organization, Alioto would have been more insulated from individual constituents. And, organizational maintenance needs would have encouraged a compromise for the long term goal of party unity. In his analysis of pressure politics and party politics, Schattschneider suggested that the pressure system cannot substitute for the party system.[49] Alioto and labor attempted to make that substitution and had temporary success, but in the end, they failed.

## GEORGE MOSCONE: LIBERAL AND CONSTITUENT POLITICS

Like Alioto, Moscone operated in a system with several potential centers of power. Through his appointments and actions, Moscone attempted to influence that system. His appointment strategy, which contained elements of Alioto's and White's, had very limited success. His promise to open up the commission system was similar to Alioto's and White's attempts to broaden representation within city government and so to appeal to liberal elements. Moscone's efforts also resembled Alioto's use of certain groups within the electorate to influence city government. But Moscone's appointments created difficulties that Alioto and White did not encounter. Further, important changes in San Francisco's political system presented the mayor with major obstacles to acquiring resources.

## Executive Leadership and the New Politics

In comparing Moscone's strategy with Alioto's, the most significant difference is that the sides of the political structure had become more fragmented. The analysis of the two experiences has broad implications, because the changes in San Francisco's political climate reflected many of the larger changes in American politics in general. The decline of political parties at the national level, for example, forced executives to become more issue-oriented in order to appeal to the electorate. Consequently, they lost a good deal of insulation and flexibility.[50] Moreover, the decline of political parties removed a crucial mechanism for centralizing influence. Jimmy Carter's rhetoric about going directly to the people, while appealing to populist sentiments, was more importantly a recognition of the absence of other vehicles through which to mobilize support.

In San Francisco, unions had approximated some of the functions of political parties: recruitment of candidates, campaigning, deflecting minor issues by taking broader positions. Thus, they helped significantly to bring manageability to a nonpartisan system. In the mid-1970s when the electorate began to splinter, however, this mobilizing and stabilizing force was on the decline. The political scene in the city was very different after 1975.

The splintering of the electorate might have been slowed by a ward system, which at least could have accommodated the increasing ethnic diversity and minimized the amount of citywide conflict for the executive. Such party-based machines contributed stability to Chicago under Daley, Baltimore under Schaefer and D'Alesandro, Sr., and Albany under Corning. Even a personal, patronage-based organization like that of White or Curley in Boston might have served. But in San Francisco, there were no mechanisms capable of localizing conflict.

Rather, the administration assembled by Moscone included many groups that were narrow in focus, issue-oriented in the extreme, and, often, in conflict with one another. Moscone's police reform policy showed the difficulty of satisfying such a fragmented constituency—it pleased the gay community, angered the black community, and agitated the media (see Chapter 3). Where Alioto had managed a coalition, Moscone was buffeted by pressure groups—none of them as effective on behalf of the mayor or itself as labor had been for Alioto. Both mayors had to expend far more in political resources than did White in Boston, but Alioto got something in return whereas Moscone got very little.

By opening up the commission system to new groups, Moscone eliminated challenges from the Left by strengthening his liberal image and co-opting groups that could have opposed him. White's similar strategy allowed him to move in new directions; Moscone's increased the demands on the mayor's office. Where most of White's early liberal appointments came from outside Boston city politics and therefore had no internal constituency, Moscone's appointments were drawn overwhelmingly from within San Francisco city politics and were very responsive to constituent demands. Indeed, the groups represented by Moscone's appointments, as well as the appointees themselves, had become highly politicized and active. The I-Hotel case illustrated the important relationship between the composition of city government and the scope and arena of issues (see Chapter 3).

The demands on the mayor's office by these groups who were now represented in city government, led to a form of "reactive policymaking."[51] Like Lindsay, Moscone often confronted issues or conflicts when he lacked the resources necessary to influence the results. Starting with weak or limited resources, Moscone found involvement in these conflicts to be an obstacle to acquiring additional resources. Where White accumulated resources through his strategy and Alioto acquired resources, Moscone experienced a constant drain of resources. And the expenditure tended to be in areas that yielded little in return. Thus, even when he was successful in a specific action, he did not increase his political capital or control.

## The Changing of the Guard

The most noticeable features of Moscone's administration were the decrease in the representation of labor and the appointment of gays, neighborhood activists, and environmentalists to city commissions.

The representation enjoyed by labor under Alioto did not last under Moscone or Feinstein. A good illustration of the changing relationship between labor and the mayor's office was the Joe Mazola incident. This case, while not an ordinary one, was noteworthy because it showed the independence of the commission system, a commissioner's propensity to serve the group he represented rather than the city, and Moscone's hard line response. Most important, it points to a major problem for the reactive mayor—the inability to pyramid resources.

Joe Mazola, head of the Plumber's Union, was an airport commissioner appointed by Alioto and retained by Moscone. During the craftworkers strike, some of the airport facilities (such as toilets) had been sabotaged and Mazola was widely believed to have engineered the incident. When Mazola refused Moscone's order to repair the facilities, Moscone initiated hearings against him and demanded his removal. The hearings, which took place before the Board of Supervisors and which were televised nightly on KQED, resulted in Mazola's removal.

It is hard to imagine such an incident of sabotage occurring under Alioto. If it had, however, it is harder to imagine Alioto publicly pursuing a union head. In many ways, the Mazola episode symbolized the end of the cozy relationship between the mayor's office and labor that characterized the Alioto administration. Coming shortly after labor's first major defeat in the craftworkers strike (see Chapter 3), the incident also demonstrated labor's declining influence in San Francisco city politics. An ILWU representative claimed that Moscone did not lose labor support because of his actions and implied that Mazola's activities were "uncalled for."[52] It seems likely that labor did not balk at Moscone's actions because they recognized their loss of popularity and especially Mazola's. In other words, they were feeling the limits of their power, and the limits were much smaller than when Alioto was mayor.

Although Moscone was successful in removing Mazola, the action did not increase his control over the Airport Commission. He was unable to persuade the commissioners to reverse their original position on airport expansion. The commissioners decided and Moscone eventually accepted their decision. By contrast, White overcame internal opposition to the Park Plaza project through his control over his appointments. But San Francisco's political structure provides less opportunity for a mayor to acquire such direct control. Alioto was very skillful and yet did not achieve the direct control that White did. Nevertheless, Alioto acquired valuable resources. But the changes in San Francisco's political system in 1975 placed more limitations on the mayor's ability to acquire power. Exacerbating these difficulties was Moscone's approach; rather than initiate or structure a situation, he would wait and react to events. As Yates suggested, one of the dilemmas of the reactive mayor is his difficulty in acquiring resources and power.[53]

## The Dilemmas of a Fragmented Administration

The appointments made by Moscone acknowledged the increasing fragmentation of the electorate. Moscone's promise to "open up the commission system" meant accommodating a wider variety of interests than Alioto had dealt with. But a fragmented and issue-oriented administration creates problems for the executive when it leads to conflict between competing interests or when it increases the demands on the mayor's office. Moscone's administration faced both these problems.

One segment of the electorate that was not politically important when Alioto was mayor was the gay community. In fact, Alioto's approach to the gay community was one of benign neglect: "I'll leave you alone, if you leave me alone."[54] By contrast, Moscone had strong support in the gay community and gave it representation in city government. The appointment of Harvey Milk, the most important political leader in the gay community and the first gay appointee to the Board of Permit Appeals, marked the recognition of the gay community as a political force and the opening up of city government to the gay community. Further, it was a meaningful appointment because of the department's power to issue permits to bars. Bars have been, and continue to be, the major thread in the social fabric of the gay community. Thus, the appointment was symbolic as well as functional.

Moscone found that attempts to appeal to one minority were not necessarily well received by other minorities. We have already seen that the black community reacted negatively to a reform police chief who improved relations with the gay section of the city. In another case, Moscone's lobbying efforts with the Board of Supervisors to elect Gordon Lau, a liberal Chinese board member, as board president, were thwarted by Ella Hill Hutch, a conservative and influential black leader. Hutch and her constituents opposed the selection because they viewed Asians as competing for scarce pieces of a shrinking pie.[55] This was a significant defeat for the mayor, becauase the board president makes committee assignments and the committees often blocked Moscone's proposals.

A fragmented constituency with broad access to city government increased the number of demands on the mayor's office. One notable problem was presented by the Officers for Justice (OFJ) suit, which illustrates the difficulties of dealing with such demands in the absence of strong resources. A significant aspect of the OFJ case was the ability of fifteen police officers to bring up an issue, expand its scope, and sustain it as a major conflict for almost six years.

The Officers for Justice case began in 1972 when several black officers complained to the Police Officers Association (POA) that the department's promotion practices discriminated against blacks. At the time there were seventeen blacks on the force. Dissatisfied with the POA's handling of the issue, 13 black officers and 2 white officers formed a group called the Officers for Justice.[56] The police investigators unit, many of whom also felt inadequately represented by the POA, simultaneously formed their own association—the Supervisors and Investigators Association (SIA), which consisted of 140 members.

At the police commissioner's request, these three groups (POA, OFJ, SIA) established a committee and designed a reorganization plan. The OFJ objected, however, because only two of their members were on the sixteen-member committee. The police commissioner then asked each group to come up with a plan. Meanwhile, the police department and the police union successfully campaigned for Proposition E, which restricted promotions to chief and deputy chief to civil service captains. Since no blacks were civil service captains, the proposition barred blacks from receiving these promotions. The OFJ, with the aid of Public Advocate attorneys, sued the department for discrimination in 1973 and requested a quota system for minority hirings and promotions. Shortly after, the U.S. Department of Justice began investigating the charges and the city admitted that discriminations existed. In 1974, the federal court placed a ban on hiring and promotions, requiring the department to establish hiring and promotion formulas for minorities and women.

Although the city was party to the suit, the mayor's office was not actively involved in the controversy until Moscone joined the side of the OFJ. His decision appears to have been an attempt, first, to mend his fences with black leaders who were angry over Police Chief Gain's dismantling of the community relations units (see Chapter 3), and second, to satisfy his minority constituency.[57]

The conflict became complicated as the participants increased to include the OFJ, the Police Department, the POA, the Civil Service Commission, the city attorney, Public Advocates, the U.S. Department of Justice, the Board of Supervisors, and the mayor's office. Many were at cross purposes. The Police Department and the POA had a vested interest in protecting the status quo, since it benefited the largest number of their constituents. In addition, both had been alienated by Moscone's appointment of Gain. The POA president also was up for re-election that year, placing him in a precarious position. While the freeze on promotions was not well received by his union, the establishment of a quota system for minorities was very unpopular with the almost all white union. Instead of quotas, the POA proposed goals. On the other side were the Public Advocates, the city attorney, the OFJ, and Moscone, all of whom had large minority support and who were being watched by their supporters. Nor was Moscone risking loss of police support, since the police already opposed him and were among the first to sign the recall petition initiated by Barbagelata in 1976 to recall all elected officials in 1978 and force them to run again (it was defeated in a referendum in 1977). In the middle were the supervisors who would have to ratify any settlement and who were under extreme pressure from the POA and the Civil Service Commission to vote for the POA's proposal. The Civil Service Commission, which was more assertive than previous ones had been, became involved when it was named as a party to the suit.[58]

The mayor, the Public Advocates, and the U.S. attorneys submitted a proposal that called for quotas and damage payments to the officers named in the suit. The board passed it, but the Civil Service Commission and the POA successfully lobbied the board to rescind its original vote. Negotiations resumed and the board scheduled another date for a second vote, but Moscone was assassinated before it was held. The case was finally resolved during Feinstein's administration with the adoption of the settlement proposed by the POA and the Civil Service Commission.

The OFJ case is important for showing the obstacles to executive leadership in the absence of resources. Even when Moscone was able to persuade the board to approve his proposal, it was defeated when others successfully exerted counterpressure on the board. Moscone's appointment strategy increased the demands on the mayor's office without providing the mechanisms necessary for dealing with them. He was reduced to a form of reactive policymaking, which further strained his resources and limited his ability to implement his own policy agenda. Moscone's relations with the Planning Commission provide a good illustration of this dilemma.

### Reactive Policymaking: The Planning Commission

By the mid-1970s, the Planning Commission had become a major factor in the city's political system. Their formal powers of approving building applications and issuing permits and zoning regulations, combined with the increased conflicts between pro-development advocates and neighborhood groups, made the Planning Commission a major target of lobbying efforts by both sides in conflicts. Moscone's appointments to the commission attempted to influence the policymaking process and thus accommodate his neighborhood constituents. Four of the five commissioners appointed by him were politically active in the neighborhoods and the fifth represented downtown interests.[59] Despite these appointments, the commission approved more high-rise applications under Moscone than it had under Alioto.[60]

Examining the activities of the Planning Commission in light of this discrepancy is illustrative. First, it points to the importance of image as a resource. The commission's liberal and neighborhood image allowed it to pursue a policy of incrementalism that involved concessions to the neighborhoods and to the pro-development advocates. Second, the process of granting the concessions reflects the larger theme of reactive policymaking. The commission, like Moscone's entire administration, was the target of many issue-oriented groups that constantly demanded concessions. Third, Moscone's appointments here again reveal the difficulties of acquiring power in a weak and fragmented political system. This part of his appointment strategy was the most effective, but it did not increase his power.

The Planning Commission's primary activities revolved around zoning, preservation, and high-rise development issues. One of the first actions of the Planning Department was a complete downzoning of all the neighborhoods to their existing densities, which was a major achievement in the anti–high-rise struggle. The remaining efforts, however, fall into the category of partial successes through compromise. Thus, although there were more high rises constructed during the Moscone administration and no applications rejected, the Planning Commission was able to exact design concessions from developers.[61] By delaying approvals, for example, they successfully forced many developers to abandon the refrigerator-box look in buildings.[62]

The access of new groups to the Planning Commission translated into pressure in the areas of housing and preservation. As in many cities, the spread of condominium conversion in San Francisco had generated considerable opposition. The Planning Commission had approved many applications for conversion but in 1977, after successful lobbying by the planning staff and neighborhood groups, they voted 4 to 3 in favor of an ordinance, drafted by the staff, to control condominium conversion.[63]

The other major area of concern for the Planning Commission was preservation. Like many older cities, San Francisco has buildings that are threatened by demolition as new development progresses. During Moscone's administration, the City of Paris building was slated for demolition in order to build a retail store. Moscone's commission temporarily delayed this action when they proposed and received approval from the board of supervisors that it be established as a landmark. The building remained during Moscone's administration, though no further plans were developed for its restoration. The building was torn down, however, during Feinstein's administration when she accepted Neiman Marcus' proposal to build a retail store on its site.

These activities suggest that Moscone's commission was both progressive, with regard to downzoning, condominium conversion ordinances, preservation of the City of Paris, and conservative, as in its approval of high rises. But when we look at the commission in a city-wide context, incrementalist becomes a more appropriate description. Like Boston, San Francisco underwent a dramatic transformation from a port city and labor town to a financial headquarters with a large service industry and a prosperous and growing private sector. Construction, especially of office buildings, has been part and parcel of the city's overall development.[64] Thus, while Moscone pledged to curb downtown development, the scope of the city's growth processes overwhelmed his efforts. The Planning Commission did not reverse the tide of the city's growth, but they did make it more responsive to the needs of the city. They approved high-rise applications but also secured compromises and amenities from developers.

The Planning Commission gained a good deal of freedom from their anti-development and anti-business image. This allowed it to approve projects without stimulating the opposition that Alioto's pro-development and pro-business commission had drawn. Business's negative reaction to Moscone's commission and the controversy surrounding his appointments drew attention away from the commission's actual policies. Similarly, their image gave them leverage in the development community. Many developers, anticipating a difficult time with the commission, were prepared to make concessions.[65] Their worries over the final decision were reinforced by the lengthy deliberations that accompanied most commission decisions.[66]

The Planning Commission well illustrates the major dilemmas of executive leadership. The executive must deal with an electorate, the majority of which fails to perceive the intricate web of connections that actions involve. As Wildavsky suggested, "policy is its own cause."[67] It is its own cause because every action has a result. The public tends not to consider the result but to focus only on the action that they want. The more radical environmentalists and neighborhood activists, in pursuing a valid objection, called only for action (stop development!) without seeing the result (loss of jobs, taxes, income). The mayor, however, looks to, and must look to, results. But the mayor must keep a delicate balance between appeasing an uninformed electorate and avoiding actions that carry potentially damaging consequences. The difficulty of maintaining balance increases as fragmentation increases. In this context, Moscone's commission served as a shield. His appointment of environmentalists and neighborhood activists appealed to his constituency but did not lead to the negative consequences that would have resulted from full compliance with their wishes. Since much of the Planning Commission's decisions did not have immediate or visible results (as in the case of downzoning), the appointments took on even more importance because they were both visible and immediate and so helped to mobilize support.

In this way, Moscone's approach to the Planning Commission was similar to White's early good government appointment strategy. Both mayors used appointments to create images that diverted attention from their actions. The significant difference is that White's strategy increased his resources and Moscone's did not. Moscone influenced the overall policy orientation of the Planning Commission through his appointments, but he did not interfere with their individual decisions (such as who would get permits or zoning changes).[68] By contrast, White's interference with the decisions of the BRA and other departments facilitated his acquisition of resources. Understanding the workings of the Planning Commission helps us to explain this difference. More important, it typifies Moscone's administration. The Planning Commission was not a very assertive body. In the cases discussed, the Planning Commission was caught in the battle between fragmented groups and responded to the pressures by making concessions to the various interests. But the process of granting concessions tends to develop its own momentum and becomes a major obstacle to acquiring resources and control. Resources are then expended rather than conserved, pyramided, and accumulated.

## DIANNE FEINSTEIN: THE POLITICS OF ACCOMMODATION

Since much of the work on this book was done in spring 1981, when Dianne Feinstein had been the elected mayor for only eighteen months, no complete assessment of her administration is possible here. Nevertheless, the type of appointments she made and certain of her policies provide support for some of the themes raised in the discussion of Moscone. Labor's influence continued to decline and the electorate to fragment; as a result, she had to accommodate a wider variety of interests, which proved an obstacle to executive leadership. Her appointments, however, created a certain image, which in turn, provided resources.

The influence of labor had declined to the extent that they did not endorse either candidate in the 1979 election between Feinstein and Kopp. This was the first time in at least sixteen years that the ILWU did not endorse a candidate for mayor and the first time in eight years that the Labor Council did not. While neither Alioto nor Morrison received the Labor Council's endorsement in 1967, the circumstances were very different. In 1967, the Labor Council was split between two candidates who were strong labor supporters. In 1979, the council did not consider

112

either candidate as pro-labor. Quentin Kopp was a fiscally conservative supervisor who, along with John Barbagelata, had taken a hard line against unions. Although Feinstein was probably more sensitive toward organized labor, as a supervisor she had supported Barbagelata's amendments to permit the city to fire striking workers. A labor representative claimed that the ILWU had lobbied Feinstein to vote against the amendment and that her failure to do so cost her their support.[69]

Since politicians are strongly motivated by the electoral imperative, it appears that Kopp and Feinstein either were not worried about losing labor's support or perceived significant benefits from taking anti-labor positions. The implications are the same in either case; labor was losing its ability to influence elected officials. Labor's loss was accompanied by the increasing influence of other, more fragmented interests. Feinstein's appointments, like Moscone's, illustrated this.

Feinstein was more conservative than Moscone and closer in orientation to Alioto, but her appointments were closer to Moscone's in the broad range of interests they represented.[70] As an elected mayor, Feinstein retained most of Moscone's appointments despite campaign hints that she would change many of them. This retention extended to the highest levels of government; Moscone's deputy for fiscal affairs held the same position under Feinstein. Apparently, Feinstein could not significantly alter the composition of Moscone's administration because of the many groups she had to accommodate. Feinstein claims to govern from the middle and some of her policies represent an attempt to balance a diversity of interests. Many observers of her administration agree that Feinstein's slogan is accurate but, as we have seen, even her own staff concedes that she has a constituency "a mile wide and an inch deep." Her tenuous support system has made her very vulnerable to pressures from a wide variety of groups, most of which she has tried to accommodate: She set up a desk in City Hall to dispense information to neighborhood groups and to process their complaints; she appointed a member of the gay community as a mayoral aide; when the Committee on the Status of Women fired the director, who was black, Feinstein, in response to pressures from the black community, fired the commissioners and rehired the director.[71] Thus, Feinstein's administration is Moscone's administration with a few changes. And the appointments she has made continue a process begun under Moscone of accommodating the newer groups in San Francisco's political system.

The most important personnel changes made by Feinstein were in the police department and on the Planning Commission. Both represented attempts to appeal to a wide variety of interests. Shortly after entering office, Feinstein persuaded the police commissioners to replace

113

Chief Gain by threatening to remove them if they did not.[72] The removal of Gain accommodated public and media negative reaction to him but was also prompted by Feinstein's major policy emphasis on the crime problem. The latter involved close cooperation between the mayor's office and the police department.[73] Keeping Gain would have strained that relationship. It should also be noted that the removal of Gain was consistent with the experience of police reform in other cities where the reform commissioners were removed once the reforms were implemented.

The second major area in which Feinstein initiated personnel changes was the Planning Commission. Her approach illustrates the difficulties faced by the executive in a fragmented system where a wide variety of interests compete. It also demonstrates the potential that image has to yield resources.

During the mayoral campaign, Feinstein agreed to remove some of the planning commissioners and the director in exchange for support from certain key developers and real estate people.[74] Feinstein did remove two commissioners and the director, but only eighteen months after she was in office. This delay appears to have resulted from an attempt to accommodate her neighborhood constituents. Moscone's Planning Commission was seen as the first neighborhood-oriented commission. Thus, altering the commission could have damaged her support among that constituency. In fact, several people to whom I talked suggest that Feinstein did lose support among environmentalists and neighborhood activists when she removed the commissioners. Her creation of a neighborhood desk and her informal meetings with neighborhood groups were moves to compensate for potential losses. Whether she will succeed is difficult to discern at this time. One thing is clear, however; her actions were viewed as supporting downtown, not the neighborhoods. Feinstein's delay appears to have recognized the risk of losing neighborhood support.

The case further illustrates the potential for image to serve as a resource. Just as the liberal images projected by Moscone and his Planning Commission allowed them to pursue pro-development policies, the more conservative images of Feinstein and her Planning Commission permitted them to pursue progressive policies. In fact, many of their policies were the final versions of proposals that Moscone's commission was developing.[75] The mixed-housing development policy, which requires developers of office buildings to either build housing or give the city money for housing construction, was developed by Moscone's commission and engineered by Feinstein's commission. In 1981, this had been only an informal arrangement involving the use of Environmental Impact Reports (EIR) and building permits to elicit commitments from developers for the housing units.[76] Since it was not a formal policy, cooperation between the mayor's office, the Planning Commission, and the development community was crucial to its success.[77] Feinstein developed this cooperation by altering the image of the Planning Commission and by ceding to the requests of the development community, especially in her appointment of a real estate person to the commission. According to Feinstein's planning director, the downtown was "not unhappy with the votes of Moscone's commission—[but] they objected to the lack of decorum of the commissioners—they did not like the treatment they received."[78] Through a cosmetic change, Feinstein was able to implement a progressive strategy.

Again, Feinstein's appointment strategy reflects the increasing fragmentation within San Francisco city politics and a mayor's attempts to accommodate the various groups. Although the conclusion remains tentative, it is more than likely that the process of accommodation will severely limit her ability to acquire resources and power. This was a major problem for Moscone and appears to be a major problem for mayors in general. Lindsay, Yorty, Bradley, Reading, and other mayors who were not able to overcome the fragmentation that they encountered were swallowed up in the process of accommodation. Moscone did not overcome that fragmentation. Feinstein at midterm was still struggling.

# FIVE

# Capturing Power:
# Mayors and the Bureaucracy

The bureaucrat identifies himself completely with the organization, confounding his own interests with its interests.[1]

To change long entrenched policy meant taking on long debilitat-
ing fights within bureaucracies, which are not generally responsive to calls for swift and sudden change.[2]

Bureaucracy is often cited as a major obstacle to mayoral leadership.
These "functional islands of autonomy," heavily guarded by civil service regulations, are held up as impediments to executive control and
coherent policymaking and as isolators of resources.[3] In a word, they are
a major source of urban fragmentation.

Douglas Yates cited this fragmentation as the most important vari-
able distinguishing the urban political system from other political systems. The fragmentation, both historical and structural—the latter reflecting the city's role as a service delivery mechanism—results in
"reactive, crisis-hopping" policymaking.[4] Because the executive is unable to command the resources necessary for comprehensive planning,
the bureaucracy becomes a policymaking body. Policies become the
products of routine procedures that feed the specific needs of bureaucracy rather than outcomes of strategies designed to achieve broad
objectives.[5]

The capture of power by bureaucracy, however, is not insurmountable. Using reorganizations and the "shrinking violet syndrome"—
the failure of other actors to exercise their authority—mayors can shift
the balance of power between the executive office and the bureaucracy.[6]
This chapter examines how the mayors used these devices to deal with
the obstacles presented by bureaucracy. An important difference among
the mayors was the focus of their efforts. While they all dealt with
bureaucracies, White and Alioto focused on areas that contained vital
resources. By contrast, Moscone and Feinstein took more of an administrative approach, using and focusing on bureaucratic difficulties as

such. Rather than acquiring resources as did White and Alioto, Moscone and Feinstein got caught up in the day-to-day business of city government in the way more appropriate to a city manager. As in their personnel strategies, Moscone and Feinstein became captives of the fragmentation that they encountered. Thus, even though they were successful in some of their undertakings, the results did not increase their resources. Like the weak state that must constantly fight just to survive, they did not build their individual triumphs into an increase in power.

## REORGANIZATION STRATEGIES

Reorganizations can be used by executives to increase power without appearing to do so. In his analysis of Richard Nixon's reorganizations, which included the creation of new jurisdictions within the executive office, Harold Seidman observed that the "major objective of Nixon's organization strategy was to contain and neutralize the bureaucracy."[7] This objective, however, was disguised by appeals to efficiency and better management. Similarly, Robert Wagner's reorganization of the budgetary process in New York City was couched in the reform language of efficiency, when, in fact, one of his objectives was to increase mayoral control over the process.[8] LaGuardia's reorganization of municipal services in New York City, while attractive to good government eyes, increased his power substantially in relation to Tammany Hall.

In Boston, White's reorganization of the BRA gave him direct access to federal money; in San Francisco, federal money remained under the control of the Redevelopment Agency. White's reorganizations in other departments shifted the balance between civil service and appointed positions, giving him more control over decisionmaking. This was furthered by reorganizations within his own office that increased the size and functions of his staff and the information available to it as well. In San Francisco, Moscone and Feinstein used reorganization in conjunction with other techniques in an attempt to increase executive control over the budgetary process.

### Taming the Lion:
### Kevin White and the Boston Redevelopment Authority (BRA)

Public authorities have often been obstacles to mayoral leadership. Designed by reformers to be free from political pressures, these authorities were usually given independent budgetary powers and their budgets were not subject to public disclosure. In New York, Robert Moses used this device to transform the Triborough Bridge and Tunnel Authority into one of the most powerful institutions in the city and state.[9] A similar role was played in other cities by the redevelopment authority. Set up by entrepreneurial mayors in the 1950s and 1960s to implement urban renewal projects, these authorities were often transformed into power centers through their substantial federal funding and strong leadership. This was the pattern in New Haven and Boston under Ed Logue and in San Francisco under Justin Herman.[10]

While the primary focus of urban renewal both in theory and practice was the central business district (CBD), there were neighborhood ventures as well.[11] But these projects often drew opposition from the local residents. In Boston, the BRA set up district planning units, which brought neighborhood representatives into the planning process, in order to soften some of this opposition. Through a reorganization, White transferred these neighborhood functions from the BRA to the mayor's office, making the BRA an instrument for the downtown or CBD area only. Abolishing the district planning units, White set up the Office of Planning and Development (OPD) and the Neighborhood Development Administration (NDA) within the mayor's office. The OPD was responsible for citywide planning and the NDA for neighborhood and community planning. The significant feature of the reorganization was the channeling of community development (CD) funds through mayoral agencies. Through skillful engineering of that resource, White extended his control in the neighborhoods.

Headed by the person who ran White's classification amendment campaign in 1978 which in style and procedure resembled a machine campaign, NDA helped to strengthen the political networks in the neighborhoods, which had been developed by the Little City Halls and expanded significantly through White's political organization. The NDA's major resource was community development funds, which were allocated according to political rather than administrative criteria. Neighborhood groups that were closely aligned with White's political organization received community development money for various projects, and groups not associated with the organization were denied requests for money.[12]

Putting neighborhood planning responsibilities in the mayor's office also increased White's patronage. The Office of Planning and Development had a staff of 130 people and the Neighborhood Development Administration had a staff of 20 people, none of them in civil service.

The NDA's highly political style was not necessarily the result of its placement in the mayor's office. In New York City, Robert Moses' Public Authority was a highly political body with most decisions made on the basis of politics rather than administration.[13] What White did

was to bring the politics of the allocation process under his control. This is in contrast to San Francisco, where a substantial portion of the allocation process was controlled by the SFRA. Unlike the BRA, the SFRA maintained projects in the neighborhoods. Under Alioto, $22 million of the $28 million of community development money received by the city was channeled to the SFRA, which became very reluctant to give it up. When Moscone wanted to divert some CD money to his constituents for housing development corporations, he was defeated by the SFRA, which would not relinquish its "established" money. Similarly, the 1981 budget hearings under Feinstein saw a large battle between the SFRA and the housing development corporations over the allocation of community development funds. In both cases the mayors were in the center of a battle between a powerful independent agency and their constituents over who would control an important resource. Through reorganizations, White answered that question in his favor.

White's control over access to city government was also made easier by the absence of district elections. Since city councillors and school committee officials did not represent district constituencies, as in San Francisco, they were less inclined to espouse neighborhood issues and challenge White's control. Further, as we have seen, the at-large electoral system, which reduced the percentage of votes needed for victory, created incentives to capture the support of a small part of the electorate rather than to build a large constituency. And councillors were not fussy about where their votes came from: they developed no relationship with a stable part of the electorate. Hence, the other elected officials in Boston did not have support systems capable of pressuring the mayor.

## Moving Down the Ranks

White extended his control over city departments by rearranging the balance between civil service and non–civil service positions. These reorganizations enabled him to overcome the obstacles to control presented by civil service protections. These obstacles also often impede service delivery. White's reorganization of the police department in 1980 created more appointed positions by reversing the roles of appointed and civil service personnel at decision-making levels. By replacing the captains with appointed superintendents, White put people in decision-making positions who were responsive to him. An important objective and result of the reorganization was an increase in the number of police on the street. According to the head of the Office of Public Safety, this increase absorbed the first round of layoffs resulting from Proposition 2½.[14]

The Residency Law and the policy management system are additional examples of White's extension of control. The first, instituted in 1976, required all new city hirees to be Boston residents and all city workers receiving promotions to move into Boston. The policy management system, instituted in 1979, required department heads to submit quarterly reports; these were used to evaluate their performance for cost effectiveness, hiring of Boston residents, and use of Boston vendors. White's emphasis—and encroachment—on city bureaucracy was a marked departure for a mayor who had been quoted earlier as saying, "I'll leave them [bureaucracy] alone, if they leave me alone."[15] As with his appointment strategy, White shifted his focus from media and audience politics to organization and constituent politics. He turned to city government equipped with strategies that increased his control, decreased some of the fragmentation, and enabled him to acquire some of bureaucracy's resources.

### Kevin White and the Reorganization Game:
### The Mayor's Office

In his 1972 article, "Title, Title, Who's Got the Title? . . . It's the Very Latest Thing," *Boston Herald* writer Robert Hannan took a somewhat jocular stab at White's reorganization strategies.[16] Portraying them as rituals of title assignments, Hannan briefly discussed the new positions on the White staff and the recruits to fill them. What he failed to discuss, however, was the significance of these reorganizations for acquisition of resources. Every mayoral election was followed by a reorganization of mayoral agencies, which included an expansion of staff. The number of employees in these various agencies went from 284 in 1967 to 584 in 1976. These post-electoral reorganizations, presented as a way to improve the administration's performance for the next four years, were at base a way to reward political campaign workers. In addition, these reorganizations substantially increased the mayor's budget. Going from $378,752 in 1967 to $6.5 million in 1976, the mayor's budget represented the largest percentage of increase of all city departments.[17]

Through his reorganization strategies, White acquired the financial and staff resources that students of urban politics deem necessary for effective leadership.[18] Once acquired, however, resources must be protected and conserved. Here again we find White using reorganizations to overcome challenges to his power. Looking at some examples reveals an important component of White's leadership—he was a power accumulator rather than a power expender.

120

In the late 1970s, the city council attacked White's programs and agencies, charging that they were largely patronage operations. When they tried to defund these programs, White used reorganizations to protect his budget and hence his resources. These reorganizations included function transfers from one agency to another, staff transfers between agencies, debit transfers (charging agencies for services performed by mayoral staff), and end-of-the-year budget transfers. By employing these administrative devices, White avoided expending resources on bargaining with the council. In the process, he undermined their primary power—budgetary review.

Expansion of mayoral agencies also increased the information and functions of the mayor's office: The Office of Public Safety had input into the policymaking of the police department; the Office of Policy and Management implemented the policy management system to exercise more control over bureaucratic policymaking; centralizing all press matters in the twenty-seven person press office increased the mayor's control over information flows and provided some insulation from the media.

White's operations sound similar to Lindsay's strategy of superagencies. But where Lindsay's strategy was not successful, White's was very successful. The different outcomes reflected the different political settings in New York and Boston (especially the size of city governments), the actors involved, the time factor, and the approaches.

Lindsay's strategy for running city govenment through his superagencies ran into two powerful blocs of resistance—the civil service bureaucracy and the unions. After several unsuccessful attempts, Lindsay discovered that the deployment of his available shock troopers could not shake up a bureaucracy composed of 374,689 employees.[19] And if the numbers had not been sufficient to thwart his strategy, the municipal unions, who were not the best of friends with Lindsay, would have brought it to a halt. In Boston, a city almost fourteen times smaller in population than New York, the bureaucracy that White faced was also about fourteen times smaller in personnel: 24,000 employees in 1976.[20] Thus, White's target was more manageable than Lindsay's target. In addition, White did not have to worry about opposition from the unions. Unlike in New York, unions have been traditionally weak in Boston, and White, unlike Lindsay, made peace rather than war with the unions.

Second, the nature of the actors involved in the two strategies differed. Whereas Lindsay surrounded himself with management-oriented reformers who were convinced that the soundness of their principles would automatically result in implementation, White relied on politi-

121

cally astute people who understood that city government was a political operation.

Third, Lindsay's strategy was to act quickly, with the creation of the superagencies beginning almost immediately. Directly confronting the inertia and established procedures of bureaucracy led to stalemate, with Lindsay the loser because he could not deliver on commitments whose implementation required bureaucratic cooperation.[21] By contrast, White's strategy evolved over time. The incremental approach permitted White to infiltrate the bureaucracy slowly with loyal appointees who would facilitate the implementation of his policies. By contrast, Lindsay used a politics of attack which fared poorly when he applied it to bureaucracy and failed miserably when he applied it to the unions.

This leads directly into the final point. It is important to fit the approach to the arena. Lindsay's politics of attack was effective as media and audience politics. But it was not effective as organization and constituent politics, especially when the organizations were powerful and well protected. By contrast, when White shifted his focus to organization politics, he shifted his strategies as well. Understanding the political environment and its participants is a crucial component of effective leadership. White's percipience was critical to the success of his strategy. And his success increased his power.

### Moscone and Feinstein: Reorganizing the Budgetary Process

Reorganization of the budgetary process in San Francisco, which was started by Moscone and completed by Feinstein, was an attempt to increase mayoral control. The case illuminates the obstacles that the political structure in San Francisco places in the way of executive leadership. In addition, it shows how the strategies of Moscone and Feinstein did not overcome those obstacles. In choosing the budgetary process as the focus of a major reorganization, Moscone and Feinstein selected a complex area where change would be slow, the process long, and the gains for mayoral resources unknown. This is in contrast to White's reorganizations, which focused on areas that offered immediate and substantial return.

### San Francisco's Budgetary Process: Mayor Keep Out

San Francisco's budgetary process contains major obstacles to mayoral control and policymaking. The city charter gives the mayor formal power to decrease but not increase the budget, in contrast to Boston where the mayor can do both. Formal responsibility for preparing the

budget resides with the controller, a mayoral appointee with a lifetime tenure. In conjunction with the department heads, the controller assembles the budget and submits it to the mayor's office for approval. It then goes to the Board of Supervisors who, like the mayor, can only decrease appropriations.

This process places several limitations on the mayor. The most obvious is the charter restriction on increasing the budget. Second, the controller's tenure is a limitation. Although appointed by the mayor, once in office the controller has no reason to be loyal or accountable to the mayor. This can be an obstacle and in fact was for Feinstein when the controller proved to be the most resistant person involved in the implementation of the new accounting system. Another limitation is the jurisdictional structure of city government. Sharing executive power with the mayor is the CAO, whose jurisdiction includes Public Health, Public Works, Government Services, Special Projects, and various other responsibilities, like hotel tax. Thus, although the mayor can expand his or her budgetary power through informal means such as pressure on departments and commission appointments, the charter puts certain key departments outside of the mayor's appointment authority. Those departments account for approximately a third of the budget. The mayor can exert informal influence, but the process is more indirect since the mayor must first pressure the CAO who then must pressure his appointments. Compounding these difficulties is the long ten-year term of the CAO. This is longer than any one person can be mayor. Thus, while the mayor has formal authority to appoint the CAO, many mayors do not get to exercise that authority.

A more recent limitation on the mayor's budgetary powers was placed by Proposition 13. This limited the mayor's power to increase the tax rate to 1 percent a year. In the past, a mayor could increase the tax rate in order to submit the balanced budget required by law, a technique often employed by Alioto.

Finally, the accounting system was a major obstacle to mayoral oversight. The difficulties in tracing expenditures, which often resulted in allocation and payment delays, were used by department heads as insulation from mayoral involvement in budget and policy matters.[22]

## The Fiscal Advisory Committee

Faced with a bureaucracy highly fragmented and lacking in incentives for responsiveness and accountability to the mayor's office, Moscone embarked on a reorganization program intended to compensate for some of that fragmentation. He set up a fiscal advisory committee, composed of representatives from the business community, to review and make recommendations for city departments whose budgets exceeded one million dollars. The committee recommended: training programs for middle and top level management; a cash management system; coordinated insurance policies; a user's committee made up of some supervisors, mayoral aides, and the controller; purchasing an accounting system and replacing the line item budget with Management by Objective (MBO). Moscone adopted the recommendations.

Using a committee of businessmen served to mitigate some of the business community's opposition to the administration and to confer legitimacy on policies intended to increase mayoral control over the budgetary process. As Banfield has suggested, the use of businessmen gives the "seal of approval" to projects.[23] Also, the use of a committee is important because of the contrast to White's more centralized approaches. Once again we find the San Francisco mayors attempting to pull power from the sides to the center. An unrelated issue may illuminate the problem. In their study of fluoridation campaigns, Crain, Katz, and Rosenthal found that in reform-oriented cities, mayors favoring fluoridation were either unwilling or unable to secure administrative adoption on their personal endorsements alone. Rather, they were forced to "get support" for their position by "submitting the issue to the public." By contrast, mayors who supported fluoridation in less reform-minded cities were able to obtain administrative adoptions.[24] San Francisco falls into the category of a reform-oriented city, with an emphasis on a participatory electorate. Lacking any mechanism for centralizing influence, the mayor must seek influence through public support. Thus, we find the San Francisco mayors "going to the public" to mobilize support more often than did White in Boston. The findings of Crain et al. support one of the hypotheses of this study: Leadership strategies will vary with how politics are organized. Unfortunately, some strategies reinforce the fragmentation and so increase the obstacles to acquiring resources and power. Reorganization of San Francisco's budgetary process proved to be an example.

## Implementing the Reorganization

The strategy that began with the establishment of the Fiscal Advisory Committee came to full bloom with the adoption of Financial Information and Resources Management (FIRM), the new accounting and budgetary system. The two major components were the Financial Accounting Management Information System (FAMIS), the computerized record-keeping system, and Management By Objective (MBO).

Through the introduction of these management techniques, the Moscone administration attempted to update and, more importantly, coordinate and centralize the city's highly fragmented budgetary and accounting systems. Partially because of the fragmentation, the mayor's office operated in an information vacuum with respect to expenditures and departmental policy.

The Moscone administration began with a trial implementation of FAMIS in the Parks and Recreation Department. The usual implementation difficulties of coordination and poor information and communication surfaced, and they were ironed out through adjustments. When the trial period was over, the implementation schedule was put into effect: seven city departments adopted the new system in 1979, followed by a restructuring of the remaining departments in 1980–1981.

Aside from the technical implementation difficulties, one major obstacle occurred during Feinstein's administration. The controller and his staff, who were central to the entire system, opposed the project.[25] The controller had not been appointed by Feinstein and she could not easily remove him. This contrasts with White's appointments, who served at his pleasure and therefore had strong incentives to follow his directives. Lacking this type of influence, Feinstein had to rely on informal pressure to persuade the controller. She persuaded the Chamber of Commerce and the press, who endorsed the policy, to pressure the controller. In addition, Feinstein and a member of the board's Finance Committee threatened to cut the controller's budget if he did not go along with the policy. The combined sources of informal pressure were effective. But securing the controller's cooperation cost the mayor time and considerable energy.

Complete implementation of FAMIS took approximately two and a half years. MBO was fully implemented in fifteen departments, which accounted for two-thirds of the total budget. MBO was to be used on a limited basis by the remaining city departments in preparing the budget for fiscal year 1981–1982.

Not enough data is in to make a technical assessment of the FIRM policy. There has been, however, one tangible result. In preparing the 1979–1980 financial report, the controller's office uncovered $30 million of appropriated but unspent funds; these were used to reduce the anticipated budget shortfall for the upcoming year. It also served as excellent public relations for the new system.

More significant, however, is the potential long term effect of increasing mayoral control over budget and bureaucracy. The new system can provide the mayor's office with more information; lack of information has been an obstacle in the past. In addition, the reforms may indirectly strengthen the executive's control over bureaucracy. As *formal* devices that were planned and implemented and are operated by the mayor's office, the new budgetary and accounting systems will give the mayor new formal tools and formal input into city budgeting. The mayor's office now has a FIRM project staff that engineers the budget and accounting systems. The strong reform bias in the San Francisco political culture gives formal titles and delineations of function a disproportionate amount of influence and significance. That is, the mayor must avoid creating the impression of overstepping the formal bounds of the office.

Thus, formally involving the mayor's office carries the potential for increasing mayoral control. Whether the reforms will lead to substantive changes, however, remains to be seen. Meanwhile, several comparisons may usefully be made. In contrast to White, Moscone and Feinstein applied reorganization strategies to an area that, because of its complexity and fragmentation, would be slow to show results and was not certain to lead to an increase in mayoral resources.[26] Had Moscone lived, his first term would have been over before the reorganization was completed. He could well have carried out a reorganization without realizing any gains. Efficiency and accuracy may have been increased, but these are the goals of the administrator, not the political leader seeking to garner resources and power before an upcoming election. Reorganizations carried out by White were motivated by and directly related to increasing his resources; through effective strategies, he achieved his objectives.

Lacking White's resources and power, however, Moscone and Feinstein had to pull power from the sides to the center in order to overcome specific obstacles that resulted from the fragmented environment. Thus, we see the cyclical relationship between fragmentation, resources, and leadership. Fragmentation is an obstacle to the acquisition of resources. Resources are necessary in order to exercise leadership. Operating without sufficient resources, Moscone and Feinstein supplemented their supply by bringing more participants into the process. But this approach sustained the fragmentation.

This relationship does not bode well for mayoral success. The reforms implemented by Moscone and Feinstein seem likely to lead to substantive changes only if the mayor has enough control to command those changes. Although dressed in procedure, the budgetary process is a political process. It involves bargaining, persuasion, coercion, and other elements of influence. Reforms of themselves will not lead to change. A mayor with the resources and power to influence others will achieve changes. But we have seen from the experiences of Moscone and Feinstein that the resources and power necessary for strong executive leadership are becoming increasingly difficult to acquire in San Francisco. Wildavsky has said, "No significant change can be made in the budget process without affecting the political process."[27] It is all too possible that, five years from now, no significant change will have been made in the budget process in San Francisco.

## THE SHRINKING VIOLET SYNDROME

In his comprehensive analysis of bureaucratic behavior, Anthony Downs cited the "shrinking violet syndrome" as a device used by bureaucracy to protect their internal ways and accustomed procedures from the disruptive effects of external pressures.[28] Anything that differs from the norm poses this threat. Hence bureaucracy will often avoid taking on a new function. This trend increased in the 1960s and 1970s as the nationalization of local politics enlarged the bureaucratic workload. Moreover, the additional work was often accompanied by numerous regulations seeking to govern the bureaucratic process.

While the shrinking violet syndrome can lead to problems as important tasks are not performed, it can also provide an opportunity for executives to gain control in areas that are outside their formal jurisdictions or in areas where control is shared with others. To the extent that executives can gain control, they can reduce some of the fragmentation in city government and thereby remove a major obstacle to leadership, policymaking, and implementation. Furthermore, the executive can break through the barrier that isolates important resources.

### Civil Service: An End to Patronage or a New Beginning?

While critics and supporters of reforms in local politics disagreed on the merits of those reforms, they shared a common belief: civil service would put an end to patronage in local politics. This would have severely hindered mayoral leadership by removing an important vehicle for gaining electoral support, attracting campaign workers, and rewarding and disciplining subordinates. In short, it would have removed the material bases of politics. But the civil service system did not always accomplish this. Perhaps it decreased the amount of patronage and made resources more difficult to acquire, but it did not eliminate them. As Theodore Lowi observed, "Reform did not eliminate the need for power. It simply altered what one had to do to get it."[29] The experiences of White and Alioto substantiate Lowi's claim. Both mayors were able to circumvent civil service obstacles and exercise control over the selection process, a possibility that reform was supposed to eliminate. While there are several explanations, one that was present in both cities was the inefficiency or "shrinking violet" behavior of the civil service commissions.

Before examining the particular events in these cases, an important distinction should be made between the two cities. In the private-regarding political culture of Boston, patronage is tolerated to a larger extent than in more reform-minded San Francisco. Thus, Alioto's use of patronage was more covert than White's and his ability to acquire this resource meant overcoming bureaucratic obstacles as well as obstacles raised by the political culture. Indeed, political obstacles prevented Alioto from pyramiding the resource as White did. Patronage was a key component used by White in building his political organization. In San Francisco, constructing such an overtly political organization would have been extremely difficult, if possible at all. Thus, although political skills are crucial for strong executive leadership, the political environment often determines how those skills can be exercised.

## Alioto

Alioto exercised a considerable amount of influence over the Civil Service Commission and Department, which he used to integrate the civil service system racially and to acquire patronage. Through the efforts of the general manager of the Civil Service Department, oral and performance exams were substituted for the standard written exams. The increased flexibility and subjectivity of the new testing devices enabled Alioto to bring minorities into temporary and permanent civil service positions.[30] During Alioto's administration, minority enrollment in city government increased from 11 to 38 percent, with black and Hispanic enrollment each increasing by approximately 1 percent a year.[31] While some of this was a direct result of federally funded programs, the civil service system absorbed a considerable number of minorities as well.

Alioto also used his influence over the civil service system to dispense patronage. Requests from the mayor's office to the Civil Service Department for jobs for specific individuals were frequent and denials were infrequent.[32]

Although the civil service commissioners have formal oversight and veto power over the department, Alioto's general manager was powerful and independent. Alioto was able to acquire this influence because of his appointments to the commission, which were drawn from his larger coalition, and the less powerful position of the commission before 1975.

Alioto's Civil Service Commission consisted of one labor representative, one Asian, and one personal friend. (After 1975, the commission had five members.) The labor representative was primarily interested in how labor faired on key issues like contract disputes, wages, and working conditions. Minority representatives were interested in making good in their communities; a policy promoting minority enrollment in city government was certainly in their interests. Given these incentives, Alioto was able to bargain with the commissioners, trading off benefits in the areas of particular concern to them in exchange for limited intervention in areas that did not directly effect them. For labor, noninterference in areas of minimal concern was a small price to pay for the larger return of good contracts and favorable strike settlements. By contrast, when Moscone was mayor, this convergence of interests between the mayor's office and the Civil Service Commission had lapsed. Labor was no longer represented and the commissioners were more assertive than Alioto's had been. Consequently, Moscone's patronage requests were usually denied.[33]

In addition to being noninterventionist, Alioto's commission had less formal power in relation to the mayor and the Board of Supervisors than it currently does. A series of legislative amendments enacted by the board and passed by the electorate in 1975–1976 gave the commission power to establish binding wage setting formulas. Previously, the commission could only recommend settlements, and formulas existed only for a limited number of categories. Moreover, the commission tended to be very passive about its recommendations and the formulas.[34] Thus, the mayor and the board had a substantial amount of flexibility, a resource forcefully used by Alioto. In addition, the board's failure to take the initiative in labor issues gave Alioto further opportunities.

While the board exhibited shrinking violet behavior in the area of labor relations, some members did perceive Alioto's power in that area and, toward the end of his administration, they attempted to alter the balance. Objecting to Alioto's influence over the civil service commissioners, Supervisor Molinari proposed an amendment in 1975 to expand the number of commissioners from three to five. Although the measure passed, the strategy ultimately backfired when Alioto ended up appointing the additional two commissioners. Molinari challenged Alioto's actions, but the city attorney upheld Alioto's right to make the appointments.[35]

## White

Like Alioto, White took advantage of the shrinking violet tendencies of bureaucracy to gain control over the civil service system. In contrast to Alioto, White did not have to bargain with commissioners and department heads to execute his strategy. He used holdover appointments to centralize his authority over his department heads. In addition, the more private regarding political culture in Boston enabled White to pyramid his resources to a greater extent than Alioto could.

White's strong and aggressive personnel office and his loyal department heads were aided in their successful attempts to bypass civil service restrictions by the inefficiency of the state Civil Service Commission, which did not monitor their actions closely. Through the narrowing of job descriptions in conjunction with department heads, the personnel office tailored job openings so that they fit only the person who was selected for the patronage position. Although this and other types of manipulations—such as not posting civil service job openings, reclassifying positions, and granting promotions for political work—were reported to the state Civil Service Commission, the failure of the state to take any action permitted these practices to continue for patronage purposes.[36]

The shrinking violet behavior of the state bureaucracy, combined with White's control over department heads, enabled him to centralize his control over patronage as well. This was an important source of control used by White to exact concessions from other people in government. For example, City Councillor Hicks supported White's proposals after receiving patronage from White to hand out to her constituents.[37]

In addition to exercising poor oversight and failing to regulate and enforce, the state Civil Service Commission was very slow in administering exams; most requests took several months and many took as long as two years.[38] White used this delay to hire provisionals, a resource that was especially useful during mayoral campaigns. In the 1975 campaign, more than 1,000 provisional slots were filled with campaign workers. In the 1979 election, the number was approximately 1,600.[39]

Controlling provisional and fulltime jobs within the civil service system complemented the patronage that White created through his mayoral agencies and programs, bringing the total number of patronage jobs at his disposal to over 4,000. Many of those jobs were used in building his political organization and strengthening the role of ward coordinators within the neighborhoods. Having patronage to dispense, they were in a better position to command loyalty and support for the administration.

Thus, using an appointment strategy that centralized his control over city departments, White took advantage of the shrinking violet syndrome in bureaucracy to acquire and control patronage. The private regarding political culture of Boston permitted White to pyramid this resource to a degree that would have shocked reform minded San Francisco.

### A Bureaucracy Stalled: San Francisco's Waste Water Project

While the shrinking violet syndrome can provide opportunities for executives to increase their power, it can also be an obstacle to mayoral leadership. San Francisco's waste water project illustrates this side of the situation. The city's sewage problem had existed for years but was left to flounder in the doldrums of bureaucracy. In 1975 it became a citywide crisis and Moscone again was pushed into reactive policy-making.

The waste water project demonstrates many aspects of how bureaucracies operate:

(1) Problems tend to be pushed along in bureaucracy;

(2) Bureaucratic policy often reflects a large gap between service providers and recipients; this is evident in the original Department of Public Works (DPW) proposal for the Sunset/Richmond districts—which also dramatized the gap between functional jurisdiction and geographical realities;

(3) Bureaucracy responds to its own internal needs. Opposition from the community did not inspire a change in the master plan drawn up by the DPW. Rather, it led to stalemate as the shrinking violet bureaucracy avoided moving to resolve the conflict;

(4) In addition to functional fragmentation, the modern mayor is faced with an enormous amount of vertical fragmentation because of the increased involvement of other governments in municipal affairs. The total number of federal, state, and regional agencies involved in the waste water project came to thirty-seven;

(5) Regardless of formal jurisdictional boundaries, most demands come to the mayor's office. The residents of Sunset/Richmond brought their opposition to the proposal to the mayor; the construction industry and the building trades expected the mayor to take action to remove a construction ban;

(6) Urban policymaking tends to be reactive.

The sewage story also provides a good contrast to White and Alioto's use of the shrinking violet syndrome. Both of these mayors took control in areas that contained crucial resources and so increased their power. By contrast, Moscone's ability to get control over the sewer project did not increase his resources. This is not to devalue his efforts. He did resolve a crisis and take action that was in the interests of the city. Moreover, through his control over the project, plans were altered in such a way that the outcomes were more acceptable and equitable. Finally, resolving the crisis avoided incurring the loss of support of those who were affected. But Moscone's achievements merely highlight a major dilemma of the weak mayor in a fragmented environment; getting control means merely keeping up. And "gains" means not incurring losses. As we have seen repeatedly, the mayor whose support is fragmented and dispersed cannot pyramid successful actions into strong resources as did White and, to a lesser extent, Alioto. Each action remains separate and each attempt to exercise control begins from the same position of weak and limited resources. Exacerbating the problem is the lack of insulation from crises and conflicts. Rather than selecting the areas to become involved in, the weak mayor is pulled into many of the issues that arise. Reacting rather than initiating, the executive ends by expending more than is accumulated.

## The Crisis Unfolds

San Francisco's sewage system had been the subject of question and debate since 1968. It was a combined system in which rain was mixed with sewage before treatment. Heavy rainfalls sent substantial amounts of raw, untreated sewage into the bay. The key question was how much discharge was permissable. On 12 December 1975, the day after Moscone won the runoff election, the Regional Water Quality Control Board (RWQCB) gave a definitive answer—San Francisco had too much. The board banned all construction in the eastern half of the city.

Although the sewage system had been a problem for several years, no concrete action had been taken toward a remedy. Lodged in the Department of Public Works, which is under the jurisdiction of the CAO, the project planning to date had generated more conflict and confusion than it had paperwork. The DPW's Master Plan represented the conflict, cited by Yates, between service providers and recipients. The plan called for a sewage treatment plant to go through Forty-sixth Avenue and Golden Gate Park (Sunset Park/Richmond areas). This set off a fierce reaction among residents of the area as well as among residents of other parts of the city who objected to the Golden Gate Park part of the proposal.[40] These plans were neither changed nor pushed. What obtained was a stalemate. The DPW had its plan, the public had its objections and demonstrations, the city had a ban on construction, and Mayor Moscone had a crisis on his hands.

Faced with a ban imposed by a regional agency, pressures from developers and the building trades for some action, and pressures from the public not to do what the DPW proposed, the new mayor called in an outsider, Richard Sklar. He had been active in Democratic party politics and ran a manufacturing firm in Cleveland, Ohio. At Moscone's request, Sklar reviewed the project and agreed to stay on for three years to run it. The project was set up as a special project and placed under Sklar's direction.[41]

Since the project was under the formal jurisdiction of the CAO, Moscone had to go through him to change the project responsibilities. This was not a problem, since the CAO was only temporary, postponing retirement until Moscone could find a replacement. Further, the CAO was not a management-oriented person and was more than happy to relinquish responsibility for what had become a major headache.[42]

A similar situation obtained with the Public Works director, who was also nearing retirement and was equally frustrated with the stalemated project. The DPW director agreed to divide project responsibilities with Sklar, the DPW maintaining responsibility for design and inspection and Sklar assuming responsibility for fiscal and public participation matters.

Once the preliminary arrangements had been made, Sklar moved to deal with the four major issues: the construction ban, site location, funding, and financing of the system. The construction ban, which was the only visible issue and the one that attracted the most pressure for resolution, was addressed first. Sklar negotiated an agreement with the Regional Water Quality Control Board to lift the ban in thirty day increments if Sklar adhered to the work schedule. The monthly progress reports submitted by Sklar to the RWQCB kept to schedule and so the ban was never enforced.

The second issue addressed was site location. According to the plans, sewage treatment plants would be placed at three sites: Hunter's Point, Richmond/Sunset, and the west side of the city. Hunter's Point, the city's major black ghetto, was slated to be the first construction site. As in any community, the residents of Hunter's Point did not want to host a sewage treatment plant. The residents also claimed that Hunter's Point had been chosen because it was a black community.[43] Sklar met with community leaders and residents and convinced them that their charges were inaccurate, since the plans also called for a plant in the middle and upper middle class white areas of Sunset Park/Richmond.

As a sweetener, Sklar promised to throw in amenities such as parks and playgrounds from the funds received for the project.[44] As a final persuasion, Sklar emphasized the number of jobs that would be lost if the construction ban were enforced and the jobs that would be gained if the project were implemented. Since there was some federal funding, project hiring would follow affirmative action requirements. Sklar's approach to the community was effective and Hunter's Point became part of the first development project, beginning within nine months of the planning and being completed in 1978. Site location difficulties in the Richmond/Sunset area, which had led to the final stalemate before Sklar was brought in, were resolved after some fundamental design alterations were made. The alterations substituted an underground tunnel for the original proposal.

After resolving the site disputes, the funding issue was addressed. The original proposal lacked provisions for matching federal money with local funds. A cost analysis of the project revealed that over a ten-year period $240 million in local funds would be required to see the project to completion. Based on these figures, a $60 million bond issue was suggested. This assumed that $60 million, the highest bond ever to be placed on the ballot, was enough to begin the project. Sklar objected to this reasoning and recommended that the entire projected cost of $240 million should go on the ballot. He felt that the issue was ripe and that, if given time, people would lose interest, thereby decreasing the chances of future bond approval. He also reasoned that once a bond proposal went over $100 million, which he admitted was a hard pill to swallow, the rest was insignificant. The decision was made to go for the $240 million.

In preparation, the city hired a consulting firm to run a campaign for the bond. Appealing to the interests of the construction industry, the environmentalists, and labor in the project, Sklar raised approximately $60,000 to finance the six-week campaign. It was very successful: the San Francisco electorate voted 73 to 27 percent in favor of the city's largest bond issue to that date.[45]

The question that remained was, who would pay for the system? If the conventional financing mechanism—property tax—were used, everyone would pay equally however much water they used or however much discharge they put into the water. To make the system more equitable, Sklar proposed a rate ordinance, or user-based system, that would base payment on the amount of water used with a surcharge on the quality of the water. Sklar lobbied the Board of Supervisors on behalf of this proposal, arguing that the project was necessary, and that the existing financing system was inequitable and worked to the disadvantage of the homeowner. This last argument was persuasive, since most of the supervisors drew their strongest support from districts overwhelmingly populated by homeowners.[46] Supervisor Feinstein, who headed the Health and Environmental Committee and was among the supervisors with strong backing from homeowners, was instrumental in supporting the rate ordinance. When the vote was taken, the ordinance passed 7 to 4.

With the major issues settled, the project moved along at a relatively smooth pace. While there were some minor problems and delays, mostly construction-related, the project kept within its basic schedule.

## The Politics of Process

The waste water project case is an example of reactive urban policy-making and the dilemmas this poses for mayoral leadership. These problems are increased when the mayor lacks means of insulation. In a strong party system, the party organization helps to keep issues localized. In a nonpartisan system, the executive is in a more precarious position because all issues gravitate to the mayor's office. Insulation from problems is hard to find. White's organization was capable of quieting opposition in Allston/Brighton, for example (see Chapter 4). But the sewage case illustrates how mayors in nonpartisan settings must deal even with crises outside their formal jurisdiction.

On the positive side, the sewage project story demonstrated how the "shrinking violet syndrome" enabled the mayor to fill a vacuum of responsibility to deal with a crisis. Recruiting someone from outside the bureaucracy with technical credentials as well as political savvy, Moscone was able to overcome some of the problems inherent in urban policymaking. Unlike the bureaucracy, which is encased in walls of routines and procedures, Sklar went out into the communities, appealed to labor and the construction industry, negotiated with the regional agencies, and lobbied the Board of Supervisors. He demonstrated a flexibility that bureaucracy lacks, but one which the decision-making process requires because, despite the reformers' attempts to disguise it, it is a political process at heart.

By contrast, the DPW behaved according to what Levy et al. termed "Adam Smith" rules, which did not "require the bureaucrat to have more contact with the public than he needs to advance his objectives."[47] Since the sewer project was embroiled in controversy, contact with the public would have meant disharmony and instability, at least temporarily. These are two phenomena that bureaucratic organizations avoid even when this means staying with an unworkable or unacceptable plan such as the DPW's original plan. As Herbert Kaufman observed,

> Since some regularities are needed, and all required regularities have unpleasant features, why risk known imperfections for unknown ones? Why gamble an established imperfect order for possible disorder? The logic of collective life thus has a conservative thrust: it lends authority to the system as it stands.[48]

Only after Moscone had taken control of the project and debureaucratized it were the risks that Kaufman mentions, and the public contact that Levy et al. cite, undertaken. And both of these factors were integral components of implementing the project.

### Shrinking Violet Mayors

Mayors as well as bureaucracies can fall into shrinking violet behavior. Mayors also may wish to avoid certain issues or areas where the return of resources will be less than the investment. In fact, the shrinking violet syndrome can be a way to conserve resources, a key component in the accumulation process. The history of the waste water project is illustrative. San Francisco's sewage system had been a problem for several years. Given the environmental consciousness of California, it was only a matter of time before the city would have to do something. Yet no concrete action was taken. Alioto did not intervene in the DPW's affairs as Moscone did.[49] And Moscone's response appears to have been largely a reaction to the construction ban. Thus, crisis-hopping is not only a result of fragmentation as Yates suggests.[50] It can also be the result of a conscious policy of avoidance.

Although it is difficult to determine what Moscone would have done in the absence of the construction ban, it seems probable that he would have avoided the issue in the same way that Alioto did and for the same reasons. Politically and economically, the issue was sticky with very little promise of political payoff. It was not a sexy issue like minority participation or little city halls; the results were not visible like parks or new schools; it did not offer disaggregatable benefits dispensable to certain people in return for their support. It was one of those benefits likely to be taken for granted. We all want clean water and feel that we have a right to it, but few want to pay for it. It is also difficult to explain project costs and technical problems to the general public. These reasons often lead mayors to avoid certain types of issues. Shrinking violet avoidance will occur when issues are unpopular, costly, deficient in visible results, and demand an expenditure of resources larger than the anticipated return. With a limited stock of resources, a mayor cannot afford to intervene in situations likely to deplete those resources.

If the incentive structure leads to avoidance of pain, it also tends to foster a myopic approach. Yates has suggested that the fragmentation inherent in urban policymaking precludes long term planning.[51] While this is accurate, it is not a complete explanation. The immediate incentives confronting a mayor, coupled with the need to acquire resources, also discourage the seeking of long term goals. Alioto's handling of the police and fire strike illuminates this issue. With only a few months left in office and limited by charter to two terms, Alioto had little incentive— perhaps none at all—to act in a way popular with the public and the media (see Chapter 4). A mayor able and planning to seek re-election would have been in a very different situation.

Even without such a structural limitation, mayors tend to make calculations based on short term objectives and immediate opportunities. The Wagner and Lindsay administrations in New York showed a similar dichotomy between the short term approaches of the mayors and the long term needs of the city. Both mayors, especially Lindsay, used inflationary spending devices in order to acquire resources for dealing with immediate situations.[52] Responding to short term political realities, both Wagner and Lindsay mortgaged the city's financial future.

One can argue that Wagner and Lindsay were operating from positions of weakness and had to go after whatever help was available. But even a strong mayor with powerful resources faces the tension between long term goals and short term needs. Banfield's observations concerning Mayor Daley discuss this precise tension:

> It seems clear that there is a tension between the nature of the political system, on the one hand, and the requirements of planning—comprehensiveness and consistency in policy—on the other. In part, this tension arises from the decentralization so characteristic of the Chicago political system. . . . In part too, the tension arises from a general premise of our political culture: the belief that self-government consists not in giving or withholding consent at infrequent intervals on matters of general principle, but rather in making influence felt in the day-to-day conduct of the public business. So long as particular interests can prevent the executive from carrying out his policy, or so long as they can place hazards and delays in the way of his carrying it out, they can

demand concessions from him as the price of allowing him to act. It is the necessity of constantly making such concessions—of giving everyone something so as to generate enough support to allow of any action at all—that makes government policy so lacking in comprehensiveness and consistency.[53]

The mayor who is caught in these demands and concessions will usually expend more resources than can be acquired. Moscone's and Feinstein's experiences illustrate this over and over. By contrast, mayors who can insulate themselves from some of these demands and concessions will be able to conserve resources. Daley's policy of "watchful waiting" was an attempt to wait out this pressure described by Banfield. Even Kevin White, ordinarily no shrinking violet, used avoidance to conserve resources. The specific cases in which White applied it lend further support to my broader thesis that he was a power accumulator rather than a power expender.

The spending of the Boston school committee, often labeled "irresponsible," had been a problem for some time. Yet, the mayor's office had taken no action to remedy the situation. Although the school committee had fiscal autonomy, their supplementary budget required mayoral approval; every year, approval was granted. For White to have clamped down on the schools during the peak of the busing controversy, when his resources were being depleted by that crisis, would have been politically costly. Similarly, it would have been politically costly to take a firm stand while the schools still served a significant white population. (As we have seen, the black vote in Boston is proportionately small.) In 1981, however, with the schools serving a predominantly black population—white enrollment was down to about 36 percent—and with the negative fallout from Proposition 2½, the time was ripe to take an austere position on school spending. White did exactly this when he refused the school committee their supplemental budget request and decried their overall spending. Thus, political realities and needs led White to allow a crisis to continue because the costs of preventive action were too high. Moreover, he did take action when there was a political gain to be made; attention and criticism were diverted from the mayor's office toward the school committee.

White's approach to the Boston Housing Authority (BHA) was another example of conserving resources through playing the shrinking violet. Although White had made attempts early in his administration to change the BHA, his unsuccessful and costly efforts led him to abandon both his policy and the BHA (see Chapter 3).

Suffering from poor management and economic and political problems, the BHA slid from one crisis to another while the administration
offered no assistance. Unable to operate in a solvent manner, the BHA
came to its final crisis in the Perez case in Columbia Point, when the
court took jurisdiction. Both before and during the court-administered
process, which included establishing a board and appointing a receiver,
the mayor's office made no attempt to prevent receivership. In fact,
White's housing advisor told the mayor, "it [receivership] was the best
thing that could happen."[54] According to a *New York Times* account,
White "hailed the decision as a step in the right direction."[55] From a
political perspective, it was indeed the best thing that could happen.
The BHA was a losing institution and was seen by many as a "pariah
institution."[56] Like the schools, public housing in Boston served a predominantly black population that had very low voter turnout.[57] Any
attempt to save the BHA from receivership would have required investment of mayoral resources with little or no return. With the BHA in
receivership, however, White could officially as well as informally
abandon it. On 25 July 1979, the BHA went into court-appointed
receivership.

In San Francisco a similar, although not identical, situation occurred. The San Francisco Housing Authority (SFHA) had also suffered
managerial, economic, and political problems. As in Boston, the crises
were tolerated with no move by the mayor's office to intervene. Twenty
percent of the units were boarded up because the SFHA could not afford
to make repairs.[58] In addition, the high delinquency rate exacerbated
the financial problems of the SFHA. The final crisis came in 1979 when
the federal government threatened to cut off funding after it was unable
to perform an audit because of the poor condition of the accounting
system.[59]

At this juncture, the story takes a different track from the one in
Boston. Unlike White, Feinstein took immediate steps to respond to the
crisis. She brought in a new director and a new management team to
shore up the housing authority. The director obtained money from the
board and some federal funds for improvements. Under the new team's
direction, the accounting system was straightened out, contracts with
unions were firmed up, and the number of vacant units decreased. Feinstein's response to the crisis so far has been effective; federal funds have
not been cut off. However, like the BHA and the Boston public school
system, the SFHA did not develop its crisis overnight. Rather, it was the
result of years of problems that had been neglected by the mayors.

Since Feinstein's actions represent a departure from White's, it is
important to ask why. First, the specifics of the two crises and White's

strategies of leadership in general put him in a stronger position politically than Feinstein. This is a crucial point, because it underscores the relationship between strong executive leadership and the acquisition of resources. In general, the strong executive will have more freedom to choose a course of action. White chose a course of action that permitted him to conserve resources. Feinstein pursued a course of action that required an expenditure of resources.

The second and equally important reason for the different approaches was the timing of the crisis. When the federal threat came, Feinstein was a newly elected mayor, still shoring up her support. With her mile wide and inch deep constituency, Feinstein was often in the precarious position of having to avoid alienating any portion of her support. Further, the media and the business community were closely watching the new mayor's handling of a crisis.

Third, the high cost of housing and the low vacancy rate contributed to an overall housing crisis in San Francisco, making the issue a volatile one.[60] For Feinstein to have ignored any part of the housing picture would have been politically costly.

Fourth, the crisis in the SFHA threatened the loss of federal funding. Unlike Boston, where the crisis resulted in a change in jurisdiction, the difficulties in San Francisco involved a loss of resources with no change in jurisdiction. The housing authority would still have been a responsibility of the mayor, in an informal sense, and she would have been forced to operate with fewer resources.

A final factor that seems to explain Feinstein's action was her attempt to create an image of involvement. While campaigning, she had pledged to be a "hands-on mayor," involving herself in the details of all administrative operations. While it is too early to determine the outcome of her strategy, staff members who have worked in, or had contact with, all three administrations reveal that she *has* sought more direct input into city departments than did Moscone or Alioto.[61] Abandoning the housing authority might have harmed her overall strategy by indicating to other department heads that she would not *always* be a hands-on mayor. Her attempt to establish a strong image would have suffered if she was perceived as running from a problem. By contrast, having already established his control, White did not have to worry about damaging his image as a strong mayor. Where White was able to abandon the BHA and conserve resources because he was already in a strong position, Feinstein became involved in the crisis in order to project her image of strength.

The larger point in the public housing crises is still valid. In both cities, housing authorities experienced difficulties that Mayors White, Moscone, and Alioto avoided addressing because the return on the investment was not promising. Because of timing and other circumstances, Feinstein was forced to act.

The Massachusetts Bay Transportation Authority (MBTA) in Boston offers another example of an institution that promises little return on mayoral investment. And White's approach to the MBTA was similar to his approach to the BHA and the schools. Early attention was replaced by abandonment as the power expender was replaced by the power accumulator.

When White first became mayor, he attended most of the MBTA meetings, but, over the years, he retreated to a position of noninvolvement.[62] With the scandals that surrounded the management of the MBTA, the indictments of MBTA advisors, and the poor service of the system, the "T" became one of the least popular institutions in Boston. Taking responsibility for the transportation system promised very little in the way of public support. Moreover, the available remedies for the ailing transportation system—increased fares, reduced services, layoffs, or a combination of the three—would arouse outraged opposition from different parts of the electorate. Nor would any of those alternatives have improved the system; they merely would have kept it alive. Thus, assuming responsibility for the "T" would have been a politically costly move. In the later part of his administration, no one could have accused White of taking such risks. In contrast to his early enthusiasm and participation, White avoided that area of public policy. In the transit crisis in winter 1980, when the system shut down for two days, White kept a very low level of visibility. Although the "T" resumed service, the crisis remained, and White still practiced avoidance.

White's success in conserving resources through inaction is seen when we consider an opposite example in New York City. In 1968 Lindsay met the transportation issue head on. Facing the powerful Transit Workers Union, Lindsay attempted to mobilize public support for his efforts through a politics of attack. His strategy resulted in a long transit workers' strike, the creation of powerful enemies, subsequent strikes by other unions, and public disenchantment. The different strategies help to explain why White was able to acquire power and resources and Lindsay was not. Like White, Lindsay operated in an environment of scarce resources, but, instead of conserving them, he expended, dispersed, and, eventually, depleted them.

## The Shrinking Violet Syndrome: A Costly Strategy

Examining the shrinking violet behavior of mayors highlights the costs associated with the acquisition of power. In the broad sense, it illustrates the tensions between the need to acquire resources and the use of those resources. More narrowly, it points to a major dilemma for urban policymaking, particularly for certain groups within the city.

The broad problem characterizes executive leadership at all levels of government. After a brief analysis of the use of resources by Presidents Roosevelt, Kennedy, and Nixon, James MacGregor Burns concluded:

> . . . the dilemma of executive power remains. In protecting themselves—their reputations, choices, resources—what are chief executives guarding? If they constantly protect themselves, to what extent are they also guarding the purpose they are supposed ultimately to be serving? How do they draw the line between preserving power for themselves and expending it for broader goals?[63]

Burns goes on to say, "If problems remain unsolved because neither President nor Congress can confront them, does this not lead to a crisis at home or abroad, in economics, politics, world stability, or national morality?" In the cases presented here, we have seen how neglect led to crises.

Turning to the narrower implication of the executive's dilemma, we must look at the costs of executive avoidance and ask who pays them. The answer points to another crisis—this one in our political system.

The cases in which the mayors acted as shrinking violets had negative effects. The sewer issue led to a construction ban; the MBTA closed for two days and had continuing financial difficulties; the BHA went into receivership; the SFHA was threatened with a cut-off of federal funds. The Boston public school system, the MBTA, and the two housing authorities provide poor services. Except for the sewage system and, to a lesser extent, the MBTA, these crisis-bound institutions serve predominantly minority populations. In fact, it was largely the composition of the clientele that enabled the mayors to avoid these areas. If they had been dealing with a white middle class population who comprised a larger percentage of the total population and of the voting population than did the blacks, the mayors would not have been able to avoid these issues at the same low cost. From a strategic point of view, perhaps the mayors' actions were sagacious. But from a social point of view, the circumstances that permitted such a strategy to be effective suggest a serious failure of our political system. In the absence of mechanisms capable of integrating all citizens into the political system, mayors and other executives will be tempted to ignore those segments of the population who remain outside the system. And, if voting statistics are indicators of participation rates, the group outside is increasing. In national, state, and local elections, the trend over the last twenty years has been a decrease in participation.[64] With the circle of participants shrinking, executives will become less responsive to larger groups of people. Because these people tend to be found disproportionately among minorities and poor people, those with the greatest needs will receive the least.[65]

# SIX

# The Irony of Executive Leadership: Charter Reform Attempts in Boston and San Francisco

Power remains strong when it remains in the dark; exposed to the sunlight it begins to evaporate.[1]

Executives can seek additional resources and power through formal mechanisms like charter changes or through informal mechanisms like personal influence. In practice, however, the formal approach faces special barriers. One of the reasons for the insufficiency of mayoral resources is the anti-power bias in the American political culture. This is a major obstacle to acquiring power at all levels of government and is especially a problem when the formal approach is employed. Thus, attempts to acquire power must often be channeled through informal mechanisms that conceal the executive's intentions.

Reform procedures tend to be effective ways of concealing the acquisition of power. The classic example is Robert Moses in New York City. Appealing to a good government audience and using reform devices like the public authority, Moses amassed a wealth of financial and political resources. The creation of the public authority was ideal because it insulated Moses from public scrutiny (his most important insulation was his nondisclosed budget), gave him independent resources, and bypassed the mechanisms of accountability. While the power acquired by reformer Robert Moses was the envy of politicians from FDR down, it was approved by his good government audience because it was developed, expanded, and protected through the seemingly apolitical device of the public authority.[2] Moreover, there was a general belief that power in the hands of the administrator would be free from the corruption associated with elected officials.

LaGuardia's administration made a similar use of reform procedures. Appealing to a "crazy quilt" coalition that included a variety of ethnic interests as well as good government voters, LaGuardia used charter reforms and extensive municipal service reforms to defeat Tammany Hall and develop power.[3]

In Chicago, reform measures were used to protect the power of the machine. After suffering a political setback from a major scandal in Edward Kelly's administration, the Democratic machine put up a reform candidate for mayor, Martin Kennelly. In an agreement of mutual noninterference, the machine waited out Kennelly's administration, which took the heat off the party. The strategy was successful and at the end of Kennelly's administration, the machine selected Richard Daley, a party regular, for office. With his election the machine began to recoup the power it had let lie dormant for eight years.[4]

These cases represent examples of the use of reform procedures to acquire or protect power. That they are drawn from different times and different cities illustrates how widespread is the problem confronting American executives: the American electorate has a low tolerance for executives who take power.

In support of the argument that reform procedures develop power because they tend to conceal the acquisition of power, this chapter examines unsuccessful attempts at charter reform in Boston and San Francisco. The hypothesis is that charter reform was defeated largely because the electorate did not perceive it as reform but rather as an attempt to increase executive power. Examining these formal attempts to extend mayoral jurisdiction and power is crucial because it points to the obstacles to mayoral leadership and so underscores the importance of political skills. Furthermore, comparing the same policy in the two cities illustrates how San Francisco's fragmented environment, its strong reform ethos, and its relatively weak mayor's office are major impediments to executive leadership and constructive action in general. Although the results were the same in both cities, the road in San Francisco was much longer, was more crowded with participants who often proved to be obstacles, had a few detours, and was usually pretty bumpy.

## CHARTER REFORM: THE FAILURE OF CONCEALMENT

Reform devices are often employed by mayors and other executives in order to acquire power. But reform does not work when the electorate fails to perceive it as reform and sees it instead as a grab for power.

This dilemma has characterized charter reform attempts in several cities. In Philadelphia, Frank Rizzo's attempt to abolish the two term limitation on the mayor's office through a charter reform was defeated by 67 percent to 33 percent of the vote in 1978.[5] Although that referendum had sharp racial overtones, the anti-power bias contributed to its defeat as well.[6] Rizzo was in his second term and passage of the proposal would have allowed him to seek a third term.

The anti-power bias is even clearer in the case of New Haven. Taking his large electoral victories as indicators of his support, Richard Lee attempted to institutionalize the power that he developed through informal means (especially his skillful use of urban renewal resources) with a charter reform proposal in 1957. Although the proposal would have increased his formal powers, Lee thought that his popularity would deflect opposition or at least make the plan more palatable.[7] He was wrong. The Republican watchdog committee criticized it, charging that Lee was motivated by "political considerations rather than a desire for 'real reform.' " The *New Haven Register* carried a five part series on the proposal entitled, "Politics Without Reform."[8] When the New Haven electorate voted on the proposal, they too demonstrated the strength of the reform bias in the American political culture. Failing to make the connection between Lee's popularity, which was tied to his early urban renewal projects, and the power required to implement those projects, the voters refused to give Lee the additional powers that he sought. The measure was defeated by a two to one margin.[9]

In Boston and San Francisco, formal attempts to increase mayoral power through charter reform were also defeated and for similar reasons. Although the objective in both cities was the same, to strengthen the mayor's office, the approaches were different. In Boston, the proposal was developed in the mayor's office and then submitted to the City Council and state legislature for approval. In San Francisco, two attempts at charter reform began with election of committees to study the existing charter and to recommend changes, which the electorate would vote on. The different approaches and their consequences support a major theme of this study: weaker, more fragmented political systems pose major obstacles to mayoral leadership.

## CHARTER REFORM ATTEMPTS IN BOSTON

In Boston, White sought to avoid the problems that Lee encountered by selecting another strategy. Rather than put a proposal for increasing the mayor's power before the electorate, White chose to go to the legislature. Despite the different strategy, public opposition did mount and was a major factor in the proposal's defeat.

Originating with White, the idea for changing the charter was worked on by a special committee of top mayoral aides. The key features of the proposal were partisan elections for mayor and City Council; change in election years to make mayoral, council, and School Committee elections coincide with state elections; district elections for School Committee officials; expansion of City Council from nine to thirteen members; formulas that would limit appropriations for general school purposes; and power to the mayor and council to appoint the school superintendent.

The school component of the reform proposal resembled a previous attempt by White of two years earlier. Plan 3, Question 7, if passed, would have abolished the School Committee and set up community school districts. In June 1974, the proposal was defeated by Boston voters in a referendum. Two main reasons for the defeat were the busing issue and the political overtones of the measure. Coming in the heart of the busing controversy, the proposal became entangled with the passions aroused by that issue. Many voters identified pro-reform with pro-busing and anti-reform with anti-busing.[10]

The second reason that the measure was defeated was the political overtones of the proposal. Had it passed, the mayor would have gained appointment power in an area that had been closed to him in the past. Voter objection to the *perceived* politicization of the schools is not surprising. In most cities, education has been seen by the general public as an area off limits to politicians. In New York City, for example, both LaGuardia and Lindsay, mayors in two different periods, were criticized by the voters for actions that were taken as political intrusions into the sanctity of educational matters.[11]

It is hard to determine which of the two considerations in Boston contributed more to the defeat of Plan 3, Question 7. Experience in other cities, however, indicates that even in the absence of busing, the political component would have been strong enough to defeat the measure.

The defeat of Plan 3, Question 7, at the polls made it seem unwise to place a similar proposal on the ballot only two years later. It was decided to send the Charter Reform proposal by a safer route. The proposal would be sent to the state legislature in the form of a home rule petition, thus bypassing the voters.[12]

When the proposal for reform was completed, it was submitted to the City Council for approval. White's staff extensively lobbied individual councillors. As an added sweetener, the mayor's office included a provision to increase councillors' terms from two to four years. The proposal passed in the council by a five to four vote.

After clearing the City Council, the proposal was sent to the state legislature. White and his lobbyists persuaded the legislative leadership to pass the measure if the Boston delegation voted for passage. While White and his staff lobbied the leadership, there was very little, if any, lobbying of Boston representatives. This was consistent with White's approach in the past, never to expend too many resources on lobbying the Boston delegation. This was partly because of the good relationship he enjoyed with the leadership, the dominance of the Massachusetts legislature by its leadership, and the increasing disunity within the legislature and within the Boston delegation.

After securing approval from the leadership, the proposal was placed before the Boston delegation for a vote, where it was defeated. White was unsuccessful here due to several factors. First, and perhaps most important, many Boston representatives viewed the charter reform proposal as antithetical to their interests. The introduction of partisan labels in local elections, combined with district elections for School Committee officials, would have created competition for legislators in their districts. By contrast, in the at-large electoral system, state representatives were the only district representatives that Bostonians could turn to. The at-large system indirectly enhanced their power. Moreover, the representatives were under public pressure to vote against the proposal. The measure had already stirred up opposition among many voters, especially School Committee officials, who objected to the school component of the package. The more vocal spokespersons used the partisan election issue to paint the entire proposal as a grab for power by White. Good government groups, such as the League of Women Voters, also criticized the partisan elections part of the proposal. After a series of public hearings throughout the city, the Finance Commission issued a negative report on the proposal and called for a new package that would exclude partisan elections.[13] In addition, the press began criticizing the proposal as well.

The opposition generated by the measure among the electorate influenced the way that the Boston delegation voted. Many representatives received phone calls and letters from their constituents urging them to vote against the measure.[14] A corollary to this point and another factor in the charter reform's defeat was the absence of "reform." White was calling for partisan elections. Thus the proposal represented a move toward politics. And politics is not reform! These sentiments were probably best reflected in State Senator Timilty's criticism of the proposal; he referred to the package as having "something for every single politician in the Commonwealth and nothing for the people."[15] With the strong public bias against the proposal, legislators hesitated to support a measure from which they had nothing to gain and perhaps something to lose. In addition, some legislators, like Barney Frank, were appealing to wider liberal audiences and therefore voted according to audience preferences.

Another factor in the defeat of charter reform was White's poor relations with the Boston delegation. Historically, relations between

Boston mayors and the Boston delegation have been poor. This situation worsened, however, with the increase in ticket splitting, which decreased the mayor's already limited ability to deliver the vote, and reforms that decreased the power of the legislature in relation to the governor.[16]

The poor relations between White and the Boston delegation, together with the resentment felt by many towards White, created incentives to veto a White proposal when such a vote would not upset their standing among their constituents. In this case, a negative vote probably enhanced their standing.

## SAN FRANCISCO: THE LONG AND WINDING ROAD TO DEFEAT

In San Francisco, charter reform failed in two separate attempts, eleven years apart. As in Philadelphia and New Haven, these proposals were put before the public, where they were defeated. But the process for devising the proposals was complex and long, in contrast to the other efforts. Moreover, the initiative did not come from the mayor's office, as in the other three cities, but rather from an external source.[17] San Francisco's second unsuccessful charter reform attempt illustrates once more the fragmented nature of San Francisco's political system and the dilemmas that it poses for action and executive leadership.

San Francisco's second charter reform attempt began in 1977. James Haas, a politically active citizen, approached several of the supervisors with a proposal to establish an advisory committee to make recommendations for charter changes. With an election pending, however, the supervisors were not very responsive.[18] Haas approached them again in 1978 and persuaded four of the supervisors to place a nonbinding policy statement on the ballot asking the electorate whether the city should elect a commission for charter change. The public approved the measure by 54 percent of the vote.[19] The next step was a ballot item asking the voters to approve passage of enabling legislation that would permit the city to establish a charter reform commission with fifteen elected commissioners.

Even at this early stage, we see how much more complex the process was in San Francisco than in Boston. In Boston, the proposal was developed by the mayor's office and so avoided committing time, energy, and resources to strictly procedural items as in San Francisco. This difference reflects the difference in political cultures. As critics of the reform movement have argued, there is a tendency in reform to place a disproportionate amount of emphasis on procedure.[20] The less reform-oriented Boston put substantially less effort into procedure than did San Francisco. Moreover, the procedure used did much to define the shape of the contest and to narrow the alternatives available to the mayor. The procedure used in San Francisco brought in more participants, whose diverse incentives, constituencies, and objectives shaped an arena characterized by substantial conflict. Disagreements among the proponents over possible changes continued until and during the actual voting. The nature of the arena gave Feinstein a brokering role and not the leadership role played by White, Lee, and Rizzo in their cities.

After the electorate passed the ballot item to elect a charter reform commission, the League of Women Voters, SPUR, good government organizations, and the Chamber of Commerce met to put together a slate of candidates. After the first meeting, the Chamber of Commerce pulled out to set up their own slate. When the election finally took place, there were 107 candidates. Of the 15 who were elected, 5 were from the good government slate, 2 from the Chamber of Commerce slate, 1 from the Chinese American Democratic Club (CADC) slate, 2 labor representatives, and 5 independent candidates.

The newly elected Charter Reform Commission addressed the preliminary issues of finances, appointment of an executive director, and the substantive issue of reform itself. When the commission began, it had no money, no staff, and no resources. The financial issue was resolved in the spring when the commission received $175,000 plus in-kind services from the city, $35,000 from the federal government for civil service reforms modeled after the Federal Civil Service Reform Act, and private foundation money, bringing their budget to approximately $300,000. The commission was divided on the choice of an executive director between a grass roots activist and a political scientist, Glen Sparrow, from San Diego State University. Sparrow was chosen by a one vote margin. The commission approached the issue of reforms by holding a series of public hearings throughout the city. Based on the response at these hearings, the commission decided to draft a new charter rather than change the existing one. The three main objectives of the new charter were to strengthen the executive, simplify the charter, and rationalize the bureaucracy.

In January, the Charter Reform Commission finally produced a first draft. This was almost two years after the supervisors agreed to put a policy statement on the ballot and approximately fifteen months after the electorate approved the establishment of the commission. The major elements of this first draft were a strong mayor form of government; elimination of the CAO, the treasurer, the controller, and the assessor; and modernization of the civil service section of the charter. In addition, the draft excluded reference to any departments like Health, Social Services, and Parks and Recreation, giving the mayor and the board the power to create these departments through enabling legislation.

The entire draft, which was between twenty and thirty pages long, was published by the *Chronicle*. With the exception of labor, the reactions were all negative. The Downtown Association, conservative segments of the business community, and the west side of the city opposed the elimination of the CAO and the controller. Neighborhood groups objected to giving the mayor and the board power to create the various city departments, especially Parks and Recreation. Labor supported the draft because it felt that some of the proposed management reforms would improve the morale of workers and some of the projected savings from these reforms would be used for additional wages, both of which would enhance labor's political power.

With the overwhelmingly negative reaction, the commission drew up a second draft, which was completed in early April—four months after the first draft, nineteen months after the vote to elect a commission, and twenty-eight months after the policy statement.

This draft reinstated the elected offices of treasurer and assessor and the administrative office of the CAO, although the CAO would serve at the pleasure of the mayor. The commissions and departments were also reinstated. The civil service section included a strike settling provision combining collective bargaining and formulas; a formula-based schedule would be established but unions dissatisfied with those wages could collectively bargain for higher wages.

This provision illustrates a special case of fragmentation within a fragmented constituency. While labor as a whole was represented on the commission, labor is not always a whole. It is composed of various unions with divergent incentives and objectives. The craft unions, which had done very well by the formulas, were opposed to collective bargaining; but the SEIU, which had less lucrative formulas, favored collective bargaining. In order to appease a diversity of interests within one constituent group, a compromise was worked out.

When this draft was presented, the reactions were similar to the earlier ones. Groups that previously had opposed the elimination of the CAO now opposed the suggestion that the CAO serve at the pleasure of the mayor. The compromise in the civil service section intended to satisfy labor was opposed by Mayor Feinstein, who felt that the unions would use the formulas as minimum rates and then bargain for higher rates.

With a second round of negative reactions, the charter commission went back to the drawing board for a third time. But they did so only after a brief detour caused by the introduction of yet another participant—the American Civil Liberties Union (ACLU). The ACLU criticized the second draft because it lacked a bill of rights and sex quotas. But the latter were opposed by the Asian community, which felt that sex quotas would decrease the number of Asians on commissions.[21] The ACLU drew up a bill of rights that would permit any citizen who did not receive adequate housing, transportation, or other basic services from the city to sue the city. The ACLU persuaded the commission to include a bill of rights; the vote was eight to four.

However desirable this step might have been, it was a long way from the commission's original objectives. And that is how it was perceived. Mayor Feinstein called it nonsense; Supervisor Molinari said it would never pass; and the *Examiner* accused the commissioners of being "out of touch with reality."[22] Four days later, the commission voted eight to four to remove the bill of rights and the quota provisions. This left the ACLU bitter but restored some of the credibility that the commission had begun to lose when they adopted the bill of rights. You can't please all of the people all of the time but, in a political system as hyperpluralistic as San Francisco's, the pressures to do so are enormous. And these pressures are obstacles to action.

After their four-day detour, the Charter Reform Commission resumed its activities and drew up a third and final draft. The proposed new charter had five key provisions:

(1) Mayoral control over the budget was increased by
    (a) limiting the controller's term to six years, with removal requiring a majority vote;
    (b) establishing a deputy mayor to prepare the budget instead of the controller; and
    (c) giving the mayor authority to increase appropriations.
(2) Mayoral control over administrative matters was increased by limiting the CAO's term to four years, with authority for removal residing solely with the mayor, and by limiting the CAO's jurisdiction to the establishment of guidelines for contracts, purchasing, permits, and inspections.
(3) Mayoral control over bureaucracy was increased by giving the mayor power to reorganize duties and functions between departments, a power previously held by the Board of Supervisors.
(4) Mayoral power in labor relations was increased by giving the mayor and the board authority to appoint a director of employee relations and a chief of labor negotiations, a power formerly held by the board only.

(5) The labor negotiation process was changed to include formulas and collective bargaining.

The proponents of the new charter, which included the Labor Council, SPUR, the League of Women Voters, and the Democratic party, conducted a three-month campaign. They raised $20,000, approximately $3,000 of which came from organized labor. Despite their electioneering, they met strong opposition from the same old groups. The Chamber of Commerce and the conservative business interests opposed the new charter because of the alterations in the position of CAO and controller. The building trades opposed it because the prevailing wage section had been removed. The *Chronicle* opposed it because the magnitude of the changes would have altered the status quo in which the paper enjoyed substantial power. It accused the commissioners of going beyond their original mandate, which was to make changes in the old charter and not create a new one. The neighborhood groups did not endorse the proposal because it did not address their primary concern, zoning matters. And Mayor Feinstein opposed it because of the labor provisions. When the proposal went to the public, it was defeated by 54 percent to 46 percent of the vote.[23]

Perhaps the moral of the charter reform story is that nothing is "just done" in San Francisco. The powerful reform bias in the political culture, which places a strong emphasis on open processes and participatory democracy, has created, as Fred Wirt observed, a "hyperpluralistic" political system which is an obstacle to action, implementation, and mayoral leadership.[24]

# PART THREE

## The Federal Arena: Additional Resources

# SEVEN

# The Nationalization of Local Politics: Opportunities and Dilemmas

Our city is a battleground among federal Cabinet agencies.[1]

In the last twenty years, the federal government became an increasingly important factor in city politics. As urban political machines faded and the parties lost their ability to deliver the local vote, national candidates began to go directly to the voters. Federal programs containing large patronage opportunities were used to gain support from urban voters.[2] Local problems as well as their solutions began to be dealt with on the national level.

This phenomenon created problems for mayors by increasing administrative burdens, by politicizing and strengthening new groups, and by creating vertical alliances between local managers and federal officials. Many observers argued that the federal presence supplanted the role of mayors and reduced the significance of local government; the federal government, not local government, was shaping local events.[3] The creation of the Advisory Commission on Intergovernmental Relations (ACIR) in 1959 and of terms like "para government," "balkanized bureaucracy," and "feudal federalism" show the widespread acceptance of the idea that local sovereignty was going if not gone.[4]

Although these new arrangements were adverse to the interests of mayors, national officials tended to favor them. Many Washington policymakers mistrusted mayors or, at best, saw them as inadequate to deal with the problems of the urban poor.[5] OEO officials, especially, bypassed mayors and went directly to the poor through the creation of Community Action Agencies (CAAs).[6]

The experience in Boston and San Francisco provides contrary evidence to both propositions—that the federal presence in local politics has undermined the mayor's role and that federal action has diminished the importance of local government. Moreover, the conclusions indicate that mayoral control over federal programs is preferable to the current alternatives.

Not all scholars saw the federal government as a monolithic actor in local politics. Jeffrey Pressman argued that the federal-local relationship was a reciprocal one. Federal programs influenced and were influenced by the local political system. Federal programs became another tool for mayors to use rather than a replacement for their leadership.[7] My analysis builds on Pressman's findings by showing how skillful mayors can create a one-way relationship with the federal presence. Through a careful manipulation of federal programs, mayors can centralize their control over those resources.

Establishing such control is essential. Uncontrolled, the federal presence tends to disrupt the local political system. Mayor Yorty's inability to control federal programs in Los Angeles resulted in a free-for-all among competing groups; battles within the black community and between blacks and Hispanics led to major conflicts that Yorty was unable to resolve. The struggles prevented an efficient use of important resources. Greenstone and Peterson have shown how the absence of consensus often is an impediment to initiating programs.[8] In Oakland, Reading's failure to exercise leadership resulted in nonelected officials controlling federal resources. This has practical as well as theoretical implications for local government. Nonelected officials are subject to fewer mechanisms of accountability and have narrower constituencies than do elected officials. Policy made by the few tends to favor the interests of the few. This adds to the fragmentation in the political system and threatens the legitimacy of democratic governance.

The failure of the mayor to control federal programs can also lead to the creation of new arenas for power struggles. This is what Pressman found in Oakland, what Greenstone and Peterson found in Los Angeles, what Sundquist found in the cities he studied, and what occurred in New York City under Lindsay.[9] But the creation of new arenas is not the same as enfranchising new groups. Pressman demonstrated how the groups in this new arena were in conflict with groups in the electoral arena.[10] Rather than setting the stage for a political competition characterized by bargaining and compromise, the result is a politics of polarization. In Oakland, Los Angeles, New York City, and many of the cities that Sundquist visited, federal programs were colored by racial conflict rather than cooperation. By integrating federal programs into the larger political system, a mayor can avoid this polarization. Mayoral control over federal programs is not only possible, but, given the alternatives, it is necessary.

## ESTABLISHING THE FEDERAL CONNECTION

During the mid-1960s a new breed of U.S. mayors arose. Younger than their predecessors, these mayors were ideological, energetic, and bent on turning cities around. The election of black mayors like Carl Stokes (Cleveland) and Richard Hatcher (Gary) held the promise of a new racial equality. Jerome Cavanaugh's establishment of the New Detroit Committee to consult with militant blacks after the riot indicated a new sensitivity to the black community.[11] White and Lindsay's pro-civil rights positions and Alioto's endorsement of the police department's community relations program contrasted sharply with tough law-and-order candidates like George Wallace or Sam Yorty (in his first term).

As did some earlier mayors like Richard Lee, many of these "new breed" mayors had ambitions for higher office. Lacking the strong local party machinery available to the earlier mayors, these rising politicos used the U.S. Conference of Mayors (USCM) and the National League of Cities (NLC) for political mobility. While political ambition was a prime motivation, these mayors had an important impact on federal legislation. Through the USCM, urban executives confronted Washington with a strong lobbying force for urban areas. Conversely, the mayors' participation gained them attention, reputations, and influence.

### The Role of the Rising Politico

Joe Alioto played the role of "rising politico" with a sophistication and charm that earned him instant recognition.[12] Elected mayor in 1967, he was chosen in 1968 to deliver the nomination to Hubert Humphrey at the Democratic Convention. Capturing the attention of everyone in the audience, Alioto established himself as a promising figure in Democratic party politics. There was even strong speculation that Humphrey would select Alioto for his vice-presidential running mate.[13]

Through the USCM and the Democratic party, Alioto acquired important influence in Washington and frequently visited there. In 1971, he used the USCM to prevent Nixon from cutting off supplemental funding for the Model Cities Program.[14] Alioto was once quoted as saying, "No mayor can really do his job unless he spends at least one day per month in Washington."[15] There is another side of the coin, however. In a 1968 editorial on the demise of Arthur Naftalin, the city's four-term mayor, the *Minneapolis Star* said, "The mayor lost press support because he spent too much time away from the city on his missions seeking federal aid."[16] Similarly, many informants in San Francisco claimed that Alioto could have been a stronger mayor had his attention and energy not been diverted by Washington and his ambitions for higher office. While this complaint was made of many 1960s mayors, the federal connection did provide an opportunity for gaining grants, resources, and a reputation.

Like Alioto, Kevin White saw the opportunities in the federal connection. Ambitious for higher office and needing to project a progressive image, White cast his lot with the USCM and NLC, identifying with the more active members like Lindsay and Alioto. One informant recalled that White referred to Lindsay and Alioto as the two best "performers" he had seen.[17] Through speeches in Washington and innovative programs like the Little City Halls in Boston, White soon earned a reputation as a rising politico with a promising future in Democratic party politics. In 1972, White was considered for vice-presidential running mate by McGovern.

By the mid-1970s, however, the rising politico role was a less effective route for acquiring federal resources than it had been in the 1960s and early 1970s. By 1976 most of the rising politicos had fallen: John Lindsay, Joe Alioto, and Jerome Cavanaugh had retired from the urban scene without obtaining higher office. Commenting on White's decreased participation in the USCM, a former aide observed, "White felt he had already played the Washington game and that those days were over."[18]

The days of acquiring federal resources, however, were not over. Acquisition now required new mechanisms. Adapting to the shift in political climate, White relied on the aid of Tip O'Neill and the recruitment of skilled grantsmen to sustain his access to federal resources. When Boston was not selected in the 1978 Entitlement grant competition for a youth employment program, Tip O'Neill and DOL personnel persuaded DOL officials to include Boston in the award.[19] As a former Carter pollster said, "When you do something for Boston, you're doing a favor for Tip—Everyone wants to do favors for the Speaker of the House."[20] Undoubtedly, this was a powerful incentive to aid Boston.

In 1976 White made federal relations an administrative priority, setting up an Office of Federal Relations under the direction of John Drew. With White as their liaison, the office established contacts with leading DOL, HUD, and White House officials. Once these contacts were made, the office pursued an ambitious planning effort, culminating in the Boston Plan: a proposal for development projects in Hyde Park, Columbia Point, Blue Hill Avenue, and the waterfront. The plan was attractive in Washington both for its originality in combining various programs and for its coordination of several local agencies, two features which were consistent with the Carter administration's emphasis on local initiative. The plan was sold in Washington, and Boston received $88 million in federal funds, Economic Development Administration (EDA) loan guarantees, and special priorities on Small Business Association (SBA) loans.[21]

The shift in strategies helps to explain why White was more successful than many post 1960s mayors in acquiring federal resources. In 1979 Boston received the highest per capita federal funding of any city in the country. With a per capita total of $109.70, Boston led the second highest city, Baltimore, by almost $10 per capita ($99.77), and the third city, Detroit, by more than $40 ($67.44). The figures for New York City and Chicago were substantially lower—$10.35 and $15.39, respectively.[22] Moscone, who was elected after the heyday of media and audience politics, was less effective in getting federal money. He did not have the contacts that White had, and the power and contacts of others in city government were often an obstacle to Moscone's ability to use federal money.

### "Up for Grabs"

As a new arena, social welfare was "up for grabs" at both the federal and local levels.[23] In his analysis of the implementation process, Eugene Bardach wrote,

> the mandate will have provided certain program elements, usually a piece of bureaucracy and a modest budget, without clearly prescribing or even envisioning what other elements might be conjoined with them and to what exact purpose. In this confused situation, the few unambiguously mandated elements are Up for Grabs by a number of different potential clientele groups to be converted into political resources that can then be used to shape the policy or program goals in ways congenial to themselves.[24]

Bardach suggested that the Up for Grabs game characterized ambiguous policies that resulted from "strong pressures on the government to 'do something' about what is generally perceived to be an urgent social problem, even though no one quite knows what ought to or could be done."[25] This describes much of the 1960s social welfare legislation. Pressured by mayors, governors, the NAACP, and the media, federal officials felt a need to "do something" about the threat and reality of urban riots. Operating in a vacuum of knowledge and understanding, they took many well-intentioned but nevertheless blind shots.

Within this situation, control over the social welfare programs was up for grabs. The major competitors in Washington were representatives of governors—the Council of State Governments (COSGO) and the National Governor's Conference (NGC)—and representatives of mayors—NLC and USCM.[26] While the mayors did not win every battle, the conference did bring many of the new programs under the control of the cities rather than the states. Control by the cities often meant control by the mayors, because their lobbying was usually stronger than that of others such as community action groups.

In pursuing federal money, which was new, mayors avoided conflicts with entrenched interests over established city funds. And, because the funding came from outside, these nationally redistributive programs were distributive at the local level. With their concentrated benefits and distributed costs, these programs attracted the support of organizations representing the target groups and very little opposition.[27]

## MAYORAL LEADERSHIP AND THE FEDERAL ARENA

Mayoral control over federal programs was not the rule in all cities. In Oakland, the shrinking violet behavior of key forces in city government was an obstacle to mayoral control over federal programs. And the mayor's own shrinking violet tendencies compounded the problem. By underutilizing the resources of his office, Mayor Reading made it possible for "federal actors to overlook City Hall and provide funds to a separate arena outside it." This federal bypass of the mayor strengthened nongovernmental groups, furthered the fragmentation of Oakland's political system, increased the obstacles to mayoral leadership, and created a politics of "separatism."[28]

Avoiding the dilemmas and capitalizing on the potential of the federal presence required a skillful mayor who established control over federal resources. The role of political skill becomes even more apparent when we consider that the political structure and the context also influence the degree of control that the mayor can exercise. Ranking the political systems from least to most fragmented we have: Boston under White, San Francisco under Alioto, and San Francisco under Moscone. Ranking the mayors from most to least control over federal programs we have: White, Alioto, and Moscone. These rankings indicate a strong correlation between fragmentation and control. Although significant, this correlation is by no means an iron law. Alioto in San Francisco and Houlihan in Oakland both overcame the obstacles of a fragmented system through forceful political action.

A favorable context is also crucial.[29] White and Alioto entered the federal arena when many of the programs were new. Not dealing with entrenched interests, they had more freedom to structure the arena than·

did Moscone, who entered when many programs were already established. A favorable context, however, does not substitute for political skill. Reading, Lindsay, and Yorty also entered when the programs were new, but they were not politically skillful enough to structure the arena to their advantage.

## Kevin White

White took an aggressive approach to federal programs, using the resources of his office to move into areas left untended by the shrinking violet behavior of other actors. He centralized his control over federal programs and used them to mobilize support. Through them he strengthened his office, his resources, and his control over other actors. Motivated by political concerns, White nevertheless used federal programs to benefit minorities, the elderly, and the poor. Moreover, by integrating federal programs into Boston's political system, White prevented the rise of new arenas of power, a development that in other cities led to major conflicts and racial politics.

Through the creation of offices and programs among minorities and the elderly, White channeled tangible benefits to important parts of the electorate. The establishment of the Office of Human Rights (OHR) and the appointment of blacks to federally funded programs strengthened White's ties in the black community and provided an important source of employment for blacks. During White's administration, black employment in city government increased from 6 percent to 20 percent.[30] Federally funded programs sponsored by the Office of Elderly Affairs, such as free lunch and bus service, solidified White's ties with the elderly and provided them with needed services. This was an important component of White's electoral support because the median voting age in Boston was sixty.[31]

Federal money was also important in permitting White to mobilize campaign workers and conflict management forces. CETA funds, which by 1976 had created more than 1,300 jobs in 38 city agencies, were used by White as political rewards.[32] White's ward coordinators dispensed CETA jobs in exchange for campaign work.[33] The Youth Activities Commission, which had approximately $2 million in federal funds in 1973–1974 and a non–civil service staff of 300, supplied campaign workers to the 1975 and 1979 mayoral elections.[34] YAC staff also aided Little City Hall managers and mayoral aides in the busing crisis. Meeting with parents of school children, YAC staff helped to limit racial violence accompanying the conflict.

Through his control over federal programs, White was able to concentrate money in politically crucial neighborhoods. Charlestown and South Boston—two conservative, working class, Irish areas that opposed White's liberal policies, his racial views, and his stand on busing—received large concentrations of CETA jobs.[35] The Boston Marine Industrial Park, a $4 million public works project undertaken in 1976 to restore South Boston's navy yard, was another attempt to concentrate resources in that electorally difficult area. As a part of the city that had been neglected by previous mayors—Collins and Hynes had focused almost exclusively on the downtown business district—the administrative presence and the 600 jobs created by the project strongly appealed to South Boston voters. In the 1979 election, White won South Boston and Charlestown.

White's first electoral victory in South Boston also owed something to his success in neutralizing important opposition. White appointed James Kelly, a powerful political leader in South Boston who had always run anti-White campaigns, to the Economic Development and Industrial Commission (EDIC). EDIC ran the public works project in South Boston, which meant that Kelly commanded a lot of patronage. Although Kelly did not campaign for White in 1979, he did not campaign against him.

White's control over federal resources strengthened his bargaining position in the business community as well. White used the federal requirement of public sponsorship for Urban Development Action Grants (UDAGs) to secure a 50 Percent Agreement from developers. This required developers and businesses occupying the buildings to draw at least 50 percent of their workers from the Boston population, 25 percent from minority communities and 10 percent from the female population. The Copley Plaza project is estimated to have provided 7,500 construction jobs and 2,000 permanent jobs when completed with the appropriate percentages going to the designated groups.[36] The bargaining potential of UDAGs was also seen by Feinstein. She forged an agreement with the Ramada Inn for the renovation of four resident hotels (460 housing units) in exchange for city approval of its UDAG application. In both cases, it is doubtful that the business community would have undertaken these important policy initiatives on its own.

In many cities, federal programs created nongovernmental arenas where powerful forces contended. This is not surprising, since the availability of federal money politicized groups who wanted a piece of the pie. If they were able to obtain some of that money, their power was increased vis-à-vis the mayor. In Oakland, when Mayor Reading underutilized his resources, OEDCI established the necessary contacts and got the federal money. As a result, they were strengthened considerably and became a major obstacle to Reading's future attempts to get and control federal money. In New York City, Lindsay's ineffective use of resources helped create powerful groups that he could not control. In an attempt to build minority support, Lindsay bargained away federal resources. By giving vocal minority leaders major roles in the Community Action Programs, Lindsay strengthened these leaders who then made demands on City Hall.[37] James Sundquist found a similar situation in many of the cities he examined. A significant finding of Sundquist's study was the problematic nature of this alternative leadership. These leaders often were either militant and in conflict with city hall, or weak and incompetent, or not well respected in their communities. These qualities made for chaotic programs, wasted resources, and poor local coordination.[38]

In the federal arena as in other arenas, the mayor must stay ahead of competitors. White's contacts with Tip O'Neill and other key Washington officials allowed him this margin. In the case of the proposed Federal Office Building, the mayor's office devised plans for locating the federally funded construction in the North Station area of the city. The federal government, however, designated the "combat zone," as the theatre district was called, to be the building site. Nevertheless, according to White's press secretary, the mayor wanted to use the Federal Office Building as an anchor for future development in the North Station area.[39] Although White's plan was challenged by local merchants and environmentalists who also favored the combat zone site, White persuaded the federal government to approve his plan through the aid of Tip O'Neill.

White's experience with federal programs illustrates their potential for increasing mayoral power. But as is shown by Lindsay's experience in New York City, Reading's in Oakland, Yorty's in Los Angeles and, as we will see, Moscone's in San Francisco, what White accomplished was not easy. Furthermore, when we place the discussion of federal programs in the context of the entire study, we see how the several strategies are interrelated. In the absence of effective personnel management, White would not have had the control over his department heads necessary to manage federal money. In the absence of favorable media attention and important contacts, he might not have had enough clout in Washington to get the federal money. And, without effective political skills, he might not have used the Tip O'Neill connection in an efficient manner. Executive leadership and the acquisition of resources is a complex subject. The variables are discussed separately in this study, but they should always be considered in the context of their interdependence.

## Joe Alioto

Like White, Alioto took an aggressive approach to federal programs that was aided by his other strategies and facilitated them in turn. He used his coalition to counter the shrinking violet behavior of other actors. Before Alioto, the Board of Supervisors had unanimously rejected a Model Cities application. And Mayor Shelley had not even tried to reverse the decision. Anticipating a similar vote, Alioto used black and Hispanic community leaders and labor representatives to lobby the board. The efforts of the first group were enhanced by the presence of one black supervisor on the board. The board voted seven to four to apply for the grant.

Alioto's use of federal programs to strengthen the mayor's office was enhanced by relativism. Before Alioto, the mayor's office was relatively weak because of its limited formal powers and the city's fragmented government. As a result, many groups bypassed the mayor's office: business interests dealt directly with the CAO and many developers negotiated directly with the powerful Redevelopment Agency. Alioto departed sharply from the practices of his two nonactivist predecessors, and moved to emblazon the mayor's office on the map of San Francisco city government. Federal programs enabled Alioto to achieve this without taking power from other parts of city government. By enlarging its functions, Alioto brought the mayor's office into more areas than it had been, thereby decreasing some of the fragmentation in city government. Housing and neighborhood development policy came under the influence of the mayor's office rather than being the sole product of the Planning Commission. Criminal justice policies, which had been formulated by the police department, were now being shaped by the mayor's office. Policy areas that had been left to private market forces, such as minority employment, were coming under the mayor's jurisdiction.

The increase in activities made the mayor's office difficult to bypass and it created an image of strength. This last factor should not be underestimated. People act largely on the basis of their perceptions. An image of power gives an executive a strong resource. This resource assumes greater importance in a system like San Francisco's, which is deficient in formal resources.

The reality as well as the image of a strong mayor's office was partially achieved by an increase in staff size. When Alioto entered office, the mayor's staff consisted of about thirty people. This number grew to almost four hundred by the time Alioto left office eight years later. Funds from HUD, the Department of Labor, and the Law Enforcement Assistance Administration (LEAA) were used to create community development, manpower planning, and criminal justice offices. Having a larger staff permitted the mayor's office to take on more activities, and it broadened the mayor's appointment powers, giving him a larger say over the composition of city government.

These resources were supplemented by the budgets attached to federal programs. The formal limitations on the San Francisco mayor's financial authority made this a crucial tool. With a budget of approximately $30 million of federal money, the mayor now had direct control over financial resources. Alioto used these new resources to increase the power of his coalition and thus, his own influence. The major components of his coalitional strategy were minorities, labor, and the bureaucracy.

Federal programs were important in cultivating support in black and Hispanic communities. This process also expanded employment opportunities for minorities. During Alioto's administration black and Hispanic employment in city government increased by 8 percent each.[40] Approximately 300 blacks received jobs in the various Model Cities programs, such as community housing and ambulatory health care. The CETA program in San Francisco provided about 1,800 jobs, most of which went to minorities. Alioto's creation of Latino Educational Centers, dance companies for children, and the Mission Housing Development Corporation provided employment, housing, and educational activities in the Hispanic community.

By integrating federal programs into his coalitional strategy, Alioto was able to handpick the leadership in the minority communities and protect his organizational base. This strategy prevented the rise of new arenas of power and the conflict that often accompanies them. Alioto's approach was similar to Daley's use of the Community Action Program in Chicago. By channeling money through the machine, Daley insured that only party faithfuls received resources, thus strengthening the organization's power against its opposition.[41] Alioto's distribution of federal resources to conservative members of the minority communities—especially ministers and black union members—strengthened their leadership positions within the community.

Eloise Westbrook, who was referred to as the grand dame of Hunter's Point, always maintained good relations with Alioto and always received funding for her programs. In one election, she delivered so many votes that Alioto appointed her director of the Bayview/Hunter's Point Educational Facility, a $45,000 a year position.[42] A crucial part of Alioto's black support came from the ministers. Alioto gained his initial access to the black community through the Baptist Minister's Union, part of the ILWU. He strengthened this bond by giving federal money to churches to expand their parish membership.[43]

By contrast, militant elements and Alioto's opponents did not receive federal money from the administration. Alioto stopped funding the Mission Economic Development Corporation after its director supported Alioto's opponent in the 1971 election.[44] When the corporation appointed a new director who supported Alioto, he restored their funding. When Dr. Arthur Coleman supported Feinstein in the 1971 election, Alioto defunded his community health center in Hunter's Point. Coleman questioned the matter and Alioto replied, "You don't bring a loser's ticket to the winner's window."[45] According to mayoral aides, this response reflected Alioto's general approach.

The Louise M. Davies Symphony Hall case illustrates Alioto's broad use of federal programs as rewards and sanctions. In 1968 Alioto created the Zellerbach Committee—named for J. D. Zellerbach, an important figure in San Francisco's financial community—to review plans for a new performing arts center and to promote a bond to finance it. Opponents denounced it as a public subsidy for the rich and, in the election, the voters defeated the bond. When the proposal came up again several years later, Alioto used a different approach. Instead of a bond, he allocated $5 million in community development (CD) money. The Neighborhood Arts Movement and some supervisors, including Feinstein, objected, claiming that public money should support community art. To defuse the opposition, Alioto gave $2.5 million in CD money to the organization to divide among the various neighborhood art groups.[46] With the opposition silenced, Alioto persuaded the CAO to release some Hotel Tax money and key financial figures in the city, like Davies, to contribute money. The project was set in motion without floating a bond, financed largely by private money.

A key factor in Alioto's coalition was the labor-dominated Redevelopment Agency. By channeling large sums of CD money to the agency, Alioto served the interests of labor. The ILWU sponsored housing developments in the SFRA's Western Addition project. Many ILWU members lived in those units. The ILWU also had its world headquarters built in the Western Addition. Using the Redevelopment Agency was also a way to give contracts to unions and union members. Local 261 received an SFRA contract to build mini-parks on SFRA property.[47] Alex Mason, a longshoreman, received contracts for developments in black communities from the Redevelopment Agency.[48] Finally, the federal money that was used for construction boosted the unions by providing jobs.

The bureaucracy formed an integral part of Alioto's coalitional strategy. Federal programs enabled Alioto to shift power from the fringes to the center without threatening the bureaucracy because these resources were new and external. The mayor's office, expanding by means of increasing the pie, was strengthened in itself and in relation to other parts of the city establishment, but bureaucracy was not weakened thereby. This distinction is important: in Moscone's time, increasing the power of the mayor's office could only be done by cutting into the bureaucracy, financially and functionally. Alioto came at a time when these programs were new and thus avoided this dilemma.

Alioto's strategy further circumvented this dilemma. Whereas Lindsay used federal programs to bypass bureaucracy, Alioto used them to make bureaucracy a working partner in his coalition. The strategy began with his appointments, which brought coalition members into policymaking areas, and continued through the allocation of federal money to bureaucracy. In the first year of CD funds, Alioto gave the SFRA 78 percent of the city's total allotment to complete its neighborhood projects. He gave the Building Inspection Department money to initiate FACE, a code inspection program, and he gave the Housing Authority money for urban renewal.

Alioto's use of federal programs to strengthen the mayor's office was an important achievement. San Francisco's city government was designed by the 1932 charter to be a government of peripheries. Through skillful use of federal resources, Alioto shifted power from the periphery to the center, transforming the mayor's office into a policymaking body.

### George Moscone

Alioto's strategy of strengthening key factions in city government made it difficult for Moscone to use federal resources. Whereas Alioto came in at the beginning of the game, set many of the rules, and chose the actors, Moscone came in the middle. As a result, he entered an arena in which the rules were fixed, the sides taken, and the actors strong.

This state of affairs increases the obstacles to mayoral control, but the difficulties are not insurmountable. White also faced a powerful organization, the BRA, with a vested interest in its share of federal money. White's predecessor, John Collins, had, like Alioto, used the Redevelopment Authority as a major source of mayoral power. By appointing Ed Logue as director and channeling all urban renewal money through the BRA, Collins created a powerful authority. But White brought that authority under his control through reorganizations and effective personnel strategies. By contrast, Moscone operated from a weak mayor's office and tended to underutilize the available resources. When he sought control over federal programs, he was usually defeated. These defeats had important consequences.

When the game of Up for Grabs is not brought under control by the mayor, it becomes open to anyone wishing to compete. This pluralist competition, however, does not lead to a wider distribution of resources. The spoils of federal programs tend to go to those participants who already have the most resources. We saw this scenario develop in the battle between the SFRA and the housing development corporations (Chapter 5). Moreover, when Moscone's aid was enlisted in the conflict, he was unable to influence the distribution of resources. This was a significant defeat, because Moscone's election had been largely a contest between pro- and anti-development forces within the electorate. Moscone's loss to the SFRA in this particular incident exemplified his larger difficulty in carrying out his electoral mandate.

The inability of elected officials to control resources results in a shift of power to nonelectoral arenas. Resources are distributed by those who cannot be held accountable to the public. The voters could not recall SFRA members. Although White's use of federal programs may have been opposed by some parts of the electorate, those groups had a form of power in the vote. The vote is not a foolproof method of accountability, but it does provide the electorate with some say in the decision-making process. Bureaucratic policymaking never has to submit to public judgment.

Bureaucratic policymaking also raises questions of equity. The decision-making criteria employed by bureaucracy tend to result in inequitable distribution. In their analysis of redistributive programs, Levy et al. suggested that professional and organizational imperatives within bureaucracy tend to create an allocation pattern of "the more, the more."[49] That is, client groups, programs, or activities that are already funded will continue to be funded. During Moscone's administration, the SFRA's client groups successfully allied with agency personnel to protect their programs.[50] By contrast, Alioto used his control to defund programs.

Alioto's actions, like many of White's, were motivated by political concerns; but bureaucracy also acts on the basis of political considerations. The difference is that the political concerns of elected officials encompass a larger number of groups than those of individual agencies. In the symphony case mentioned earlier, Alioto gave federal money to the neighborhood groups to defuse their opposition. Without the broader goal of constructing the symphony hall, he might not have allocated this money. Similarly, White's electoral goals led him to create jobs and improve service delivery in poor areas of the city that had been neglected in the past. The point is that the wider political concerns of the mayor force him or her to respond to a wider range of interests than does the bureaucrat. And the more resources the mayor controls, the more responsive the mayor can be. White and Feinstein both used their control over UDAGs to gain employment and housing concessions from the business community. White and Alioto used federal money to increase minority employment in city government and to create programs in minority communities. The key in each case was mayoral control over federal programs.

The absence of mayoral control combined with constituency demands for allocation of resources can lead to negative policy decisions as well. Again, the SFRA case is illustrative. Caught between constituent demands for housing development corporations and the SFRA's refusal to give up its federal money, Moscone responded by using city money.[51] This was similar to Lindsay's approach in New York City. Both mayors were in a weak position in relation to constituents who had been politicized by the existence of federal money. When they could not deliver the federal money, the mayors used city money. In New York, this tactic was a major contributor to the city's fiscal difficulties.[52] The existence of additional resources, the competition for those resources, and the inability to wrench "established" money from powerful competitors, tends to decrease mayoral resources. Moreover, it can lead to negative consequences for the city as it did for Lindsay.

The housing development corporations also illustrate the role played by political skill and executive ability in mayoral success. Pressman argued that Houlihan's forceful approach in Oakland partially explained why he was a stronger mayor than Reading. This observation also is applicable to Alioto and Moscone. According to former administration members, Moscone did not deny constituent requests for federal money. He approved all of the six requests for housing development corporations, two of which were in Chinatown.[53] Alioto, however, funded only two such requests—from the Mission District and Hunter's Point. And his motto, "You don't bring a loser's ticket to the winner's window," carried the message that tapping into federal programs had a price. Approaching these programs with the forcefulness that he brought to all areas, Alioto clearly indicated that he was in charge. Moscone's approach lacked that forcefulness, often seeming merely reactive. As with Reading, this impression formed an obstacle to his establishing control and acquiring resources. A former Moscone aide referred to the community development program as a "hodgepodge of every type of neighborhood idea rather than a specific proposal."[54] This perception did not create an image of a mayor in charge.

171

The inability to control federal resources can lead to vertical fragmentation or what Terry Sanford called "picket fence federalism."[55] The CETA case highlights this problem, as well as Pressman's point on the underutilization of resources. The CETA director in San Francisco was perceived by many people as insensitive and racist because she defunded many programs. Despite these local perceptions, she had very good ties with key officials in DOL's regional office. When Moscone tried to remove her, the regional office threatened to decrease the city's allotment of CETA money.[56] Moscone quietly dropped the issue and the director remained.

This recalls Reading's unsuccessful competition with Percy Moore, the OEDCI director, for federal money. Pressman showed how Moore used press conferences to emphasize the need for federal funding whereas Mayor Reading "endured his defeats in silence."[57] Like Reading, Moscone did not seek out means to mobilize support in his favor and thus forfeited control to an outside official. By contrast, White successfully countered all opposition to enforce his priority with the Federal Office Building. The key in both cases was contacts; the major difference was who had them. In Boston, White had the contacts and used them. In San Francisco, other parties had the contacts. And Moscone never found a way to alter the balance of power in the federal arena. In the absence of an effective exercise of political skills by the mayor, the federal presence created a separate arena which increased the fragmentation in San Francisco's political system and the obstacles faced by elective leadership.

As a consequence, the city found important decisions being made by federal officials. This was a problem because the motivations and viewpoints of federal and local officials differed. A mayor has a larger stake in a city than any federal official does, even if the concern is only to secure a personal political base. Federal officials tend to be less knowledgeable about the city and less sensitive to its character than are local officials, so that federal decisions do not always serve the best interests of the community. Both these points were cited by Pressman and Wildavsky as major factors in the fiasco that overcame a $23 million EDA project begun in 1968 in Oakland: they argued that the federal planners had insufficient knowledge of Oakland's political and economic structure and had different incentives from those of local officials.[58] Analyses by Martha Derthick of the unsuccessful New Towns program and by James Sundquist of OEO's National Emphasis programs came to similar conclusions.[59] And, as we have seen, outside decision making in San Francisco's CETA case resulted in the retention of a director who was perceived as racist by many of her black clients.

## THE FEDERAL CONNECTION: A LOOK BACK

Since this study sets out to explore the acquisition of power by mayors, discussion of federal programs has focused primarily on this aspect. Given the Reagan administration's cuts in federal programs, however, an important further question must be examined: What is the legacy of the social welfare programs of the 1960s and early 1970s?

Perhaps the most important spinoff of federal programs was giving mayors increased access to the minority communities. Although White and Alioto won the endorsement of the minority communities through their earlier strategies, federal programs broadened that access and strengthened those initial ties. This access became vital in light of events in the black community in the 1960s. In San Francisco there were riots in Hunter's Point, demonstrations by blacks in the Western Addition, and protests by minority students at San Francisco State University. In Boston, racial tensions were exacerbated by the Racial Imbalance Act. The assassination of Martin Luther King, Jr., in 1968 led to ghetto riots throughout the country. Mayors—like White, Alioto, and Lindsay—who had access to the black community were better equipped to handle the racial troubles that swept U.S. cities than were mayors like Roman Gribbs of Detroit, who was identified with racist policies, or John Reading, who lacked any effective communication with the Oakland black community.

Lulled by the relative peacefulness of U.S. urban centers in the 1970s, many of us have forgotten that the primary task of many mayors a decade ago was riot prevention. Among the forgetful must be counted the current administration's policymakers who have ignored the role that federal programs played in keeping the recent peace.

Implemented at the local level with external resources, the programs took on a distributive appearance and avoided many of the battles that often surround redistributive policies. A major resource provided by these programs was jobs for minorities. Federal programs enabled mayors to recruit minorities into city government without incurring union or civil service opposition. During White's administration, black employment in city government increased from 6 to 20 percent. Under Alioto, minority employment in city government increased from 11 to 38 percent with black and Hispanic employment increasing by approximately 8 percent each. A substantial percentage of these increases was due to federally funded jobs. Moreover, federally funded projects led to further employment gains by minorities. The Boston Plan's public works project mandated 18 percent minority hiring and minority firms in San Francisco were given SFRA contracts for redevelopment work.

In addition to facilitating the peaceful opening up of economic opportunities to minorities, federal programs broadened political enfranchisement. Programs that emphasized community participation contained an implicit recognition of the political rights of minorities, rights that had been systematically denied in the past.[60] Thus, federal programs provided an adaptive mechanism that allowed the American political system to accommodate a wider variety of groups.

PART FOUR

# When Arenas Collide: The Private Sector

# EIGHT

## Tackling the Private Sector: The Master Builder Strategy

> Without large-scale public projects, it is quite clear that the entrepreneurial style will be difficult to reproduce in the 1970s.[1]

The private sector is an important arena in city politics. This is especially true in Boston and San Francisco. Among large U.S. cities, they have the fourth and fifth largest amounts of office space in their Central Business Districts (CBD) and their current construction rates are among the highest.[2] Many resources are found within the private arena. Chief among them are taxes; the larger the tax base, the greater the mayor's budgetary resources. We have already seen the importance of campaign contributions by business. The private arena also holds the resources of jobs, expertise, and prestige: attracting major corporations to the city can enhance a mayor's prestige and the informal influence of the office. As federal programs at the local level are eliminated and local budgets shrink because of decreasing federal aid and tax-cutting measures (such as Proposition 13 in California and Proposition 2½ in Massachusetts), the resources of the private sector will become even more important to the mayor and to the city as a whole. The mayor who has more control in this arena will be in a stronger position.

"The master builder strategy" has been effectively applied in the past. The logic was to use the "available political and financial resources to provide large-scale public projects and other new public services to build and consolidate political support."[3] This approach was especially popular in the 1950s and early 1960s when federal urban renewal legislation provided new resource opportunities at the local level. Mayors like Lee in New Haven, Collins in Boston, Daley in Chicago, Dilworth and Clark in Philadelphia, and Allen in Atlanta perceived and mobilized the opportunities offered by this strategy for building political fortunes.

Although potentially effective, the master builder strategy is very difficult because it requires that the mayor operate and have significant influence in a variety of arenas—the formal arena of city government and in the public, private, and intergovernmental arenas as well. The drying up of urban renewal money has placed an even greater emphasis on the mayor's skills in these arenas. White's and Alioto's attempts to use the master builder strategy illustrate what happens when efforts in these different arenas collide. We will see that different arenas require different strategies, that resources within the arenas differ, and that selection of arenas is an important tool of mayoral leadership. The mayor's previous strategies, however, will influence what resources are available and the mayor's ability to choose arenas. Further, as we have already noticed, the political system helps to determine the resource opportunities.

## KEVIN WHITE: THE ARRIVAL OF THE MASTER BUILDER

The Park Plaza project in 1970 was White's first major attempt to use the master builder strategy to enhance his reputation and to increase his control within Boston's private sector. At various stages in the project, it was featured in the *New York Times* and national magazines, giving White welcome exposure in view of his ambitions for higher office. The project gave White an opportunity to extend his influence in the private sector; he formed an alliance with Mortimer Zuckerman, a rising figure in Boston's business community, who had developed the proposal. The two men became strong friends and Zuckerman acted as an important fundraiser for White.[4] White was able to use the project to demonstrate his access to resources and his willingness to use them to secure power and control.

Such personal and symbolic factors figured prominently in White's private sector activities. Although the project was not implemented at the time, White's actions strongly advanced his capacity for dealing with the private sector. A Boston businessman who had opposed White's site for the Federal Office Building commented, "If Lafayette Place takes on a gray pallor, that will lie at the city's doorstep, and they know it. But it's better for us to work something out with the mayor than to complain, both because North Station isn't a bad idea, and because if we do throw stones at [the mayor], he'll get even. And we need him."[5] This perception of White as a strong mayor who "gets even," which was shared by many businessmen, gave White a significant measure of control and facilitated his use of the master builder strategy.

### Park Plaza

The Park Plaza project included a hotel, apartments, a parking garage and an office complex to be built near the Commons with private fi-

nancing and under the direction of the BRA. The project was complicated by the numerous arenas and opponents that it involved. In the
governmental arena, there was opposition from the BRA; in the private
sector, there was opposition from area businesses; in the public arena
there was opposition from environmentalists; and in the intergovernmental arena there was opposition from the governor and a state office.
A *Boston Globe* reporter called the project a "nightmare" and observed
that "the worst assignment for a reporter next to a three alarm fire at
three in the morning was covering the Park Plaza project."[6] The controversy continued for four years until the developer finally pulled out.

## The Long Battle

In 1970, the BRA director informed White that Westinghouse in Pittsburgh was interested in developing the Park Square area near Boston
Commons. White instructed the BRA director to draw up an adver-
tisement for bids for the development. While the ads were being drawn
up, the Westinghouse negotiator sent White a $10,000 campaign con-
tribution via the BRA director. Taking the motto "The buck stops
here" literally, the director never turned the money over to White. Discovering this interception, White immediately fired the director.[7] Relations between White and Westinghouse grew distant.

Shortly after, Mortimer Zuckerman, a young businessman who had
just left the major firm of Cabot, Cabot and Forbes, submitted an
alternative plan that would serve his and White's political interests.
Like the achievements of earlier master builders, the project would establish White as a giant nationally. The accomplishment would stand
out because Park Plaza would be the first major urban renewal effort
undertaken without federal money. The project would enhance Zuckerman's reputation in the development community since it was his first
major independent undertaking.

When the proposal was submitted to the BRA, poor relations between the BRA director, Robert Kenney, and Zuckerman gave rise to
internal opposition. Using his appointment authority, White hired
Stewart Forbes, a planner recommended by Zuckerman, to head the
project. Although the BRA director remained, White made it clear that
this official was not autonomous and that the staff would be controlled
by the mayor. White delivered this message through his firm treatment
of BRA staff and by publicly expressing his disagreements with the BRA
in the media.

Hiring Forbes eliminated internal opposition, but the plans also
aroused external opposition. Given the scale and timing of the project,

179

this is not surprising. The earlier master builders had federal resources to use in dealing with their opponents. The promise of large sums of federal money to rebuild downtown appealed to business and created initial support for the program, giving the mayor a tool for countering opposition. Lee used the Citizen's Action Committee, composed of businessmen, civic leaders, and other early supporters to co-opt, neutralize, and defeat opposition.[8] Further, when Lee, Collins, and Allen began, their programs were new and untainted by all of the criticism of urban renewal that later arose.

Park Plaza, however, met the backlash created by Collins's urban renewal programs and drew opposition as soon as the plans were announced. The major opponents were business interests, the state, and environmentalists (the last not a major factor in early urban renewal programs). Nor did White have the carrots of federal funds that Collins and Lee had to buy off opposition. But White did have control over key resources in city government, most notably taxing and assessing powers, which he used to further the project. Through effective pyramiding of resources, White combined formal authority with informal influence to overcome much of the opposition.

To enhance the legitimacy of Zuckerman's proposal, it was presented as the result of a competitive bidding process. Using his control over taxing, acquired through his personnel strategies, White pressured developers to submit bids higher than Zuckerman's. One of the developers to submit a losing bid was Cabot, Cabot and Forbes.[9] Their vice president, Gerald Blakely, was on poor terms with Zuckerman, but had several important interests in the city, including the Ritz Carlton, that he wanted to protect.[10] Blakely also sent the manager of the Ritz to testify that Park Plaza would benefit his hotel. The testimony led the Back Bay Businessmen's Association to endorse the project.[11]

In his discussion of the entrepreneurial leader, Eugene Bardach cited "maneuvering for arenas" as an important tactic.[12] Successful leaders place issues in arenas where their resources are the greatest. Early on, White used the resources of city government to keep the Park Plaza controversy out of the legal arena. Important opposition was mounted by the landowners in the area. Several of the landlords, including the heads of Avis and the R. M. Bradley Company, hired an attorney— Charles Francis Mahoney—to fight the project. White called a meeting with them, which also was attended by the building commissioner, the BRA director, and the assessing commissioner. White heard the landowners' complaints and warned them that he would use the full powers of his office to get Park Plaza through.[13] This show of force was largely effective in discouraging the opposition from shifting the battle to the legal arena. Mahoney did get several injunctions that caused minor delays, but he did not bring a full suit against the project.[14]

If choosing the arena is an important tactic in entrepreneurial leadership, doing so often requires that the mayor have access to other resources. White was successful here because of his access to key resources within city government, which was a result of his effective personnel strategies.

As an urban renewal project, Park Plaza required state approval. In the intergovernmental arena, White encountered further opposition. Dealing with a Republican governor who had decisively beaten him in the last general election put White at a disadvantage. Furthermore, Governor Sargent's strong support from the liberal community made him sensitive to opposition groups like the environmentalists. When the project came up for state approval, Sargent directed his Department of Community Affairs (DCA) chairman, Miles Mahoney, to kill it. White enlisted the aid of the Plasterers Union head, who was on his payroll, to get five thousand construction workers to march on the state house protesting Sargent's decision. With another election year approaching, Sargent did not want to alienate the labor vote; he said that he would now approve the project. His DCA chairman, however, vetoed it when it came up for approval the second time. Sargent dismissed Mahoney and replaced him with Lew Crampton. To insure that Crampton would approve the project, Sargent had him sign his resignation in advance.[15] Crampton approved the project but with strict modifications, which involved scaling down the project. The scaling down and modification of the project required by the state, the delays in getting approvals, and his partner's skepticism finally led Zuckerman to pull out.[16] Some observers have speculated that Zuckerman withdrew because he lacked the financial ability to carry out the project.

## The Emergence of the Master Builder

Although the original project did not go through at the time, Park Plaza illustrates how a skillful mayor pyramids resources. White used his formal appointment authority to overcome the internal opposition of the BRA; he used taxing and zoning powers to defeat the external opposition of the business community, choosing the most advantageous arena in doing so; and he used informal influence to pressure the governor. Acquiring such wide-ranging resources and control is difficult but is necessary in developing strong mayoral leadership.

Perhaps the most important development to come out of the Park Plaza controversy was Kevin White himself. Through his strategies in pursuing the project, White introduced himself in the development community as a mayor who possessed, and was willing to use, resources. He began by altering the relationship between the mayor and the BRA; he served notice that the BRA was no longer going to be the powerful, independent planning agency that it had been under Ed Logue.

## Strengthening the Message

In the Waterfront Hotel project, White strengthened the Park Plaza message. In Park Plaza, White demonstrated his willingness to use his resources to see a project through. In the Waterfront Hotel, he established his ability to extend his control within the development community by politicizing the selection process.

When bids were being accepted for the Waterfront Hotel, the BRA director, Robert Walsh, suggested to White that an outside architectural advisor be called in to aid in the selection. Since the site was one of the most attractive on the east coast, Walsh wanted to make the process as objective as possible.[17] White agreed to recruiting an outside advisor.

The selection criteria used included architectural design, tax payments to the city, adequacy of financing by the developer, and quality of hotel operator. Among the bids submitted was one from Zuckerman. The BRA staff and the outside advisor gave Zuckerman's bid the lowest rating.

After the evaluation and the BRA's rating, White called in Peter Blake, an architect from the Boston Architectural Center, to review the proposals. Walsh was asked to participate but refused, declaring that a decision had already been made, based on a fair and objective review. White and Blake then reviewed the bids and, according to Walsh, considered only four of the eight bids, one of which was Zuckerman's.[18] Despite the BRA's evaluation, White selected Zuckerman as the developer for the project. When White asked Walsh to give the job to Zuckerman, Walsh refused. Although Walsh was the BRA director, his term had expired and he was on hold-over status. White fired him and replaced him with an old-time political associate. White's new appointment, a less independent personality than Walsh, accepted the bid of Zuckerman.

Awarding Zuckerman the contract over the objections of BRA planners and subsequently firing the director and accepting the resignations of some planners was a highly visible demonstration of White's increased power in the development area. In the Park Plaza project, White had demonstrated his willingness to use his resources to implement a project. In the Waterfront Hotel case, the issue was not opposition but competition: who would get the contract. By intervening in the selection process, White demonstrated that he and not an independent planning agency would have final say over the planning and selection processes. With the firing of Walsh, the BRA, for all practical purposes, was no longer an independent agency.

## Reaping the Benefits

White's strategy concerning the BRA and the development process demonstrated two important things; the effective use of tools to centralize control in key areas and the accumulation of power rather than the expenditure of resources. A mayor who can do both of these things will have sufficient resources to approach other actors from a position of strength.

An important resource that White was able to use by taking control over the BRA was the 121A agreement. This was the state statute enacted in the 1950s to persuade the Prudential Insurance Company to locate its headquarters in Boston. Its two main components are a provision for waiving zoning requirements and the formula for determining tax liability. Prudential was wary of locating in Boston because of the city's arbitrary assessing practices. The 121A protected the company by establishing, in advance, a payment in lieu of taxes that was based on a percentage of income. The BRA was given sole authority for granting 121As.

Through his control over the BRA, White gained control over 121As, a powerful bargaining device, which he used to exact further resources. A good example is the 121A that was granted to Jordan Marsh. As one of the largest, if not the largest, advertisers in the city, Jordan Marsh had substantial influence with the media. When Nevis and Cole, two television newsmen, were attacking White, White used Jordan Marsh's influence to pressure the station. Nevis resigned and Cole was fired. Both were replaced by less critical newsmen.[19] A similar bargain, which came out of the 121A agreement for Lafayette Place (an expansion of Jordan Marsh and a parking garage), was struck with the *Boston Globe* in which the paper agreed to tone down its articles somewhat.

Access to the 121A also strengthened White's negotiating position with the Copley Plaza for the 50 Percent Agreement (see Chapter 7). The ability to secure such agreements will become more important as federal programs and local budgets, two major sources of jobs for city residents in the past, are cut. Thus, the mayor who has influence and control in the private sector will be in a better position to exact concessions to benefit the city's residents. The Boston Compact, signed by City Hall, the School Department, and Boston's business community in September 1982, is another example. The business community agreed to give hiring priority to Boston graduates if public school attendance figures and basic skills levels improved. City Hall sources stated that half of the 1982 graduates who sought full time employment received entry level positions.[20]

These cases suggest that having power and using power are two different, but not unrelated, issues. There is no guarantee that the strong mayor will direct power toward goals that benefit the public. In fact, resources will often be used for increasing mayoral power. But the weak mayor is not in a position to deliver. Many of the 1960s mayors had benevolent intentions, but lacked the power to implement their proposals. They often did more harm than good by creating a politics of rising expectations without any viable way to deliver. This hurt the city by creating a conflict-ridden environment, as in New York under Lindsay or Cleveland under Kucinich, and it hurt the mayors by widening the gap between demand and supply.[21] Through his strategies, White bridged that gap. Furthermore, the mayor, as an elected official, will have more incentive than private sector actors to initiate programs that benefit the electorate. The proposal for the 50 Percent Agreement came from White's office, not the private sector. The proposal was implemented because of the power and resources that White had accumulated and his demonstrated ability to use these tools to see his proposals through.

## JOE ALIOTO: DILEMMAS OF THE MASTER BROKER

Alioto used the master builder strategy as an active broker who convened the necessary actors, conducted the negotiations, and forged agreements. But because of Alioto's prior strategies, San Francisco's fragmented political system, and the existence of powerful groups on the sides, the cost of his strategy was high. Alioto's prior strategies limited his ability to select arenas or to operate in the ones available to him. Applying the master builder strategy in a decentralized system containing strong groups prevented Alioto from accumulating power. According to the literature, the master builder uses the resources acquired from each project to facilitate successive projects.[22] This was the strategy employed by White, Collins, Lee, and Moses. Alioto's attempts, however, signally failed to further his control or resources. Each attempt was like a first one, in the resources required to execute it. This expenditure limited Alioto's ability to parlay his policy successes into an increase in power and, in general, made success more difficult to achieve.

### Yerba Buena: The Rocky Road to Resolution

The original plans for Yerba Buena, conceived by the late Ben Swig in 1954, included a convention center, a sports stadium, a high-rise office building, and a 7,000-car parking garage in the South of Market area. Stalled by opposition from Mayor Christopher, the federal urban renewal agency, and the city planning director, Swig temporarily dropped his plans in 1956.[23] When Mayor Christopher appointed Justin Herman to be executive director of the SFRA in 1959, however, the project picked up momentum. In 1962 the city received a $600,000 planning grant from the U.S. Housing and Home Finance Agency (HHFA), and in 1965 HHFA set aside a $19.6 million grant for Yerba Buena (YBC). The grant was finalized in 1966 in an agreement between the SFRA and HUD, HHFA's successor.

When Alioto entered office, demolition and population displacement were occurring. This caused opposition from the heavily unionized labor in the area businesses and from the residents who would be displaced by the project. In addition, Justin Herman's unwillingness to compromise led to delays and conflicts with other parts of city government. Overcoming the obstacles was a long process, and final resolution and implementation did not occur until Moscone's administration.

### Managing the Opposition: Alioto and Labor

In his analysis of the entrepreneurial leader, Bardach discussed the importance of mapping as a preliminary step.[24] This involves identification of the necessary actors, the sources of support and opposition, the motives of the actors, and the tools required for dealing with the actors. Alioto's first moves to further the Yerba Buena project included such mapping. Once the information is gathered, however, the mayor must deploy enough resources and effective strategies to act. Alioto's resources and strategies were sufficient to deal with organized labor but not sufficient to deal with the residents.

Labor's opposition to SFRA policies in general and to YBC in particular centered on the threat implicit in altering the city's economic base. San Francisco's shift to a financial and service headquarters business base decreased the number of blue collar jobs in the city. In 1963 leading union officials were saying, "It may suit the purpose of some to make San Francisco a financial and service center, but it destroys the jobs of working people and weakens the City's economic foundations."[25]

Although organized labor opposed the changes in San Francisco's economic base, it was a trend that, as in most cities, organized labor was unable to reverse. In response, many of San Francisco's leading union officials, facing declining memberships, consolidated their power around city hall, exacting the spoils of the political system.[26] Because his personnel policies and wage settlements facilitated this movement, Alioto was not dealing with a hostile opposition. He also had strong ties with the ILWU, a leading spokesman for the city's labor movement.

Nor did all unions oppose projects like YBC. The Building and Construction Trades, for example, stood to gain from such projects. To transform opposition into support, Alioto had to bring disorganized interests into a pattern of interest convergence, using bargaining and persuasion to convince opponents that implementation was in their interests.[27] In the case of YBC, Alioto met with the heads of the Building and Construction Trades Council (BCTC), the bartenders and culinary workers, and the cooks unions, all of whom had an interest in construction and hotel development. The BCTC became one of the strongest supporters of YBC and of redevelopment in general. Through his negotiating skills, Alioto turned labor into a source of intrinsic (BCTC and others) and extrinsic (ILWU) support.

In endorsing YBC, labor joined the SFRA and the media as a major critic of all opposition efforts. When the residents brought suit against the proposal, the Labor Council, the BCTC, and the ILWU issued a pamphlet entitled, "What Ever Happened to Those 30,000 Jobs!"[28] Labor's turnaround denied the residents a potentially strong ally but it did not destroy their opposition efforts. In fact, the area residents became the major obstacle to the YBC project.

### Effective Opposition, Weak Mayoral Resources: Alioto and the Residents

Between 1969 and 1973, the relocation issue was in the forefront of the YBC controversy. The residents wanted adequate replacement housing within the project area; Herman and the SFRA wanted to remove low income housing from the area. Unlike White, Alioto did not control his redevelopment agency. This limited his ability to choose the arena in which the issue would be fought. Another limitation came from the media. Although the media was instrumental in mobilizing public support, their endorsement of the project limited Alioto's ability to bargain with the opposition.[29] Thus, tools that are effective in one arena are often counterproductive in another. Finally, the autonomy of other governmental actors was an obstacle to acquiring resources within the formal arena for use in dealing with the opposition. These factors enabled the residents to delay YBC for more than three years in the courts, an arena in which Alioto had few, if any, resources. And, their activities encouraged others to use the legal arena to create further delays.

In summer 1969, the merchants and residents in the South of Market area formed TOOR (Tenants and Owners in Opposition to Redevelopment).[30] Many of the residents were retired trade unionists who had not forgotten the tactics of organizing. The issue around which they organized was adequate replacement housing in the same area.[31]

In November 1969, TOOR filed a formal complaint with Federal District Court Judge Weigel. Weigel issued an injunction halting all demolition and relocation and set 1 July 1970 as the date for suspending all federal project funds unless a satisfactory relocation plan was devised. Several days later Alioto, representing the SFRA in court, requested that the injunction be modified to permit some relocation and demolition to continue. Weigel was on vacation and so the request was made before a close friend of Ben Swig, Judge George Harris, who scheduled a new hearing.[32] Feeling that the cards were being stacked against them, TOOR requested a delay, which was denied, and then asked to meet in chambers, to which Harris agreed.

Aided by planners and architects, TOOR devised a plan for 2,000 units of new and rehab housing within the YBC area. The plan was endorsed by California's ex-governor, Pat Brown, who was appointed Special Master to oversee replacement housing activities. This plan ran counter to the objectives of Herman and the SFRA, however, who wanted to change the demographics of the area. They rejected Brown's report and submitted their own plan, which called for replacement activities to be conducted by the San Francisco Housing Authority (SFHA). Herman and Alioto persuaded the SFHA to give YBC displacees special priority in exchange for additional urban renewal money.[33] HUD approved this plan and Weigel lifted the injunction, with the proviso that the SFRA would provide 1,500 to 1,800 new or rehab units of low rent housing by 1973. The legal battles were over and the project proceeded. But not for long.

TOOR objected to the SFRA's plan because it did not guarantee replacement housing within the project area. In 1971 TOOR supplemented its legal efforts with a political approach; its co-chairman,

Peter Mendelsohn, decided to run for supervisor in the upcoming election. To counter this challenge, Alioto and Supervisor Robert Mendelsohn, an ally of Alioto's who was up for re-election, met with Peter Mendelsohn, TOOR and its attorneys, and city officials. An agreement was reached in which the city made a commitment for the rehab and retention of four hotels in the area and Peter Mendelsohn withdrew from the race.

Thus, using his negotiating skills, Alioto worked out an agreement consistent with TOOR's objectives. The agreement was quickly defeated, however, by opposition from the SFRA and the media. The SFRA accused TOOR of "chipping away at the integrity and viability of the project."[34] The *Examiner* carried an editorial describing TOOR's plan as "building a lovely garden without removing a pile of rusty tin cans stacked in one corner of it."[35] An editorial in the *Chronicle* referred to the proposal as "Good Money after Bad" and declared that the retention of the hotels "would certainly blight the whole Yerba Buena project."[36]

With the two sides split, TOOR asked the Board of Supervisors to apply for HUD funds to rehabilitate the four hotels. The board's Planning and Development Committee passed the resolution, but the SFRA persuaded the full board to exclude all references to the specific hotels in the resolution. Thus, Alioto's attempts to settle the dispute were defeated by the SFRA, and TOOR was left with the earlier court-approved plan for replacement housing anywhere in the city.

Although TOOR lost the political battle, the slow pace of the relocation refueled their legal fight. The following incident once again shows the fragmentation of San Francisco's government and the obstacles this poses to a mayor who lacks central control over the key decision-making points. In 1971, the Housing Authority removed the special priority status of YBC displacees. Its action was triggered by pressures from other city residents, who had been pushed further down the already long waiting lists, and by strained relations with the SFRA. The SFHA had twice requested a site in the YBC area for a public housing development and both times had been refused by the SFRA. The Housing Authority's decision on priorities prompted TOOR to go back to Judge Weigel to complain that the relocation plan was not being implemented. This new development encouraged the active participation of another actor—HUD. Reviewing the plans, HUD concluded that the SFRA was not meeting the relocation needs of the residents and issued an administrative injunction.[37]

This was a departure for HUD: they had approved all of the SFRA's previous activities. There was speculation that HUD's action was prompted by Nixon's anger over Alioto's federal court suit for the release of impounded funds (see Chapter 7).[38] Whether or not this speculation was correct is unimportant, for the power of Herman and the SFRA, combined with the media's attack on TOOR, were enough to defeat Alioto's attempt to settle with TOOR outside of the legal arena. Furthermore, Alioto's inability to enforce his policy with the Housing Authority brought in a new participant, another obstacle, and more delays.

Although HUD finally approved the third plan submitted by the SFRA, TOOR continued its legal battle. This threatened additional delays that would further increase project costs. More important, TOOR's success again drew other opponents of the project into the legal arena as a stalling device. In 1972, two separate suits revolving around the financing issue were brought against YBC. The plaintiffs, Alvin Duskin and Gerald Wright, charged that the financing plan was illegal because it had not been placed on the ballot. They claimed that the plan called for a general obligation bond which, under California law, requires approval by two-thirds of the electorate. Construction was again delayed, as bonds cannot be sold when their legality is the subject of litigation. Thus, we again see the importance of Bardach's key tactic, the selection of arenas. The problem with YBC, however, was that the opposition, rather than the mayor, were effectively using the device.

Alioto approached TOOR's challenge first. He now had more freedom to maneuver because, in summer 1971, Justin Herman had died. Alioto enlisted William Coblentz, a prominent attorney and University of California regent, to settle the dispute. After several weeks of out of court negotiations, the city agreed to construct 400 new units of housing, in addition to the earlier commitment of 1,500 to 1,800 units, in or near the project area; and TOOR agreed to drop its lawsuit with prejudice (without possibility of reinstituting it). This agreement was not very different from the one between Alioto and TOOR three years earlier. The most important difference was the absence of Justin Herman to block the settlement.

Three years of courtroom battles ended with TOOR emerging as a proponent of YBC. Further attempts to halt the project over the financing issue were publicly denounced by TOOR. The financing suit, however, remained a difficulty through the remainder of Alioto's administration.[39]

As we observed at the beginning, the master builder strategy is difficult to execute. It requires the mayor to operate successfully in a variety of arenas. This ability depends partly on prior strategies and partly on the political system. Alioto's previous strategies had not centralized his power as White's did, and the political system in San Francisco provided less opportunity for achieving control than Boston's did. In the Park Plaza project, White's access to key resources within city government enabled him to keep the issue out of the legal arena. Lacking White's control, Alioto was forced to operate in an arena in which he had few, if any, resources.

### Transamerica

A comparison of YBC and Park Plaza again supports the themes of this study. First, the fragmented nature of San Francisco city government was an obstacle to the mayor's acquisition of resources. Second, Alioto's failure to reduce that fragmentation limited his ability to use the master builder strategy effectively. Third, these two factors prevented Alioto from accumulating power as White did. As a result, Alioto constantly had to bargain and negotiate with his appointees. In the Transamerica project, we can see all of these factors at work.

In 1969 the chairman of the board of Transamerica approached the city with development plans for his corporation's new headquarters building. The architectural design, a strict pyramid contrasting sharply with San Francisco's skyline, created a major controversy within the Planning Department. Even now, almost ten years later and many buildings later, the pyramid stands out amid the architectural contours of the financial district. To some it is a brilliant design, to others an eyesore, and to all, a conversation piece.

Although there was a court suit over the closing of a street, the real battle centered on the design. The Planning Department was overwhelmingly opposed to the architectural plan. The Planning Commission, which consisted of five commissioners appointed by the mayor and two ex-officio members (the CAO and Public Utilities manager), was split. Transamerica conducted a major public relations campaign while Alioto extensively lobbied the Board of Supervisors and the Planning Commission. Through promises of electoral support, Alioto and Transamerica secured a ten to one approval from the board. The campaigns were also persuasive with the Planning Commission. After design concessions by the architect, the commission approved the project by a four to three vote.

The need to secure board and commission approval is one more way that San Francisco's political system is more fragmented than Boston's. The Boston City Council did not have any authority in development projects whereas the San Francisco board had formal authority in all of them. This factor may or may not have significance by itself, but Alioto's failure to centralize his authority gave it extreme significance. By not eliminating the power of other actors, Alioto had to deal with each one whenever he undertook a project. Where White was able to conserve resources by eliminating actors, Alioto constantly had to expend resources.

The planning function also was structurally different in the two cities and affected the strategies employed by Alioto and White. Boston does not have a planning commission. Under Collins, city planning was conducted by the BRA. Under White, the BRA had responsibility for city planning along with the Office of Planning and Development and the Neighborhood Development Administration, both of which were in the mayor's office. By locating these functions within his own office, White acquired more control over the planning process than Alioto had in San Francisco. Through his personnel and reorganization strategies, White set up a structure that facilitated his use of the master builder strategy. By contrast, the commission system in San Francisco was relatively autonomous. Alioto's personnel strategies did not significantly reduce the fragmentation. Thus, Alioto still had to deal with an implementing vehicle that was independent of his office.

The infrastructure of San Francisco's Planning Commission was also more fragmented than the BRA, its Boston counterpart, which was another obstacle to using the master builder strategy. The BRA under Collins and Logue, and the BRA, OPD, and NDA under White were hierarchically structured. With decisions being made from the top down, White and Collins had to control only those at the top, which they did. In San Francisco, decisions were made by the department's civil service staff and almost always ratified by the commissioners.[40] In the Transamerica case, the commissioners were reluctant to go against the decision of the Planning Department staff. When they did, the planning director and several planners, who objected to the proposal, resigned. The change in personnel, however, did not increase Alioto's control over the Planning Commission. In contrast to the dominant-subordinate relationship that White established with his appointees, Alioto still had to lobby his appointees for approval of his proposals. Not having White's control, Alioto's attempt to use the master builder strategy was more costly than White's and less successful.

### U.S. Steel and the Waterfront: A Battle of Commissioners

U.S. Steel's proposal for a waterfront development further illustrates San Francisco's fragmented political system and the obstacles it presents to a mayor. An important feature is the power of the commission system; the entire waterfront proposal turned into a struggle among commissioners.

In spring 1969, representatives of the San Francisco port offered the U.S. Steel Corporation waterfront property for development. The site was between the Old Ferry building and the approaches to the Bay Bridge. U.S. Steel hired an architectural firm to design plans for a $200 million complex that would include an office tower, a shopping center, and a large hotel. The site that was selected carried an 84-foot height limitation with 10 percent of the site eligible to have the limitation raised to 175 feet.[41] The plans, however, called for a 550-foot tower. Since it exceeded the maximum, the proposal required a majority vote in the Planning Commission and on the Board of Supervisors. Alioto, the Port Commission, the Chamber of Commerce, the Labor Council, and the Building and Construction Trades Council (BCTC) conducted an extensive lobbying campaign to influence the decision makers.

The first lobbying effort was directed to the Planning Commission to obtain approval to raise the height limitation to 400 feet. At the end, Alioto summoned the commissioners into his office individually to discuss the proposal just before the vote was taken.[42] The combined lobbying was successful. As in the Transamerica case, the commissioners went against the advice of the Planning Department staff and approved the increase. Shortly after, U.S. Steel and the Port Commission successfully lobbied the Planning Commission to raise the limitation to 550 feet.

The second clearance point—and under ordinary circumstances, the final one—was the Board of Supervisors. But proposals for the waterfront required approval from the Bay Conservation and Development Commission (BCDC). The BCDC is a regional agency with regulatory powers over dredging and filling projects in San Francisco Bay. Appointments to this commission are made by the Board of Supervisors.

While the BCDC reviewed the U.S. Steel and Ferry Port Plaza (another prospective waterfront development) proposals, the Board of Supervisors prepared to vote on the 400-foot limitation. They were lobbied by the same bodies who lobbied the Planning Commission. As the time to vote drew near, only two supervisors—Boas and Feinstein—decidedly opposed the increase. Four supervisors favored lifting the limitation and the remaining five had not voiced an opinion.

Encouraged by the favorable lineup of votes, the proponents pushed for a 500-foot limitation. This new development created room for bargaining. Boas was approached by some supervisors who agreed to come down from the Planning Commission's 550 feet if he went along with the 400 feet. Boas was prepared to agree when one of the supervisors called for a postponement. By a six to four vote, the postponement was granted, giving the Port Commission and U.S. Steel three months to work on getting the desired 550 feet.[43]

The BCDC was still reviewing the Ferry Port Plaza application, using the criteria of project appropriateness to the waterfront and net loss of water area in the bay. To settle the second issue, the BCDC proposed to rely on the "rule of equivalencies." This theory stated that the Port Commission could undertake a project involving a net loss of water if an equivalent area of water was opened elsewhere. The latter could be achieved by tearing down an old pier.[44] The BCDC asked Attorney General Thomas Lynch to study the proposed rule, thus bringing yet another party and another hurdle into the picture. As it turned out, this was the crucial juncture. Lynch declared the rule of equivalencies inconsistent with the commission's fundamental principles. Two weeks after Lynch's decision, the BCDC voted twenty-two to one against granting fill permits for the Ferry Port Plaza.

Although the supervisors still had to vote on U.S. Steel's height limitation, the BCDC's ruling on Ferry Port Plaza sounded the death knell of the U.S. Steel proposal. The chances of the BCDC reversing their position on the rule of equivalencies for U.S. Steel were small. At the least, their ruling halted the momentum built up by the supporters of U.S. Steel. Amid opposition, the proposal cleared the Planning Commission twice, received the endorsement of SPUR, and was very close to passing the Board of Supervisors, at least with the 400-foot limitation.

When the board voted on the proposal, the original dissenters had acquired two more allies, Pelosi and Mailliard, who agreed to vote against the 550-foot limit. With the increased strength of the opposition, Supervisor Terry Francois, who was usually a sure vote for Alioto, unsuccessfully moved for another postponement. Angered by his failure, Francois accused the supervisors of "trying to kill the Port" and moved for a 40-foot limitation in order to "really kill it."[45] Resentful of Francois's charges, one of the four dissenters proposed a 175-foot limitation, which was the Planning Department's recommendation. This proposal attracted two other supervisors and the final vote was six to four in favor of the 175-foot limitation. This was the end of the U.S. Steel proposal.

The proposal's defeat testifies to the obstacles that autonomous forces and a fragmented environment create for mayoral leadership. The fragmentation, combined with Alioto's failure to centralize his control, allowed more parties, who were independent of the mayor, to take leading roles in the controversy. As a result of their autonomy and the fragmentation, these decision makers were vulnerable to pressure from sources other than the mayor. Thus, Alioto had to compete with many actors in an environment full of counterpressures. In such a context, the number of actors, or decision points, becomes critical. Pressman and Wildavsky have demonstrated mathematically how only a marginal increase in the number of participants significantly reduces the chances for implementation.[46] The U.S. Steel project provides a fine illustration of their point. Alioto was able to persuade the Planning Commission to go against the decision of the planning staff, which, as in the case of Transamerica, was an unusual accomplishment. But he was unable to add this success to his resources in a way that would benefit the rest of the project.

# Conclusion:
# Mayoral Leadership
# and the Acquisition of Power

# NINE

# Mayoral Leadership and the Acquisition of Power

The folly of searching for a single factor to explain leadership effectiveness has become a well accepted dictum of leadership research.[1]

The preceding analyses have demonstrated the extent of this "folly." The cases have illustrated the integral relationship between political systems and cultures and the development of leadership. This relationship calls for broader analysis and more clearly focused theories. The study of mayoral leadership must be conducted within an integrative framework.[2] Outputs alone do not determine whether a mayor was successful. Such a determination may miss the even more fundamental question of why the mayor was successful or not. Similarly, classifying mayors' acts on the basis of styles gives insufficient importance to the contexts in which they function.

These shortcomings have two major implications for theory building. First, leadership strategies must be examined in the context in which they are executed. That is, the relevant variables must be recognized and made part of the integrative framework. Second, there can be no *single* theory of executive leadership. We can, perhaps, develop some broad conclusions that will apply to executive leadership in all settings and at all levels of government. But to be truly useful, our theories of leadership must be related to specific settings. This requires that we analyze leadership in different political systems and in different arenas within the same system. Such a dual approach will allow us to identify the strategies that work best in a given set of conditions: When will innovative strategies be the most effective? In which arena is conflict strategy a viable approach? Under what circumstances are organizational strategies needed?

This comparative approach has positive implications for policymaking as well. Once we understand how institutional factors constrain and promote strong leadership, we can effectively target reforms. Reform efforts, however, must be accompanied by a careful examination of the costs and benefits of strong executive leadership and of the alternatives to that leadership. This study has clearly demonstrated that acquiring resources can be costly. However, the absence of strong executive leadership also carries costs. This study has been biased in favor of strong mayoral leadership. The reader is invited, and even encouraged, to disagree. But first, I must strongly urge that the full range and complexity of the issues be considered.

In sum, leadership analysis must integrate all the relevant factors. For purposes of theory building, this requires consideration of the context. For purposes of policymaking, this requires examination of costs, benefits, and alternatives. By examining mayoral strategies in the context of political systems and political cultures as well as in different arenas, the preceding analysis represented a move in that direction. The themes identified by the comparative analysis may provide a basis for developing theories of mayoral leadership that will be able to explain and predict its outcome. The remainder of this chapter will survey some of those major themes, examine the costs and benefits of strong mayoral leadership, consider the alternatives, and look at the implications for policy and future research.

## REQUIREMENTS FOR STRONG EXECUTIVE LEADERSHIP

### Political Culture

This study has demonstrated the significant role played by political culture in determining the leadership opportunities. A private-regarding political culture—which emphasizes the personal side of politics, divisible outcomes, and material incentives—is favorable to strong executive leadership. By contrast, a public-regarding or reform ethos—which defines politics as a form of public service, is preoccupied with issues, and emphasizes rational purposes and procedures—is often a limiting factor on the executive. Of the San Francisco mayors, Alioto's approach to the mayor's office was the most closely akin to White's. Yet Alioto's exercise of political skills was often hindered by San Francisco's strong reform ethos. By contrast, Boston's private-regarding political culture enabled White to actively, even brazenly, use the strategies traditionally associated with the boss pattern of leadership. Building a political machine increased his control in the bureaucracy and in nongovernmental arenas. The possibility of replicating this strategy in San Francisco, however, is sharply limited by the reform ethos there. Thus, although White and Alioto both acquired a key building block of a political organization—patronage—only White was able to parlay that resource into a larger achievement.

Efforts to acquire resources in a strong reform ethos run counter to this culture's anti-power bias and must be carried out covertly. When White appealed to a liberal suburban audience, he also faced a reform political culture. By keeping his more political actions out of suburban view as much as possible, however, he minimized the inhibitive effect of the political culture. The need for concealment strategies and the resources they can deliver is further illustrated by the activities of San Francisco's Planning Commission. Under Moscone, the commission's liberal image permitted it to pursue policies that would have been viewed as conservative during Alioto's administration. Similarly, the conservative image of Feinstein's commission diverted attention from the progressive nature of its policies. Concealment strategies in general are workable ways to acquire resources. In reform political cultures, they become a necessity.

## Political System

In this book, we have also seen the importance of the political system in determining resource opportunities. The key considerations in a system are its degree of fragmentation, its orientation, and its kind of organization. The individual effects and the interaction of these factors determine the location of resources and the strategies necessary for acquiring them.

The fragmentation of authority limits the mayor's formal control in key areas of city government and makes it necessary to pyramid what resources the mayor has or can create. The particular strategies employed depend largely on the degree of fragmentation. Weaker, more fragmented systems demand informal mechanisms. As Alexander George argued, "The pluralistic structure of dispersed, decentralized power requires a political leader who can accumulate personal influence to supplement his limited formal authority."[3] The comparison between White and Alioto supports this thought. Operating in a less fragmented system, White used formal tools to centralize his control within city government; Alioto, operating in a more fragmented system, used brokering strategies, such as mediating labor disputes, to accumulate personal influence.

In selecting strategies, the executive must also consider the orientation of the political system: highly political participants are more receptive targets for an exercise of political skills than are less political ones. The strong political orientation of people in Boston's government enabled White to use material incentives such as patronage to achieve a centralized control. White also established a dominant-subordinate relationship with his appointees that gave him access to their resources; he used this to extend his control to the neighborhoods, the federal arena, and the business and development communities. By contrast, in the weaker political orientation of San Francisco, participants in government were not so interested in material incentives. They were interested in pursuing political goals of their own or of the groups they represented. Far from being subordinate to the mayor, they were equal in power. As a result, the mayors sought resources in the public and private arenas, which they then attempted to convert into influence in city government. Consolidating influence in this way, however, requires a constant expenditure of resources; influence is a more nebulous commodity than control. Where White was able to rely on his department heads to carry out his priorities, San Francisco mayors usually had to lobby and bargain with their appointees, and not always successfully.

This last factor points to the major flaw in the strategy of consolidating influence. Effective use of this strategy requires that the sides contain powerful groups. But if the groups are strong, it is difficult for the mayor with weak resources to gain control over the groups. Moreover, when these groups comprise a mayor's major resources, the mayor has a vested interest in maintaining and increasing their power. Rather than heading an executive-centered coalition the mayor often becomes captive to groups of supporters, as Alioto seemed to be in his settlement of the police and firefighters' strike.[4]

The strategy is equally problematic when the sides are weak and fragmented. The groups within Moscone and Feinstein's constituencies were too weak to provide the resources that labor and business provided for Alioto. Further, when the groups are issue-oriented and divided, fragmentation becomes a major obstacle to concerted action. Moscone's attempts at agenda setting were often thwarted by the fragmentation of his constituency.

These cases indicate the significance of political organization. The important consideration is how the electorate is organized. Boston and San Francisco supply three models. First, Boston's informal arrangements were characterized by the absence of strong organizations and a predominately non-ideological, non–issue-oriented electorate. Second, San Francisco's informal arrangements under Alioto were characterized by the presence of strong labor and business organizations and the beginnings of an issue-oriented electorate. Third, during Moscone and Feinstein's administrations, the electorate was ideological, activist, and organized into many narrow, issue-oriented groups. Such arrangements influence mayoral leadership in general and, more specifically, the strategies that attempt to pull power from the sides to the center.

Political organization also influences the mayor's agenda. Attempts to pull power from fragmented groups removes some of the mayor's insulation and diminishes his or her ability to manage conflict. Alioto's coalition provided a measure of insulation, but Moscone's constituency threw him into the thick of controversial issues which he then had to resolve. This difference is analogous to the difference between political parties and interest groups as support systems at the national level. In directing appeals through political parties, candidates are able to take broad positions and deflect many divisive issues. Appeals to interest groups, however, must be narrower and more numerous and are often conflicting.

By contrast, Boston's electorate, which lacked strong organization and was not issue-oriented or ideological, presented fewer obstacles than did San Francisco's electorate. White did not have to bargain away key resources to strong groups or continually mediate the conflicts generated by an issue-oriented electorate. Through an effective exercise of political skills, White helped to further this favorable political environment. Through good wage settlements, White bought off labor early in his administration. Through the Little City Halls and his subsequent political organization, White forestalled the rise of powerful groups in the neighborhoods. Thus, political organization helps to shape the resource opportunities, but the organization is also influenced by mayoral strategies.

The issue of political organization bears directly on the theme of innovative leadership. The quest for innovation has been seen as counterproductive to mayoral leadership because it requires support from a broad range of groups, many of whom are in conflict with one another.[5] My analysis suggests a more optimistic view. The success of innovative attempts depends largely on the political organization of the target. White, Alioto, and Moscone all pursued innovations in city government, but Moscone was much less successful. His active acknowledgment of groups that had previously been excluded from city government was an innovative move. But once recruited, issue-oriented individuals with constituencies outside of city government created problems for him that limited his ability to acquire resources. This suggests that there is often an important trade-off between innovation and acquisition of power.[6] When the target of innovative appeals is fragmented and not easily bought off, the strategy increases the demands on the mayor's office and decreases the mayor's ability to respond to them.

This also highlights the dilemmas of a weak political system; in order to gain power, the executive must give up some resources. But as the cases in this study demonstrate, this trade leads to the downward

201

spiral of the weak mayor. The executive is often unable to recapture the power that is given up. While innovation is highly celebrated, change cannot be implemented or maintained without the expenditure of power. Moscone's ability to achieve innovative goals was sharply limited by the obstacles of a fragmented target and a weak political system. Important changes are occurring in San Francisco as a result of demographic and political shifts. Perhaps history will credit Moscone with facilitating some of these changes. In the long run, they may take hold and be institutionalized. But in the immediacy of his own administration, Moscone was unable to acquire the power necessary to secure his goals.

By contrast, when White and Alioto broadened representation within city government, they did so by focusing on groups that were relatively disorganized, powerless and nonideological. These groups were not independent but needed the executive's favor. Using federal and mayoral programs, White and Alioto co-opted these groups, a strategy which enabled them to implement innovative policies without sacrificing any control. This approach characterized White's innovative neighborhood policies as well. In contrast to the many activist neighborhoods in Moscone's San Francisco, Boston neighborhoods were nonideological and many were politically weak. White reinforced these favorable conditions by dealing with the neighborhood issue as a matter of basic service delivery and then following up with policies and programs that dispensed these services.

The differences in political organization, structural arrangements, and orientation between San Francisco and Boston and within San Francisco early and late in the 1970s explain why certain strategies were used and why they came out as they did. Most important, they illustrate the difficulties of developing strong executive leadership at the local level.

### Effective Political Skills

To draw on the resource opportunities shaped by the political system and the political culture, the mayor must employ effective political skills. Strong executive leadership is developed by accumulating, pyramiding, and conserving resources. This requires that the mayor identify the resource opportunities, select strategies, and choose the arena in which to operate. Since the effectiveness of strategies varies by arena, the selection is critical. (We have seen the difficulty of trying to use an electoral coalition in the governing arena.) Moreover, strategies interact with other participants and with other strategies. This ties the mayor's future ability to acquire resources to the outcomes of past strategies. White's ability to acquire more power than the San Francisco mayors was largely a function of this, his ability to establish the conditions for the exercise of strong leadership. Bardach made a similar observation:

> The political entrepreneur . . . must initiate and complete various political activities in a temporal sequence. How effectively he can perform a given activity at a given time depends in part, therefore, on how well he has created the conditions that make the present activity feasible and productive.[7]

But times change and adaptability is an essential mayoral skill. As resources and the mechanisms for acquiring them vary, mayors must alter their strategies in order to make the most of opportunity. Disraeli's observation, "There is nothing in which the power of circumstances is more evident than in politics," is certainly true of White's administration and reflects one of the major reasons that he was able to acquire power in a time of dwindling resources. By the mid-1970s, it seemed hardly plausible that Kevin White had begun his administration as the Boston version of John Lindsay. But it was precisely because of his shift from media and audience politics to organization and constituent politics that White was able to survive and, more important, to thrive.

The use of political skills and the attempt to acquire power is further complicated by the anti-power bias in the American political culture. Although the electorate expects much of executives, they are reluctant to grant executives the power necessary to function effectively. As a result, mayors often must develop power without appearing to do so. Charter reform, as an open attempt to increase mayoral control, has failed while more covert devices such as reorganizations, personnel strategies, and the creation of new agencies has succeeded. The defeat of charter reform in cities with different political cultures and different political systems indicates the prevalence of the anti-power bias.

These indications of the importance of political skills run counter to models of executive leadership based on business and managerial principles.[8] Such models tend to reflect an administrative orientation. They favor efficiency, scientific management, and rational planning and procedures. The anti-political nature of these models was aptly summed up by Douglas Yates: "The managers demonstrated little taste for and mastery of the give and take of politics, as if accommodation and compromise interfere with good administration."[9]

These models are badly flawed in not recognizing that dealing with other political actors makes accommodation and compromise essential. Both in implementing policy and in the daily business of city government, the executive encounters many and diverse actors who are competing for the same scarce resources. To assume that compromise and accommodation can be eliminated is to take a naïve and, more important, an ineffective approach to executive leadership. In order to acquire the power necessary to govern, the executive must be skilled in the art of politics. The evidence in this study is supported by data from other administrations as well. Mayor Reading's apolitical orientation led him to conclude that the soundness of his principles would be sufficient to sustain him in the political arena. Failing to utilize the tools available to him, Reading lost many battles and forfeited crucial resources to more politically minded actors. Lindsay's attempt to overhaul city government through superagencies and management information systems was defeated by political resistance from bureaucracy. The long term relationship between local Democratic leaders and career civil servants, combined with established civil service patterns of procedure, proved too strong a match for Lindsay's team of management experts. This relationship was understood by Abe Beame, who successfully combined political skills with management techniques to gain control over the bureaucracy. Curiously, Beame's political skills in the organizational arena were undercut by his weak political skills in the public arena. Lacking the charisma to mobilize public support, Beame failed to convince the public that he was an effective mayor, even though he was able to make city government work both politically and managerially.[10] By contrast, Kevin White the mayor was able to acquire power in ways that many of his counterparts could not because of the success of Kevin White the politician.

Experiences drawn from these several administrations suggest that the strong mayor is the exception. Moreover, when strong executive leadership arises, it often seems to be unique. White's skill as a politician was the substance of his strength as a mayor. But skillful politicians cannot be cloned. Even if they could be, they would still face problems where the political system and the political culture place limitations on the development of leadership. Cities where strong mayoral leadership developed—such as Chicago under Daley, Baltimore under D'Alesandro, Jr., and Schaeffer, Pittsburgh under Lawrence and Barr, and Albany under Corning—contained systemic and cultural conditions favorable to strong leadership. But such cities tend to be exceptions. Moreover, their being partisan cities suggests a positive correlation between partisanship and the exercise of strong executive leadership.

In nonpartisan and reformed cities, the combination of political skills, political system, and political culture necessary for strong mayoral leadership does not often develop. Most western cities (San Francisco, Los Angeles, San Diego, Portland, Seattle), many of the emerging Sunbelt cities (Phoenix, Atlanta, Houston, Dallas, Miami), and many midnorthern cities (St. Paul, Minneapolis, Duluth, Madison, Milwaukee, Denver) are characterized by a strong reform ethos. Cities like San Francisco, New York, Los Angeles, Oakland, and Miami have highly fragmented political systems. Finally, the combination of limited resources within city government and a strong reform ethos in cities like Oakland, Milwaukee, and Seattle tends not to produce skillful mayors.

## IN DEFENSE OF STRONG EXECUTIVE LEADERSHIP

This study has explored the conditions under which strong executive leadership is developed. Some of the examples examined may raise the question whether such leadership is desirable in the first place. Strong executive leadership does not, as we have seen, guarantee that power will be directed toward substantive ends that benefit the public. On the other hand, the weak mayor is not in a position to deliver benefits at all, and a weak mayorality often carries costs for the entire city. But strong executive leadership also has costs. This dilemma points to important concerns about the desirability of mayoral power, the costs of acquiring power, and the alternatives to mayoral leadership.

The cases presented in this book indicate a relationship between strong executive leadership and achievement of goals. In order to influence the distribution of resources, a mayor must either control those resources or be able to influence those who do control them. White's use of taxing and zoning agreements created a favorable climate for expansion of the private sector. Through his control in the development community, he directed many of those new jobs to Boston residents. Similarly, his power over department heads enabled him to implement policies to send municipal jobs and contracts to Boston residents and vendors.

Through skillful Washington activities, White and Alioto acquired substantial federal funding to provide jobs for minorities, economic assistance for small businesses and poorer sections of the city, additional funds for public transportation, money for cultural activities, and programs for the elderly and handicapped. By integrating federal programs into their broader political strategies, they forestalled the rise of new arenas of power, a cause of major conflicts in other cities. The ability of both mayors to manipulate the civil service system was crucial to increasing minority employment in city government. Both mayors used control over key resources and negotiating skills to create and expand employment opportunities for minorities in the private sector as well (the 50 Percent Agreement in Boston; affirmative action programs with the airlines in San Francisco).

In contrast to his predecessor, John Collins, White made city government more responsive to the neighborhoods and effectively implemented innovative programs there. White's political organization, although set up for electoral purposes, served as well to facilitate contact between residents and bureaucracy and to localize conflict. The latter contributed a high degree of stability to the city and the city government. This was crucial since the lack of stability often impedes executive responsiveness and, hence, effective government. Moscone was not successful in his attempted innovations; he was unable to move the bureaucracy and he helped to politicize neighborhood and reform groups by his appointments. Consequently, minor issues were often expanded to citywide scope with Moscone actively participating but unable to influence the outcome.

During White's administration, Boston enjoyed a peaceful labor climate, in contrast to San Francisco, New York City, Memphis, and Detroit, where major strikes severely disrupted municipal operations. In contrast to New York City and Cleveland, Boston averted a full fiscal crisis in the mid-1970s. Boston and San Francisco did experience fiscal difficulties because of statewide tax cutting measures (Proposition 2½ in Massachusetts and Proposition 13 in California). But in contrast to New York City and Cleveland, these difficulties were brought on by voters' desire to cut taxes and not by elected officials in general or by governments' expending more than their income. Moreover, the extent to which Boston actually had a fiscal crisis is questionable. As one would expect, the media played up the "plight" of Boston's municipal finances. White also emphasized the fiscal crisis but apparently as part of a political strategy to undercut the School Committee's power and to create new sources of revenue for Boston.[11]

Developing the power necessary to influence the distribution of resources, however, involves costs. The tension between the need to protect resources and the need to use those resources is often resolved by sins of omission; mayors will minimize their involvement in areas where there is little or no political payoff. These areas overwhelmingly affect the lives of poor people and minorities. In the later part of his administration, White avoided taking a firm stand on the race issue; he allowed the Boston Housing Authority (BHA) to deteriorate so badly that it was placed under court-appointed receivership; and he neglected the public school and public transportation systems. These costly omissions raise two important questions: How much can a mayor do in these areas? What are the conditions that permit such costly omissions to occur?

The race issue in Boston resulted from a combination of deep-seated prejudices caused by class, cultural, and educational factors; the exploitation of those prejudices by local politicians (especially school committee members); and the avoidance of the issue by other politicians. White masterfully redefined the issue as one of public safety and minimized trouble, but the larger question remains—to what extent can a mayor influence or change human behavior, and at what cost in time and resources? The answers are likely to be complex—and pessimistic. Although Boston's race relations deteriorated in the mid-1970s, they started out worse than in many other cities. Within this unfavorable climate, White managed to increase minority employment substantially in city government. Moreover, in the late 1970s and early 1980s, race relations in the political arena seem to have improved. Blacks have been elected to the School Committee and one has been president. Blacks have also been elected to the City Council.

Many experts agree that public housing is a national problem that is beyond the city's ability to resolve.[12] Nevertheless, White did make early attempts to reform the BHA. In contrast to previous mayors who used the BHA as a patronage operation, White appointed public housing tenants to the board to increase its responsiveness to the population served by public housing. His efforts failed, however, when he could not control his appointees. After an unsuccessful attempt to remove one of the board members, White abandoned that area of public policy.

The Boston public school system is under the jurisdiction of an elected school committee. It has fiscal autonomy, with only their supplemental budget requests requiring mayoral and council approval; it appoints the superintendent; and it negotiates with the teachers union. The School Committee's ineffective leadership resulted from the electoral process, not mayoral mismanagement. White attempted to change the electoral process so that the committee would be more representative and more responsive. Plan 3, Question 7 in 1974 and the charter reform proposal in 1976 would have replaced at-large elections for School Committee officials with district elections. Both of these measures were defeated: the first by the voters, the second by the state legislature. (White finally achieved some changes in School Committee behavior by manipulating public concern over its fiscal practices.) Furthermore, Boston public schools, like their counterparts in other cities, experienced significant "white flight" after federal court decisions in busing were implemented. Federal court intervention was brought on by the extreme intransigence of the School Committee.

Finally, despite the extreme economic and social importance of education to an area, the issue has traditionally been off limits to politicians. In New York City, reform mayors LaGuardia and Lindsay were severely criticized for attempting to influence educational policy. This underscores a major dilemma of executive leadership: the public does not give the executive the formal tools or the informal permission to do the job that they expect done. Nevertheless, they blame the executive when things go wrong, even when they occur in areas where the executive has no influence. Conservative South Boston residents were angered by White's implementation of the court's busing order while many blacks in Roxbury argued that he did not take a strong enough enforcement stand.[13] In San Francisco, Moscone was criticized for keeping a low profile in handling the craftworker strike even though the public had just voted to reduce the mayor's power in that area.

Boston's public transportation system is a similar example. The entire system was controlled by a regional authority (MBTA) and served seventy-eight cities and towns. Although White had some influence, it was diluted by the authority's broad composition and power. Further, public transit difficulties, like public housing problems, primarily result from inconsistent national policy. The emphasis on highway construction in the 1950s and 1960s dealt a serious blow to public transportation and created major financial difficulties for urban mass transit systems. Within this context, a mayor's ability to improve transportation service is very limited. In the latter part of his administration, White minimized his involvement in MBTA affairs.

By contrast, Lindsay met the transportation issue head-on in 1968. But his action resulted in a long transit workers strike, public discontent, and hostility among other unions leading to further strikes. More recently, Mayor Koch publicly criticized striking transportation workers. He successfully mobilized public support but the antagonisms he created among union leaders and the governor, Hugh Carey, resulted in a contract settlement higher than the city could afford.[14] Moreover, Lindsay and Koch's actions were attempts to gain power. Both mayors used the transportation issue to mobilize support. The key difference between the two New York City mayors and Mayor White is that White's strategies worked and the others' backfired.

The executive's ability to be a shrinking violet—that is, to avoid taking on unpleasant or unprofitable responsibilities—is facilitated when institutional mechanisms for integrating all citizens into the political system are absent or not working. V. O. Key's analysis of southern politics indicated a direct link between institutional weakness and irresponsible and unaccountable executives. Without strong representative institutions, the system of checks and balances is seriously weakened. In Boston, there were no effective institutional challenges to White's acquisition and use of power: there was no political party to demand accountability; the City Council represented only a few interests and was often irresponsible in its demeanor and performance; the School Committee was even less representative, often anti-black, and had a poorer image among the public.

The combination of this institutional failing, the tensions involved in acquiring power, and the mayor's personal ability will lead to further sins of omission. The serious problem addressed here is epitomized in a statement alleged to have been made by Mayor Koch. When criticized for neglecting the black community, Koch responded, "They [Blacks] don't vote anyhow."[15]

Acquiring power also involves sins of commission. The strong mayor will often develop power first and worry about the public's good later. White and Alioto's attention to minorities was largely encouraged by their ambitions for higher office and the need to attract favorable media notice. Their activities, however, increased employment opportunities for minorities and services provided to them. White's reorganizations within city government were designed to increase his power over department heads and broaden his access to municipal resources. Without such control, however, he would not have been able to improve municipal services with policies such as police reform and the policy management system. Thus, politically inspired actions often result in outcomes beneficial to the public. Further, we must ask what the alternatives are. The patronage dispensed by White was intended to secure his political base. Perhaps some, or even many, of those jobs did not go to the best qualified individuals. But neither has the civil service system proved to be an effective recruiter of talented personnel. In fact, it has developed a reputation for protecting mediocrity. The point is not to justify self-serving patronage or to denigrate the bureaucracy. Rather, it is to indicate the complexity of the leadership issue. Power is necessary, but its acquisition is costly.

The issue of executive leadership at the local level is further complicated by the costs of weak leadership. The power that the mayor fails to acquire is often captured by participants outside the electoral arena. But these other actors cannot provide alternatives to mayoral leadership. San Francisco saw the rise and active participation of reform and neighborhood groups. But we saw how narrow their focus was. In the Charter Reform campaign, these groups had the opportunity to change the governmental structure, but they dropped out of the process because the initiative did not address their specific concern—zoning matters.

Another group that showed a narrow focus was organized labor, especially in the police and firefighters strike. By pushing for immediate benefits, they undercut their own power and hurt the city as well. The craftworkers strike demonstrated the potential for irresponsible and destructive behavior by union officials. Although the city's labor leaders did not publicly condemn the sabotage of the airport facilities, neither did they privately condone it.[16]

When the media took a leadership role, it too behaved as a pressure group. In the Yerba Buena case, the San Francisco *Chronicle* and the *Examiner* had strong financial interests in the project and used their resources to pursue those interests. They attempted to discredit the residents' opposition by depicting them as "winos" and "bums" when, in fact, many were retired trade unionists living on meager pensions.[17]

In both cities, we saw the dilemmas created when higher governments imposed their decisions on local matters. In San Francisco's CETA case, a director was retained who was perceived as racist by many of her black clients. State government and federal court intervention in Boston's public school system resulted in a busing plan completely at odds with the interests of the city. Rejecting the plan drawn up by the city, the federal judge adopted the state's plan, which paired Roxbury and South Boston High Schools. South Boston is the city's most conservative and most anti-black neighborhood. Much of the violence that accompanied the busing occurred in South Boston.

The busing case, however, also illustrates the ineffective leadership of Boston's other elected officials. Had the School Committee behaved responsibly and implemented the Racial Imbalance Act, they could have avoided judicial intervention. Rather than devise a plan consonant with local needs, the committee exploited opposition to the act to gain political support. In doing so, they contributed to a dramatic increase in the city's racial tensions.

Under a weak executive, power is often captured by the bureaucracy. Banfield and Meyerson's analysis of Chicago's public housing controversy in the late 1940s and early 1950s directly linked the weakness of Mayor Kennelly and the capture of policymaking by the Chicago Housing Authority. The authority's decisions, however, led to citywide conflict and stalemate in a policy area that was very important at the time.[18] Pressman's analysis of Mayor Reading in Oakland saw a cause-and-effect relationship between a weak mayor and the forfeiture of policymaking control to nonelected actors.[19]

These two studies are important for their treatment of the problems of accountability and equity when policy is made in the nonelectoral arena. Bureaucratic policymaking is based on the internal needs of the organization rather than on clients' concerns. Because they are not elected, bureaucrats have more insulation than the mayor, tend to be less familiar with outside concerns, and, hence, have less incentive to compromise. In the Yerba Buena case, Alioto's negotiations with TOOR were a response to external demands. By contrast, Herman's actions were based on the concerns and needs of the SFRA. Alioto's inability to control Herman resulted in decisions that were in the interests of the SFRA rather than the residents. Similarly, when the waste water project was controlled by the Department of Public Works, it made no attempt to compromise with the residents who opposed the plans.

Bureaucratic policymaking also raises the question of equity. When issues are defined administratively rather than politically, questions of social and economic equality are seldom considered.[20] In fact, bureaucracies' decision-making criteria tend to produce inequitable distribution patterns. The motto "The more, the more," is characteristic of the bureaucratic approach.[21] Resources are allocated according to existing patterns. Groups that received resources in the past continue to receive, often at increased levels. And distribution is biased toward groups that can make the most effective demands—the better educated and the higher income groups.[22] Moreover, when the agencies are professionalized, the gap between server and served is widened, as the perception of what is needed and what is actually desired differs.

The failure of the mayor to acquire power over other civic actors can also result in a hyper-pluralistic competition for scarce resources. Moscone's inability to deflect issues, combined with the broad access that he provided to city government, increased the number of actors in the competition. Democratic bias would incline us to believe that this is a positive good. But E. E. Schattschneider has observed, "The flaw in the pluralist heaven is that the heavenly chorus sings with a strong upper class accent."[23] When newer groups attempt to enter this pluralist heaven, they may be left in limbo. And, without a strong center, which the pluralist model does not provide, there is no mechanism to achieve or protect the goals sought by these new groups. The result is often a stalemate, which is a victory for the status quo. Although there was considerable competition in the federal arena, Moscone was unable to alter the existing balance of power. The fluoridation campaigns in the 1950s and urban renewal programs illustrate the same pattern.[24] In cities where power was highly fragmented, executives were either unwilling or unable to take initiatives. Consequently, issues were either stalled or, as in urban renewal, were directed by nonelected officials.[25]

This relationship between fragmented power, pluralist competition, and stalemate is supported by studies in organizational theory as well. These studies revealed that highly decentralized organizations produce more innovative proposals than centralized organizations, but have few adoptions. Conversely, organizations with centralized power have many adoptions.[26]

When stalemate occurs in redistributive areas, the costs are borne by poor people and minorities. Michael Parenti's study in Newark showed how difficult it is for these two groups to alter the status quo, a point confirmed by Sharon Krefetz's study of welfare policymaking in San Francisco.[27] Examples drawn from protest politics, considered by some to be the only resource available to these groups, showed how the status quo is often used as a weapon against these groups.[28] My study provides further evidence for the weakness of the pluralist model and the costs of stalemate. The International Hotel case and the Officers for Justice suit became major public issues and had strong mayoral support during Moscone's administration. In both cases, the proponents lost. Thus, weaker groups had more access to city government during the Moscone administration than during the Alioto or White administrations, but when they got through the door, the room was empty. While the *process* may appear more democratic in the pluralist model than in the strong centrist model, the outcomes are similar; politically weaker groups are at a serious disadvantage in both systems.

The problems associated with strong and weak executive leadership pose serious challenges to democratic governance. The issues of accountability and equity are obvious problems. But a more subtle and dangerous phenomenon is at work. Almond and Verba discovered that Americans turn more to elected political leaders than to administrators when they wish to influence local government.[29] This predisposition, which contrasts with that of Germans, Italians, and Mexicans, is indicative of certain expectations that we have of our elected officials. We expect them to be responsive, credible, competent, trustworthy, and reliable. But if the executive cannot deliver because of a lack of power, or is unwilling to deliver because of a need to protect power, a gap is created between expectation and outcome. This gap is filled with apathy, as evidenced by the decline in voter participation, or with frustration. Although seemingly opposite, apathy and frustration stem from the same root: the perception of a government divorced from its citizenry.

This is a serious threat to democratic government. A working democracy requires an active citizenry and a leadership strong enough to respond to that citizenry.

## POLICY IMPLICATIONS

As political scientists, the most important questions that we face are who gets what, when, where and how? The search for equitable solutions must focus on developing strong executive leadership at the local level. This study has explored the conditions that promote such leadership. It has indicated the difficulties and costs of developing that leadership in the absence of an institutional base. Indeed, the most important lesson is that we need to shift our focus to institutions. An effective institutional framework can facilitate the development of executive leadership and minimize the costs of acquiring power.

Ironically, the reform movement in American politics amply demonstrates the need for power. The history of reform is largely an attack on the abuses of power. Rather than devise mechanisms to foster an accountable exercise of power, however, the reformers instituted measures to thwart power. But Lowi has observed, "Reform did not eliminate the need for power. It simply altered what one had to do to get it."[30] But this alteration increased the costs of acquiring the power necessary to govern while it weakened the institutional checks and balances on the acquisition and use of power. The outcome is often that power is developed for its own sake. The fine line between necessary power and self-aggrandizing power is blurred and there are no institutional mechanisms to redraw it. Many have argued that this was the tragic flaw in Kevin White's administration: the power to improve the quality of public service was replaced by an obsession with power. Indeed, the last years of the White administration appear to have been almost completely overwhelmed by such an obsession.

As reform did not advance the cause of executive leadership, reforms of the electoral process did not result in increased citizen participation and rational voting behavior.[31] Rather, they decreased voter participation and often created racial, demagogic, and personality politics. Municipal civil service reforms did not achieve their goal of increased governmental efficiency. Civil service systems tend to protect inefficiency, to contribute to stasis, and to promote narrow, specialized interests that serve the agency rather than the public.

This record teaches that reform should be directed toward the responsible accumulation, not the thoughtless destruction, of political power. As Lowi accurately observed, "Lack of power can corrupt city hall almost as much as the possession of power."[32] Using the criteria of accountability, responsiveness, and representation, we must discover which institutions are capable of producing effective leadership and move to strengthen those institutions.

A major component of our institutional structure has been the two-party system. A re-introduction of partisan elections would provide a mechanism of accountability that is currently lacking. At least the executive would be accountable to the party. As an institution, the party has a larger stake in long term survival than does the individual candidate. An observation by Thomas Sowell is suggestive:

New York City's financial crisis of the 1970s grew out of policies and practices adopted during the administrations of one of its most charismatic and independent mayors during the 1960s [while] the contrasting financial solvency of Chicago at the same time was maintained in one of the last bastions of municipal machine politics.[33]

Further, the party's organizational needs encourage it to perform valuable screening and recruitment functions. Without such screening, the chances for irresponsible individuals to enter and win elections is increased. Local electoral behavior in the South in the first half of this century provides an excellent illustration. Based on an exhaustive study of this behavior, V. O. Key concluded that,

Not only does a disorganized politics make impossible a competition between recognizable groups for power. It probably has a far-reaching influence on the kinds of individual leaders thrown into power and also on the manner in which they utilize their authority once they are in office. Loose factional organizations are poor contrivances for recruiting and sifting out leaders of public affairs. . . . In an atomized and individualistic politics it becomes a matter of each leader for himself and often for himself only for the current campaign.[34]

By contrast, a two-party system can generate the competition that produces effective executive leadership. Democracy, as a political system, requires conflict, competition, organization, leadership, and responsibility.[35] The key here is organization. Without it, the competition is between individuals, who substitute either the personal conflict of personality politics or demagogic appeals to avoid the major issues of economic, political, and social justice.[36] In such a situation, the public is the loser. A competitive two-party system in Boston would have fostered a more responsive and more accountable exercise of power by White. This speculation is based on the experience of cities that did have strong two-party competition. When New Haven was gripped by intense party rivalry in the 1940s and 1950s, Republican and Democratic officeholders initiated major programs in education and redevelopment.[37] When Chicago's Democratic party leaders faced a serious Republican challenge in the late 1940s, they focused on housing issues.[38] When scandals in Daley's administration opened the door for strong interparty competition, Daley implemented a major police reform. In Philadelphia, the Democratic party's efforts to counter Republican challenges in the 1940s and 1950s produced the Dilworth and Clark administrations that accomplished budgetary and managerial reorganizations and major urban renewal, housing, and traffic control programs.[39]

These examples suggest that similar challenges in Boston would have forced White to direct his political skills toward more substantive ends. But Boston's electoral process did not create that type of competition. Rather, it produced demagogic appeals like those of Hicks in 1967 and 1971 and personality conflicts exemplified by Timilty and City Council elections.

The electoral processes in Boston and San Francisco, as well as in other nonpartisan cities, indicate the need for an institutional framework to support executive leadership. Some pieces of framework already exist, but in their current form, are malfunctioning. The legislative bodies in Boston and San Francisco are potential sources of institutional leadership. The potential has been thwarted, however, by the system of at-large elections which encourages personality politics and irresponsible behavior. District-based elections would probably foster more accountability and more stability. Representing only one constituency—and a definite one—legislators could rely less on personal appeals and concentrate more on the substantive needs of their constituents. Encouragingly, Boston has recently voted to reinstitute district elections for city councillors and School Committee officials after thirty-one years of an at-large system.

While district-based elections traditionally have accompanied partisan systems, they become even more important in nonpartisan and weak party systems. Morris Fiorina and Richard Fenno observed an increasing trend of district-orientation among members of the U.S. Congress.

The decline of political parties has encouraged legislators to increase their less controversial activities such as case work, pork barrelling, and ombudsmenship.[40] While this supports predictions of a dim future for political parties at the national level, it is an optimistic sign at the local level. As spokespersons for groups presently ignored by the executive, district-oriented legislators can put pressure on the executive, which is currently lacking, to show responsiveness to those groups. When San Francisco had district elections between 1975 and 1978, the board's composition changed from predominantly white and middle and upper middle class to include gays, Chinese, and neighborhood representatives. Consequently, the nature of the issues changed, reflecting the interests of these newer groups.

If their votes came from only one district, legislative candidates would be forced to bring more people into the political system. In at-large systems where all candidates run against one another and require only a small percentage of the vote to win, there is no incentive to mobilize any one group or even significant numbers of voters. The turnout for the Boston City Council election in 1977, for example, was only 34 percent. Those who suffer the most from this situation are minorities and poor people whose low voter turnout makes them a negligible influence. As Berkeley observed, "By the mathematics of the situation, at-large councils cannot help but exaggerate the representation of the majority and minimize the representation of the minority."[41]

The electoral imperatives of a district system can make legislative bodies more representative and responsive. But incentives must be accompanied by resources sufficient to perform the job. The current part-time status of supervisors in San Francisco limits their resources. Making the job a full-time one would increase the supply of resources and better equip the supervisors to meet their tasks.

Similarly, the mayor's office in San Francisco would benefit from abolition of the two-term limitation. Mayors have much less incentive in the second term to perform in a responsive manner. We saw this in Alioto's handling of the police and firefighters strike. With only four months remaining in his administration, Alioto was less vulnerable to the checks and balances of public and media pressures.

Another consequence of the two-term limitation is that other actors have less incentive to cooperate when a mayor approaches the end of the second term. Alioto's cordial relationship with the board deteriorated toward the end of his second term as it began vetoing his proposals. Some observers attributed this to resentment of Alioto's settlement of the police and firefighters strike, but his status as a lame duck provides at least a partial explanation.

The final prescription for improving executive leadership—a broad, theoretical one—calls for putting politics where it belongs, in the electoral arena. Currently, too many important decisions are made in non-electoral arenas and so are divorced from the needs and demands of the voters. This has resulted, as we have seen, from the depoliticization of many issues and from the mistaken idea that participatory democracy is only an extreme form of representative democracy. It does not necessarily follow that direct citizen participation leads to a wider representation of interests. Nevertheless, this notion has influenced our institutional development, as witness the proliferation of local boards, commissions, advisory councils, and referenda.[42] But those who participate tend to be disproportionately drawn from the leisured, educated, and propertied classes. San Francisco's boards, commissions, and citizen advisory committees resembled blue ribbon panels, a trend that continued even after minorities were appointed to those positions. What is civic responsibility and public obligation to the leisured classes is a luxury to the poorer classes—a luxury they cannot afford.

Participatory proliferation often results in what Thomas Sowell calls an "incremental trade-off of the public's right to decide by elected representatives for a self-selected constituencies' opportunity to be insiders."[43] The size of this trade-off varies in direct relation to the strength of the executive. Moscone's proposals were often thwarted by such "self-selected constituencies." What appeared to be participatory democracy was actually a shift of power from the electoral to the nonelectoral arena.

This imbalance can be partially corrected through structural changes limiting the number of nonelected boards and commissions and increasing mayoral control over policymakers. This study has demonstrated that executives tend to be more familiar with and responsive to the needs and demands of the citizens than do nonelected officials. Abolishing the office of the CAO in San Francisco, for example, would remove some of the bureaucratic insulation from key areas of city government. Transferring the CAO's authority over public health, public works, government services, and special projects to the mayor would move these important jurisdictional areas closer to accountability. The mayor would have more incentive to be accountable to the electorate than does the CAO, whose tenure does not depend upon public acceptance. Similarly, decreasing the controller's term from life to four years would restore important policy areas to public review.

These last two structural changes would strengthen the executive office both formally and informally. Formally, they would increase the authority of the mayor. Informally, they would put the mayor in a stronger position because there would be fewer actors to bargain with. As a result, the executive would not have to expend so many resources in enforcing priorities. This is important in a weak political system, because the executive's initial stock of resources is so limited. We saw how Feinstein had to delegate power to the business community to persuade the controller to implement the budgetary reforms. The necessity of doing this, a case of pulling power from the sides to the center, was an obstacle to centralizing authority and to executive leadership.

Undoubtedly the recommendations made above will be criticized by reformers as overly political. But every decision, theirs included, is both political and partisan.[44] Decisions are political and partisan when they influence the rules of the game. Reforms in urban government that ushered in nonpartisan systems and placed vital functions in the administrative arena significantly altered the rules of the game by decreasing the access of poor people and minorities to city government. If we follow James Q. Wilson's advice and ask, "What difference does it make?"[45] rather than "Who governs?" we learn that the structure of government does make a difference!

In a democracy no less than in any political system, effective government is a necessity. Despite the anti-power bias in the American political culture, when we call for effective government, we are in essence calling for strong executive leadership. Discovering and building an institutional framework for this leadership is an overdue task. The changes advocated here represent only a beginning. The job now is to re-examine our institutions. The call to revive political parties may be criticized as infeasible. Although Minneapolis re-instituted partisan elections, the barriers to resurrecting parties at the local level are high. But that does not diminish the important role that parties can serve as models to guide our actions and inform our decisions.

Constructing these models will require careful research, proper questions, and intensive soul searching. These efforts can effectively be led by political scientists. Through our work we help to determine what issues are examined and debated. Douglas Arnold has suggested that the current allocation of scholarly resources neglects important areas that he calls "undertilled fields." In a similar argument, Nelson Polsby cited important transformations that are occurring in American politics that need to be researched.[46] Many of the transformations, especially those in communications, are extremely complex. While both men have valid points, they seem to be caught up in the whirlwind called future shock. In our race to keep up with a technological sophistication we cannot comprehend, we have paid only lip service to the basic questions that a democratic society must constantly probe. The first undertilled field that must be approached concerns the fundamental questions: What do we mean by "participatory democracy"? What do we mean by "representative democracy"? Are our definitions of democracy compatible with our conceptions of justice? How do we reconcile competing claims of freedom and equality? The fundamental questions must be continually raised. The type of institutions we build depends on how we answer them. As John Rawls observed, the social contract is not just an historical fiction, but rather, an on-going process.[47]

The rise of so-called big government has made another type of questioning essential. We must ask ourselves what we expect from government and what price we are willing to pay for it.[48] Avoidance of these questions will continue the trend of contradictory demands, contrary politicians, misplaced hopes, and extreme frustrations.[49] Confronting them, however, we begin to resolve the tensions between the anti-power bias in the American political culture and our high expectations toward the government. We must either define the government's role more narrowly or grant our executives the power required to do their job. My strong speculation is that we will reject the first option. Therefore, we should not fear power but, rather, make it accountable and responsive, within the standards established in the on-going social contract.

# Notes, Selected Bibliography, and Index

# Notes

CHAPTER 1

1. Douglas Yates, "The Mayor's Eight-Ring Circus: The Shape of Urban Politics in Its Evolving Policy Arenas," paper delivered at the annual meeting of the American Political Science Association, New York, 1978, p. 5.
2. Ibid.
3. Michael Lipsky, "Toward a Theory of Street-Level Bureaucracy," in Willis Hawley and Michael Lipsky, eds., *Theoretical Perspectives in Urban Politics* (Englewood Cliffs, N.J.: Prentice-Hall, 1974), pp. 196–213.
4. Mayors Impellitteri, O'Dwyer, LaGuardia, Wagner, and Lindsay. For a good discussion of Robert Moses' reign, see Robert A. Caro, *The Power Broker: Robert Moses and the Fall of New York* (New York City: Random House, 1975).
5. Wallace S. Sayre and Herbert Kaufman, *Governing New York City: Politics in the Metropolis* (New York City: Russell Sage Foundation, 1965).
6. Theodore J. Lowi, "Machine Politics . . . Old and New," *Public Interest* 9 (Fall 1967): 86–87.
7. Jeffrey L. Pressman, *Federal Programs and City Politics: The Dynamics of the Aid Process in Oakland* (Berkeley and Los Angeles: University of California Press, 1975).
8. Yates, "The Mayor's Eight-Ring Circus."
9. Ibid., p. 17.
10. See Martin A. Levin, *The Political Dilemmas of Social Policymaking* (forthcoming).
11. Aaron Wildavsky and Jack Knott, "Jimmy Carter's Theory of Governing," in Walter Dean Burnham and Martha Wagner Weinberg, eds., *American Politics and Public Policy* (Cambridge: MIT Press, 1978), pp. 55–76.
12. Dukakis was defeated in the 1978 Democratic primary. He was re-elected in 1982, but his strategy was based on a very effective state-wide political organization. This approach differed substantially from that of 1978 when he barely campaigned at all.
13. Andrew McFarland, *Power and Leadership in Pluralist Systems* (Stanford, Calif.: Stanford University Press, 1969), p. 154.
14. Jeffrey L. Pressman, "Preconditions of Mayoral Leadership," *American Political Science Review* 66 (June 1972): 511–24.
15. See Charles Levine, *Racial Conflict and the American Mayor: Power, Po-*

*larization and Performance* (Lexington, Mass.: D. C. Heath, 1974), for a detailed analysis of these limitations.

16. Peter Bachrach and Morton Baratz, "Two Faces of Power," *American Political Science Review* 56 (Dec. 1962): 947–52.

17. This literature includes Douglas Yates, *The Ungovernable City* (Cambridge: MIT Press, 1977), and John P. Kotter and Paul Lawrence, *Mayors in Action* (New York City: John Wiley, 1974).

18. Levine, *Racial Conflict and the American Mayor*, p. 5.

19. Edward M. Levine, *The Irish and Irish Politicians* (Notre Dame, Ind.: University Press of Notre Dame, 1966), p. 171.

20. Samuel Huntington develops a similar point in his analysis of American politics and the American political culture. He argues that the anti-power ethic is so strong that the concealment of power is the most effective exercise of power. *American Politics: The Promise of Disharmony* (Cambridge: Harvard University Press, 1981), esp. chap. 4.

CHAPTER 2

1. Alan Lupo, Frank Colcord, and Edmund P. Fowler, *Rites of Way: The Politics of Transportation in Boston and the U.S. City* (Boston: Little, Brown and Company, 1971), p. 2.

2. As a result of a referendum, San Francisco had district elections for supervisors from 1976 to 1980. It went back to an at-large system after the electorate voted to repeal district elections in a subsequent referendum in August 1980. In Boston, the electorate voted in 1981 to reinstitute district elections beginning in 1983.

3. "Private-regarding" refers to the more traditional ethnic-oriented politics of northeastern and older industrial cities of the United States. It is characterized by a strong personal component and an emphasis on tangible rewards. For an historical analysis, see Edward Banfield and James Q. Wilson, *City Politics* (Cambridge: Harvard University Press, 1966).

4. Between 1900 and 1950, San Francisco was the most ethnic and Irish of the Western cities.

5. 1970 Census, U.S. Department of Commerce.

6. The small size of the black populations in the two cities is only one reason for the slower political development. More significant is the absence of political parties in the two cities to integrate blacks into the political system. I discuss this point later in this chapter.

7. Although Dorchester was 45.2 percent black in 1980 (U.S. Census), the housing was fairly segregated. In fact, recent attempts by blacks to move closer to white parts of Dorchester were met by resistance that was often violent; black families were threatened and several black homes were vandalized.

8. 1980 Census, published in *New York Times*, 9 June 1981.

9. 1980 Census, published in *Boston Globe*, 25 Feb. 1982.

10. In 1981, San Francisco had the highest median cost of housing in the

continental United States at $129,000. Los Angeles was second at $118,000, and New York third at $90,000. *New York Times,* 9 June 1981. See Tables 3 and 4 for comparative housing data.

11. Oakland's early transition to containerized docks and San Francisco's much slower move sent a great deal of shipping business to Oakland.

12. David Dalin, "Public Affairs and the Jewish Community: The Changing Political World of San Francisco Jews," Ph.D. diss., Brandeis University, 1977.

13. Swig owned the Fairmont and St. Francis Hotels, two of San Francisco's most exclusive hotels. He was also the prime mover behind the Yerba Buena project, San Francisco's major convention center (see Chapter 8).

14. Schorenstein is president of Milton Meyer, Inc., one of the largest real estate outfits in San Francisco. For his fund-raising activities, see Dalin, "Public Affairs and the Jewish Community."

15. Irish control over San Francisco's Democratic party was an obstacle to Jewish membership. It is important to realize, however, that although the Irish were powerful within San Francisco's Democratic party, they did not control the political machinery as did their counterparts in Boston. Several factors account for this. First, the Irish in San Francisco did not encounter strong anti-Catholicism like the Boston Irish. (Rather, San Francisco was marked by strong anti-Chinese sentiments, in which the Irish played a leading role by the end of the nineteenth century.) Thus, the San Francisco Irish did not form small protective associations, which could have formed the basis of political clubs. Second, since the political system was not dominated by any one group, the Irish who came to San Francisco entered a more open system with diverse employment opportunities; the Irish entered construction, civil service, the Roman Catholic church, and union politics. Moreover, the diversity of employment was matched by the diversity of skills that the Irish brought with them. In contrast to the Irish in northeastern cities, who came straight from Ireland, San Francisco's Irish population mostly came from northeastern cities, where they had picked up skills and been partially assimilated into American culture. Third, and relatedly, the political machinery in San Francisco was not the central means for economic and social mobility as it was in Boston and many other cities of the Northeast.

Thus, while the Irish in San Francisco did have strong political predilections, politics was not a matter of survival for them as it was for their counterparts on the Atlantic coast, especially Boston. Because neither the Irish nor any other one group dominated San Francisco's political system, it developed in a more open fashion than Boston's. Consequently, a much wider diversity of groups exerted influence on San Francisco's political system, which is a major reason that San Francisco's political system tends to be less protectionist, more tolerant, more liberal, and more diversified than Boston's.

For an analysis of the Irish in San Francisco city politics, see Fred Wirt, *Power in the City: Decision-Making in San Francisco* (Berkeley and Los

Angeles: University of California Press, 1974), chap. 9. For Boston, see Thomas H. O'Connor, *Bibles, Brahmins, and Bosses: A Short History of Boston* (Boston: Boston Public Library, 1976); see also Edgar Litt, *The Political Cultures of Massachusetts* (Cambridge: MIT Press, 1965).

16. Dalin, "Public Affairs and the Jewish Community."
17. Edward Banfield referred to this as the "private regarding" political ethos. Banfield and Wilson, *City Politics*.
18. For a good discussion of Irish political behavior, see Edward M. Levine, *The Irish and Irish Politicians* (Notre Dame, Ind.: University of Notre Dame Press, 1966). See also Milton Rakove, *Don't Make No Waves, Don't Back No Losers: An Insider's Account of the Daley Machine* (Bloomington: Indiana University Press, 1975).
19. In 1976, San Francisco's population was 32 percent of its metropolitan area; Baltimore's was 39 percent; Philadelphia's was 37 percent; Chicago's was 44 percent; and New York City's, 66 percent. ACIR, *Central City–Suburban Fiscal Disparity and City Distress—1977.*
20. With only a few exceptions, Boston has had only Irish mayors since the turn of the century. Most city councillors and school committee officials have been Irish. See Thomas H. O'Connor, *Bibles, Brahmins and Bosses.*
21. In 1885 the first Irish mayor was elected in Boston (Hugh Roe O'Brian). The Yankees, through their control over the state legislature, placed control over the Boston police with the state. The city did not regain control until 1962. The state also took over liquor licensing and, by means of "Except Boston Bills," city finances. In subsequent years, major parks and roads and the water system were placed under the control of the Metropolitan District Commission. The Finance Commission was set up as a watchdog agency to oversee city spending.
22. Russell B. Adams, *The Boston Money Tree* (New York City: Thomas Y. Crowell, 1977), pp. 269–70.
23. James Michael Curley was first elected in 1913. Opposed to his spending patterns, the business community banded together to defeat him. With the help of Lomasney, they ran two Irish candidates, which split the Irish vote. Andrew Peters, the business community's candidate, defeated Curley. This was only temporary. Curley was elected again in 1921, 1929, and 1945. For an account of the 1917 election, see Frank Levy, *Northern Schools and Civil Rights: The Racial Imbalance Act of Massachusetts* (Chicago: Markham, 1971), chap. 1.
24. *A Decade of Development in Boston*, report prepared by the Boston Redevelopment Authority, 1979.
25. Boston Redevelopment Authority, *Outlook for Boston.*
26. Adams, *The Boston Money Tree*, p. 270.
27. For a good exposition of the conservative-liberal dichotomy, see Alan Lupo, *Liberty's Chosen Home: The Politics of Violence in Boston*, 1st ed. (Boston: Little, Brown, 1977). See Chapters 3 and 4 for details on mayors' attempts to appeal to both groups.
28. In 1978, California voters passed Proposition 13, a statewide tax-cutting

measure that prohibits cities and towns from levying new taxes and that permits only a one percent increase in the property tax each year. A similar measure, Proposition 2½, was passed by the Massachusetts voters in 1980. Under this measure, cities and towns must decrease the property tax rate by 15 percent each year until it reaches 2½ percent.

29. *New York Times*, 9 June 1981.
30. Planning Department Records.
31. San Francisco controls its public transportation system (excluding BART), its police, its major parks and roads, its water system.
32. Philip B. Heyman and Martha Wagner Weinberg, "The Paradox of Power: Mayoral Leadership on Charter Reform in Boston," in Walter Dean Burnham and Martha Wagner Weinberg, eds., *American Politics and Public Policy* (Cambridge: MIT Press, 1978), p. 292.
33. The main source of revenue is the property tax. Before Proposition 2½, passed by the Massachusetts voters in November 1980, the mayor set the tax rate each year. Proposition 2½ removed that discretion by requiring cities and towns to reduce the tax rate by 15 percent a year until it reaches 2½ percent.
34. V. O. Key, *Southern Politics in State and Nation* (New York: Vintage, 1949).
35. Election Department Records.
36. *Boston Globe*, 3 Nov. 1981.
37. All purchasing for city government is done within the Department of Government Services; Special Projects includes the Moscone Convention Center (formerly the Yerba Buena Convention Center), the waste water project, and the solid waste disposal system.
38. Alioto, Moscone, and Feinstein all inherited their CAOs. Mellon stayed on as Moscone's acting CAO until Moscone found a replacement.
39. The mayor appoints two out of four to BART, one out of nine to the Golden Gate Bridge Highway and Transportation District, and one out of two to the Bay Area Pollution and Control District.
40. Terry Francois was appointed by Shelley; Robert Gonzales and George Chinn were appointed by Alioto; Gordon Lau was appointed by Moscone.
41. Police commissioners are an exception to the term appointment; they serve at the pleasure of the mayor. Removals must be made for cause and require approval of two-thirds of the board of supervisors. Parks and Recreation commissioners cannot be removed even for cause.
42. This 74 includes 11 supervisors, 19 municipal court judges, 24 superior court judges, 7 board of education officials, 7 members of the community college board, the assessor, the city attorney, the district attorney, the public defender, the sheriff, and the treasurer.
43. While lagging far behind San Francisco, Boston and Massachusetts voters are increasing their use of the referendum, as witnessed by the classification campaign in 1978 and Proposition 2½ in 1980. The future of this trend is impossible to foresee.

44. See Richard M. Abrams, *Conservatism in a Progressive Era: Massachusetts Politics, 1900–1912* (Cambridge: Harvard University Press, 1964). See also James R. Green and Hugh Carter Donahue, *Boston's Workers: A Labor History* (Boston: Boston Public Library, 1979).
45. Interviews, 25 Feb. 1981, 22 May 1981, and 5 June 1981.
46. Martha Wagner Weinberg, "Boston's Kevin White: A Mayor Who Survives," *Political Science Quarterly* 96 (Spring 1981): 87–106.
47. Daniel Pool, "Politics in the New Boston, 1960–1970: A Study of Mayoral Policy-Making," Ph.D diss., Brandeis University, 1974.
48. Dianne Paul, *Politics of the Property Tax* (Lexington, Mass.: D. C. Heath, 1975), p. 79.
49. Ibid.
50. The state legislature passed a statute, the 121A agreement, which consisted of a zoning provision and a taxing component (6a). The latter sets the tax rate in advance, based on a percentage of profits, and so avoids discretionary decisions.
51. Gary Orren, "The Cycle of Black Political Impotence: School Politics in Boston," paper delivered at the annual meeting of the Midwest Political Science Association, Chicago, 1978.
52. See Key, *Southern Politics*; Banfield and Wilson, *City Politics*; and Willis D. Hawley, *Non-Partisan Elections and the Case for Party Politics* (New York City: John Wiley, 1973).
53. Mark R. Levy and Michael S. Kramer, *The Ethnic Factor: How America's Minorities Decide Elections* (New York City: Simon and Schuster, 1973), p. 68.
54. Although Newark was 54 percent black in 1970, Gibson won the run-off election with the aid of white voters: he got approximately one out of every six. It should also be noted that his opponent, Hugh Addonizio, was under federal indictment for extortion and tax irregularities at the time and has since been convicted. Levy and Kramer, *The Ethnic Factor*, p. 70.
55. Two of the components of the "cycle of black political impotence" that Orren discusses, for example, are at-large electoral systems and low voter participation by minorities. Nonpartisan systems tend to depress minority participation. As a result, at-large candidates do not direct their appeals to minorities, which further depresses minority participation because they feel excluded from the system. Orren, "The Cycle of Black Political Impotence."
56. Blacks accounted for a larger percentage of New York City's population than of Boston's, but compared with Chicago, Cleveland, Newark, and other cities, they were still a relatively small minority.
57. Interestingly, the first black elected to the school committee, John O'Bryant, had an Irish name and was elected when the schools had become primarily black.
58. Robert L. Crain, *Politics of School Desegregation: Comparative Case Studies of Community Structure and Policy-Making* (Chicago: Aldine, 1968), pp. 143–44.

59. See Levy, *Northern Schools and Civil Rights.* See also Orren, "The Cycle of Black Political Impotence."
60. White did not win on the strength of his liberal stand on race, however. See Chapter 3.
61. In 1973 white enrollment comprised 55 percent of the public school student body. By 1980 it had declined to 36 percent. See Robert A. Dentler and Marvin B. Scott, *Schools on Trial: An Inside Account of the Boston Desegregation Case* (Cambridge, Mass.: ABT, 1981). The authors do not conclude, however, that desegregation caused the decline in white enrollment.
62. Cambridge has a significant working-class population as well, but it tends to be overshadowed by the more vocal and politically active professional class.
63. Walter Bean, *Boss Reuf's San Francisco: The Story of the Union Labor Party, Big Business, and the Graft Prosecution* (Berkeley and Los Angeles: University of California, 1967), p. 12.
64. Sharon Perlman Krefetz, *Welfare Policy Making and City Politics* (New York City: Praeger, 1976).
65. Chester Hartman, *Yerba Buena* (San Francisco: Glide Publications, 1974), p. 59.
66. Banfield and Wilson, *City Politics.*
67. Election Department Records.
68. In 1976, 64 percent of eligible blacks were registered to vote, compared with 77 percent of eligible whites. Extrapolated from election data in Coro Foundation, *District Handbook.*
69. Interview with ILWU representative, 5 June 1981.
70. In 1976, 58 percent of eligible Spanish-speaking people were registered to vote, compared with 64 percent of eligible blacks and 77 percent of eligible whites.
71. Research conducted for Supervisor Silver, 1979.
72. Extrapolated from data in Coro Foundation, *District Handbook.*
73. The vacancy rate is reported in a survey of the Community Design Center, 1969.
74. Interview with political lobbyist for Moscone, 17 June 1981.
75. It would appear that some of these developments, especially among the younger Chinese, help to explain the large disparity between high Chinese turnout and low voter registration rates. Although a breakdown of the Chinese voters was not available, a possible interpretation is that the younger Chinese account for the high turnout, while the low registration reflects the Chinese community as a whole. If this argument, which is basically an assimilation theory, is accurate, then it will be quite a while before the Chinese acquire significant influence within San Francisco's political system.
76. Figures for 1967 from *San Francisco Chronicle,* 29 Sept. 1967; 1979 figures from COPE Records.
77. Interview with ILWU representative, 5 June 1981.

78. 1980 Census, published in *New York Times*, 9 June 1981.
79. The comparable figure in Boston was 34 percent. Although it is close to San Francisco's, the number is distorted by Boston's large student population, many of whom are counted in the census. Although some are politically active from time to time, they tend to act more on national issues than on Boston issues. In addition, Boston's student population is rather segregated (residentially and socially) from the permanent Boston population. By contrast, San Francisco's young population, many of whom are professionals, have moved into neighborhoods like North Beach, Haight-Ashbury, Western Addition, and Castro where they have become very active in city politics.
80. Population figures are from Manuel Castells and Karen Murphy, "Cultural Identity and Urban Structure: The Spatial Organization of San Francisco's Gay Community," p. 1; voters estimate is from Hugh Schwartz Public Opinion Research, San Francisco, 1979.
81. Interviews with political pollster and consultant, 17 June 1981; and aides to Moscone, 2 June 1981.
82. Election Department Records.
83. Walter Robinson, "A Bay Stater's California Notes," *Boston Globe*, 25 July 1982, p. 81.
84. *Boston Globe*, 19 Sept. 1981, p. 13.
85. David S. Broder, *Changing of the Guard: Power and Leadership in America* (New York City: Simon and Schuster, 1980), pp. 339–40.
86. I elected not to examine John Collins's administration because it precedes the era of dwindling resources. The literature on mayors who struggled and sometimes failed to acquire power focused primarily on the Lindsay era of charismatic, crusading, audience-seeking executives. By contrast, Collins falls into the bricks-and-mortar era of mayors like Lee in New Haven, Allen in Atlanta, and Clark and Dillworth in Philadelphia—an era whose literature stressed the availability of resources. See, for example, Robert A. Dahl, *Who Governs?* (New Haven, Conn.: Yale University Press, 1966), and Raymond Wolfinger, *The Politics of Progress* (Englewood Cliffs, N.J.: Prentice-Hall, 1973). Thus, Collins's experience does not illuminate the question that I pose: How does a mayor acquire power in a time of dwindling resources?
    For an analysis of John Collins's administration, see Daniel Pool, "Politics in the New Boston."
87. This excludes Albany and Milwaukee, both of which have mayors with longer tenures than White—Erastus Corning and Henry Maier, respectively.
88. In *A Life in Our Times: Memoirs* (Boston: Houghton Mifflin, 1981), John Kenneth Galbraith claimed that he was actually responsible for McGovern's change of heart. This runs counter to the widely held belief that it was Ted Kennedy who blocked the nomination. For whatever reason, however, White lost a chance to run in a national election.

CHAPTER 3

1. E. E. Schattschneider, *The Semisovereign People: A Realist's View of Democracy in America*, rev. ed. (Hinsdale, Ill.: Dryden Press, 1975), p. 65.
2. For a good analysis of party development and shifting alliances, see James L. Sundquist, *Dynamics of the Party System: Alignment and Realignment of Political Parties in the U.S.* (Washington, D.C.: Brookings Institution, 1973); William Nisbet Chambers and Walter Dean Burnham, eds., *The American Party Systems: Stages of Political Development* (New York City: Oxford University Press, 1967); and Schattschneider, *The Semisovereign People*.
3. V. O. Key, *Southern Politics in State and Nation* (New York City: Vintage, 1949).
4. Henry Fairlie, *The Kennedy Promise: The Politics of Expectation*, 1st ed. (Garden City, N.Y.: Doubleday, 1973).
5. Schattschneider, *The Semisovereign People*; Key, *Southern Politics*.
6. Douglas Yates used the first phrase in his *The Ungovernable City* (Cambridge MIT Press, 1977); the second is from his paper, "The Mayor's Eight-Ring Circus: The Shape of Urban Politics in Its Evolving Policy Arenas," delivered at the annual meeting of the American Political Science Association, New York, 1978.
7. Schattschneider, *The Semisovereign People*.
8. The electoral incentives were very strong. Four wards of the city were usually decisive in school committee elections: East Boston, South Boston, Hyde Park, and West Roxbury. All four had conservative constituencies. Robert Wood, "Professionals at Bay: Managing Boston's Public Schools," *Journal of Policy Analysis and Management*, 1982.
9. Edward C. Banfield and James Q. Wilson, *City Politics* (Cambridge: Harvard University Press, 1966).
10. This point is developed very well by Douglas Yates in *The Ungovernable City* and by James Q. Wilson in "The Mayors vs. the Cities," *The Public Interest* 16 (Summer 1969): 25–37.
11. New York City figures from 1970 Census, U.S. Department of Commerce, and *American Jewish Yearbook*, vol. 75 (Philadelphia: Jewish Publication Society, 1974). Boston figures from 1970 Census, U.S. Department of Commerce; Jewish population estimate extrapolated from data on Boston neighborhoods. Neighborhood data was compiled by the United Community Planning Corporation in Boston, June 1975. This figure differs from the one in the *American Jewish Yearbook* (23 percent) because theirs is for the larger metropolitan area whereas mine is for the city of Boston only.
12. Election Department Records.
13. Daniel Pool, "Politics in the New Boston, 1960–1970: A Study of Mayoral Policy-Making," Ph.D. diss., Brandeis University, 1974.

14. *San Francisco Chronicle*, 19 Sept. 1967; interviews with ILWU representatives, 22 May 1981 and 5 June 1981.
15. *San Francisco Chronicle*, 29 Sept. 1967.
16. Chester Hartman, *Yerba Buena: Land Grab and Community Resistance in San Francisco* (San Francisco: Glide Publications, 1974), p. 59.
17. *Ibid.*
18. Interview with ILWU representative, 5 June 1981.
19. Hartman, *Yerba Buena*, p. 62.
20. This phrase has come to symbolize Feinstein's administration. Participants in San Francisco's city politics, observers, journalists, and high officials in the Feinstein administraton itself all referred to her constituency in this fashion.
21. Robert H. Salisbury, "Urban Politics: The New Convergence of Power," *Journal of Politics*, 26 Nov. 1964; Wallace Sayre and Herbert Kaufman, *Governing New York City* (New York City: Russell Sage Foundation, 1965), p. 658.
22. Yates, "The Mayor's Eight-Ring Circus," pp. 17–18.
23. Interview, 11 June 1981.
24. Interview with Alioto's deputy mayor, 1 June 1981.
25. *San Francisco Examiner*, 5 Jan. 1976.
26. Interview, 7 May 1981.
27. Edward C. Banfield, *Political Influence: A New Theory of Urban Politics* (New York City: Free Press, 1961), p. 282.
28. Interview with CAO, 28 May 1981. Interview with Market Street Development Corporation head, 27 May 1981.
29. Interviews with CAO, 28 May 1981; Corporation head, 27 May 1981; SFRA personnel, 28 May 1981; and journalists, 5 May 1981 and 12 May 1981.
30. For a good analysis of Lee's advocacy, see Raymond E. Wolfinger, *The Politics of Progress* (Englewood Cliffs, N.J.: Prentice-Hall, 1973), and Robert A. Dahl, *Who Governs?* (New Haven, Conn.: Yale University Press, 1961). For Houlihan's stand, see Jeffrey L. Pressman, *Federal Programs and City Politics* (Berkeley and Los Angeles: University of California Press, 1975), p. 50.
31. This point must be looked at in relation to San Francisco and California labor. Historically, they were very active (prone to strike). Thus, while San Francisco had more labor unrest than Boston under White, for example, it was relatively quiet compared with the potential for labor unrest in that city. It was also relatively quiet compared with areas like Memphis or Florida that did not have histories of labor unrest but were experiencing labor difficulties in the 1960s.
32. Bureau of Labor Statistics, *Analysis of Work Stoppages*, 1967–1970, Annual Bulletin nos. 1611, 1646, 1687, 1727 (Washington, D. C.: Government Printing Office, 1969–1972).
33. Interview with ILWU representative, 22 May 1981.

34. Election Department Records.
35. Interviews with journalists, 5 May 1981 and 8 May 1981; Moscone's deputy mayor, 26 May 1981; and review of newspaper coverage of the strike.
36. *Boston Globe*, Sunday Magazine, 6 Mar. 1969.
37. James Q. Wilson developed this point very well in "Mayors vs. the Cities." For an in-depth analysis of Lindsay's audience dilemmas, see Yates, *The Ungovernable City.*
38. *Boston Phoenix*, 22 May 1978.
39. *A Decade of Development in Boston*, report prepared by the Boston Redevelopment Authority, May 1979.
40. For a good discussion of the contribution that new agencies make to effective implementation, see Martin A. Levin, *Political Dilemmas of Social Policymaking* (forthcoming).
41. For most of the twentieth century, Boston politics was dominated by the Irish. In fact, there was a saying that "even the walls in city hall were painted green."
42. In the 1967 election White lost ward 2 (Charlestown), wards 6 and 7 (South Boston), and wards 15, 16, and 17 (Dorchester). Together these wards cast 26 percent of the total vote in that election.
43. White won only seven out of twenty-two wards in the election, four of which were predominantly black.
44. Survey of the Community Design Center, 1969: Chinatown had a .5 percent vacancy rate, and two-thirds of the dwellings in the core area were substandard.
45. Sixty-seven percent voted against it, 33 percent for it: Election Department Records.
46. Banfield and Meyerson's analysis of a 1940s public housing controversy in Chicago shows how outcomes may differ when there is a solid support system and when there is a fragmented constituency. The public conflict, unusual for machine politics, was the result of party weakness at the time. Martin Meyerson and Edward C. Banfield, *Politics, Planning and the Public Interest: The Case of Public Housing in Chicago* (Glencoe, Ill.: Free Press, 1955).
47. Gays constituted approximately 21 percent of the city vote. Research done by Richard Schlachman for Carol Ruth Silver (supervisor), 1979.
48. Interview with former policeman under Gain, 12 June 1981.
49. Interviews with aides to Moscone, 11 May 1981, 20 May 1981, and 26 May 1981.
50. Interviews with aides to Moscone, 20 May 1981 and 26 May 1981; and with reporters, 7 May 1981 and 8 May 1981.
51. Wolfinger, *The Politics of Progress.*
52. Good examples of this literature are Yates, *The Ungovernable City*, and Wilson, "Mayors vs. the Cities."
53. See Murray Burton Levin, *The Alienated Voter: Politics in Boston* (New

York City: Holt, Rinehart and Winston, 1960). His study of the 1959 mayoral election in Boston concluded that there was a high degree of alienation and a strong sense of powerlessness.

54. The managers sought to avoid "embarrassing" the mayor. He also suggested that their dual role (part of the administration and part of the community) created tensions that they resolved by concentrating on service delivery and avoiding issues. In rating the performance of the LCHs, he gave issue advocacy a moderate rating in contrast to the high rating that direct services, complaint referral, and community catalyst received. *Decentralizing the City*, esp. chap. 7.

55. For a thorough analysis of Lindsay's approach to the community action program, see J. David Greenstone and Paul E. Peterson, *Race and Authority in Urban Politics: Community Participation and the War on Poverty* (New York City: Russell Sage Foundation, 1973).

56. Interviews with former Little City Hall managers, 9 Jan. 1981 and 19 Jan. 1981.

57. Election Department Records.

58. Schattschneider, *The Semisovereign People*.

59. Banfield, *Political Influence*.

## CHAPTER 4

1. Warren F. Ilchman and Norman Thomas Uphoff, *The Political Economy of Change* (Berkeley and Los Angeles: University of California Press, 1969), p. 211.

2. For an analysis of how Mayor Lee pyramided resources in New Haven, see Robert Dahl, *Who Governs?* (New Haven, Conn.: Yale University Press, 1966), and Raymond Wolfinger, *The Politics of Progress* (Englewood Cliffs, N.J.: Prentice-Hall, 1973). For a more general discussion of this theme, see Jeffrey Pressman, "Preconditions of Mayoral Leadership," *American Political Science Review* 66 (June 1972): 511–24, and Alexander George, "Political Leadership and Social Change in American Cities," *Daedalus*, Fall 1968. For an analysis of how legislators pyramid resources, see Eugene Bardach, *The Skill Factor in Politics: Repealing the Mental Commitment Laws in California* (Berkeley and Los Angeles: University of California Press, 1972).

3. Ilchman and Uphoff, *The Political Economy of Change*, p. 211.

4. Alan Lupo, *Liberty's Chosen Home: The Politics of Violence in Boston*, 1st ed. (Boston: Little, Brown, 1977), p. 119.

5. All respondents who discussed this time period mentioned Frank and the large role he played in the administration. See also Lupo, *Liberty's Chosen Home*, and *Boston Globe* and *Boston Herald* articles from this period.

6. Although Sullivan was deputy mayor, he was not so visible as Frank or the other top aides.

7. Frank, Kiley, Jackson, Weinberg, and DeGrazia, three years; Schwartz, five years; Delmonico, six years.
8. *Boston Globe,* Sunday Magazine, 9 Mar. 1969.
9. *Boston Herald American,* 23 Apr. 1972.
10. Ibid., 30 Apr. 1972.
11. *Boston's Fiscal Crisis: Origins and Solutions,* special report prepared by the Boston Municipal Research Bureau, Dec. 1976.
12. Interview with former press secretary, 22 Dec. 1980.
13. *Report on Holdovers Who Serve on Boston's Boards and Commissions,* Boston Finance Commission, 5 Jan. 1978.
14. Hugh Heclo, "Issue Networks in the Executive Establishment, " in Anthony King, ed., *The New American Political System* (Washington, D.C.: American Enterprise Institute, 1979), pp. 87–124.
15. Interviews with former Little City Hall manager and OPS director, 9 Jan. 1981; and with former deputy mayor, 25 Feb. 1981.
16. Interviews with former BRA directors, 28 Jan. 1981 and 11 Feb. 1981.
17. Interview, 9 Feb. 1981.
18. James Q. Wilson, *Varieties of Police Behavior: The Management of Law and Order in Eight Communities* (Cambridge: Harvard University Press, 1968).
19. Some observers of Boston city politics suggested that White felt the liberals abandoned him as early as 1970, when a majority of them voted for Republican Francis Sargent in the governor's race.
20. References to the "1960s pattern" of mayoral leadership and the obstacles in that pattern are made throughout the study. For good analyses of this pattern, see Douglas Yates, *The Ungovernable City* (Cambridge: MIT Press, 1977), and James Q. Wilson, "Mayors vs. the Cities," *Public Interest* 16 (Summer 1969): 25–37.
21. *Report on Holdovers,* p. 13.
22. Interview with former press secretary, 22 Dec. 1980; former OPS director, 9 Jan. 1981; and former deputy mayors, 26 Jan. 1981 and 25 Feb. 1981.
23. "Bossism by the Book," *Boston Phoenix,* 18 Nov. 1980. Frank Kent's book was *The Great Game of Politics: An Effort to Present the Elementary Human Facts about Politics, Politicians, and Political Machines, Candidates and Their Ways, for the Benefit of the Average Citizen.*
24. The comment on the Kerner Report was made in Mar. 1968. Quoted in "Faces of Change," *Boston Phoenix,* 2 May 1978.
25. Martha Wagner Weinberg, "Boston's Kevin White: A Mayor Who Survives," *Political Science Quarterly* 96 (Spring 1981): 103.
26. Interview with head of White's political organization, 4 Mar. 1981.
27. Interviews with former Little City Hall managers in Jamaica Plain, 15 Dec. 1980; North End, 9 Jan. 1981; and East Boston, 19 Jan. 1981.
28. Interviews with Brighton ward coordinator, 6 Mar. 1981; Back Bay precinct captain, 13 Mar. 1981; and organization head, 4 Mar. 1981.
29. Interviews with members of Brighton Civic Association, 9 Feb. 1981; city

councillor, 3 Feb. 1981; and director of South Boston Information Center, 16 Feb. 1981.

30. Charles Levine, *Racial Conflict and the American Mayor: Power, Polarization and Performance* (Lexington, Mass.: D. C. Heath, 1974), p. 14.

31. Interviews with former BRA director, 11 Feb. 1981; and Office of Federal Programs director, 13 Feb. 1981.

32. Interview with White's 1979 campaign manager, 26 Jan. 1981.

33. Ibid.

34. James MacGregor Burns, *Leadership* (New York City: Harper and Row, 1979).

35. Levine, *Racial Conflict and the American Mayor*.

36. For a good discussion of the reform view of government, see Edward C. Banfield and James Q. Wilson, *City Politics* (Cambridge: Harvard University Press, 1966).

37. Cyril Magnin was president of the Chamber of Commerce when Alioto was mayor.

38. Banfield and Wilson, *City Politics*.

39. Sharon Perlman Krefetz, *Welfare Policy Making and City Politics* (New York City: Praeger, 1976).

40. Interviews with members of opposition movement, 2 June 1981; and journalist, 8 May 1981.

41. Interviews with Alioto's deputy mayor, 1 June 1981; and SFRA consultant, 5 June 1981.

42. Interviews with ILWU representatives, 22 May 1981 and 5 June 1981.

43. For an elaboration of Daley's strategy, see Milton Rakove, *Don't Make No Waves, Don't Back No Losers: An Insider's Analysis of the Daley Machine* (Bloomington: Indiana University Press, 1975). See also J. David Greenstone and Paul E. Peterson, *Race and Authority in Urban Politics* (New York City: Russell Sage Foundation, 1973).

44. Interviews with SFRA personnel.

45. Interview with ILWU representative, 5 June 1981.

46. *San Francisco Redevelopment Program*, report prepared by San Francisco Redevelopment Agency, 1981.

47. The vote was 126,538 in favor and 60,989 against: Election Department.

48. E. E. Schattschneider, *The Semisovereign People: A Realist's View of Democracy in America*, rev. ed. (Hinsdale, Ill.: Dryden Press, 1975), p. 34.

49. Ibid.

50. See Martin A. Levin, "A Politics of Institutions," in Vincent Davis, ed., *The Post-Imperial Presidency* (New York City: Praeger, 1980).

51. Yates, *The Ungovernable City*.

52. Interview with ILWU representative, 5 June 1981.

53. Yates, *The Ungovernable City*.

54. Interviews with Alioto aides, 18 May 1981.

55. Interview with lobbyist for Moscone, 18 June 1981.

56. Interview with OFJ spokesman, 12 June 1981.

57. Ibid.

58. Interview with Civil Service commissioner who served on Alioto and Moscone's commissions, 2 June 1981.
59. One of the neighborhood activists, for example, was a chief organizer in the city's anti-freeway campaign in 1966.
60. Moscone had even written a letter to the *San Francisco Chronicle* (7 Nov. 1978) explicitly pointing to his high-rise record in an attempt to diffuse the controversy surrounding his appointments.
61. Interview with one of Moscone's Planning Commissioners, 21 May 1981.
62. Design concessions were mentioned by developers in interviews, 26 May 1981 and 2 June 1981.
63. There are seven commissioners: five appointed and two ex officio (the CAO and the Public Utilities General Manager).
64. During this time period, San Francisco had the fifth largest amount of central business district (CBD) office space of all large U.S. cities and one of the highest construction rates. See John Mollenkopf, *The Contested City* (Princeton, N.J.: Princeton University Press, 1983).
65. Interview with Planning Director, 10 June 1981.
66. Interviews with Planning Director and commissioner, 10 June 1981 and 21 May 1981.
67. Aaron B. Wildavsky, *Speaking Truth to Power: The Art and Craft of Policy Analysis* (Boston: Little, Brown, 1979).
68. Interviews with commissioner, 21 May 1981, and director, 10 June 1981.
69. Interview with ILWU representative, 5 June 1981.
70. Feinstein's voting record as a supervisor showed her conservative bent. She supported anti-union legislation; she tried to reverse the decision on the International Hotel; she voted against Moscone's revenue package that would have taxed downtown business; she voted against district elections.
71. Interview with Planning Commissioner, 21 May 1981.
72. Interview with aide to Feinstein, 8 June 1981. Police commissioners can be removed by the mayor without board approval.
73. Interview, 12 June 1981.
74. Interview, 14 May 1981.
75. Interview, 10 June 1981.
76. EIR is required by state law for all new construction. It is used by the city to determine how many additional units of housing will be needed as a result of the construction of new offices. This figure is then used by the Planning Department to determine how many units of housing it will require the developer to build. As an informal arrangement, the process is a negotiable one.
77. It had not been submitted to the Board of Supervisors for approval.
78. Interview, 12 June 1981.

CHAPTER 5

1. Robert Michels, *Political Parties: A Sociological Study of the Oligarchical Tendencies of Modern Democracy* (New York City: Free Press, 1962).

2. John V. Lindsay, *The City* (New York City: W. W. Norton, 1969).
3. The phrase is from Wallace Sayre and Herbert Kaufman, *Governing New York City* (New York City: Russel Sage Foundation, 1965).
4. Douglas Yates, *The Ungovernable City* (Cambridge: MIT Press, 1977).
5. Peter Bachrach and Morton S. Baratz referred to this type of bureaucratic policymaking as "non-decision making." Peter Bachrach and Morton S. Baratz, "Two Faces of Power," *American Political Science Review* 56 (Dec. 1962): 947–52. See also Frank Levy, Arnold Meltsner, and Aaron Wildavsky, *Urban Outcomes* (Berkeley and Los Angeles: University of California Press, 1974).
6. The "shrinking violet" phrase is from Anthony Downs, *Inside Bureaucracy* (Boston: Little, Brown and Company, 1967).
7. Harold Seidman, *Politics, Position and Power: The Dynamics of Federal Organization*, 2d ed. (New York City: Oxford University Press, 1975), p. 108.
8. Natale Cipollina, *No Past and No Future: The Politics of Accountability and Structure in New York City* (forthcoming).
9. For an exhaustive account of Moses' use of the Authority's budget to gain power, see Robert Caro, *The Power Broker: Robert Moses and the Fall of New York* (New York City: Random House, 1975).
10. Logue was director of New Haven's Redevelopment Authority before going to Boston.
11. In Boston there were urban renewal projects in the residential West End and South End; in San Francisco there were two major urban renewal projects in the residential Western Addition; in New York City the residential area around Lincoln Center underwent urban renewal.
12. Interviews with city councillor, 20 Feb. 1981; and community leaders, 8 Feb. 1981.
13. Caro, *The Power Broker.*
14. Interview, 5 Jan. 1981.
15. "The Faces of Change," *Boston Phoenix*, 2 May 1978.
16. *Boston Herald*, 30 Apr. 1972.
17. *Boston's Fiscal Crisis: Origins and Solutions,* special report prepared by the Boston Municipal Research Bureau, Dec. 1976.
18. See Jeffrey Pressman, "Preconditions of Mayoral Leadership," *American Political Science Review* 66 (June 1972): 511–24; Alexander George, "Political Leadership and Social Change in American Cities," *Daedalus,* (Fall 1968), pp. 1194–1217; Raymond Wolfinger, *The Politics of Progress* (Englewood Cliffs, N.J.: Prentice-Hall, 1973).
19. 1970 Census, U.S. Department of Commerce.
20. Ibid.
21. Diana Gordon details several cases in which Lindsay's policies were thwarted by bureaucratic inertia or resistance: *City Limits: Barriers to Change in Urban Government* (New York City: Charterhouse, 1973).
22. Interview, 8 June 1981.
23. Edward Banfield, *Political Influence* (New York City: Free Press, 1961).

24. Robert Crain, Elihu Katz, and Donald B. Rosenthal, *The Politics of Community Conflict: The Fluoridation Decision* (Indianapolis: Bobbs-Merrill, 1969), pp. 201–2.
25. Interview with member of Feinstein's budget office, 8 June 1981.
26. In New York City, Wagner's budgetary reforms actually decreased his control over the budget. See Cipollina, *No Past and No Future*.
27. Aaron Wildavsky, *The Politics of the Budgetary Process*, 2nd ed. (Boston: Little, Brown and Company, 1974), p. 132.
28. Downs, *Inside Bureaucracy*.
29. Theodore Lowi, "Gosnell's Chicago Revisited via Lindsay's New York," in Stephen David and Paul Peterson, eds., *Urban Politics and Public Policy: The City in Crisis* (New York City: Praeger, 1973), p. 25.
30. Interview, 11 May 1981.
31. Civil Service Department records.
32. Interviews with civil service commissioner, 5 June 1981; and former head of Local 400, SEIU, 11 June 1981.
33. Interview with commissioner who had served on both Alioto's and Moscone's commission, 5 June 1981.
34. Interview, 5 June 1981.
35. Civil Service Commission reports.
36. Interviews with Finance Commission personnel, 11 Feb. 1981; Office of Federal Relations personnel, 27 Feb. 1981; and city councillor, 20 Feb. 1981.
37. Interview with former mayoral aide, 10 Dec. 1980.
38. Interviews, 11 Feb. 1981.
39. Martha Wagner Weinberg, "Boston's Kevin White: A Mayor Who Survives," *Political Science Quarterly* 96 (Spring 1981): 97.
40. Review of newspaper coverage.
41. Interview with Richard Sklar, 9 June 1981.
42. Interviews with former aides to Moscone, 2 June 1981 and 20 May 1981.
43. Interview with Richard Sklar, 9 June 1981. Sklar's views inform the rest of this section.
44. Ibid. and interview with former aide to Moscone, 20 May 1981.
45. Election Department records.
46. Extrapolated from neighborhood data in *District Handbook*, Coro Foundation, 1979.
47. Levy, Meltsner, and Wildavsky, *Urban Outcomes*, p. 229.
48. Herbert Kaufman, *The Limits of Organizational Change* (University, Ala.: University of Alabama Press, 1972), pp. 9–10.
49. Interview with aide to Alioto and Moscone, 20 May 1981.
50. Yates, *The Ungovernable City*.
51. Ibid.
52. Cipollina, *No Past and No Future*.
53. Banfield, *Political Influence*, p. 325.
54. Interview with White's housing advisor, 23 Jan. 1981.
55. *New York Times*, 26 July 1979.

56. Martin Levin used the phrase in a discussion, 10 Dec. 1980.
57. Approximately 75 percent of the tenants were black. Extrapolated from Turner's article, "This Was the Year That Was," *Boston Globe,* 21 Dec. 1980, p. B5.
58. Planning Department records.
59. Interviews with Feinstein's deputy mayor, 9 June 1981; and planning commissioner, 21 May 1981.
60. Planning Department Records. See Chapter 2 for details.
61. Interviews with press secretary for Alioto and Feinstein, 12 May 1981; and budget director for Feinstein and Moscone, 29 May 1981.
62. Interview with former head of MBTA advisory board, 27 Jan. 1981.
63. James MacGregor Burns, *Leadership* (New York City: Harper and Row, 1979), p. 396.
64. Boston and San Francisco exemplify this trend. The 1979 Boston mayoral election had the lowest voter turnout in the previous twenty years; in San Francisco the 1979 mayoral election had the lowest voter turnout since 1906.
    At the time of this study, voter decline was the trend. The 1984 Democratic presidential primary, and particularly the Jackson candidacy, appears to have reversed this trend, especially among minorities. While this is certainly a positive indicator, it is still too early to tell whether this is a temporary or a definitive change.
65. This argument on the costs of strong executive leadership is developed more fully in Chapter 9.

CHAPTER 6

1. Samuel Huntington, *American Politics: The Promise of Disharmony* (Cambridge: Harvard University Press, 1981).
2. When Robert Moses began his public career, he did believe in the principles of the good government reform movement. Nevertheless, his actions did substantially increase his power, and his belief in good government principles waned as his career progressed.
3. Arthur Mann, *LaGuardia Comes to Power, 1933* (Philadelphia: J. B. Lippincott, 1965).
4. For a good discussion of the administrations of Kelly, Kennelly, and Daley, see Edward Banfield and James Q. Wilson, *City Politics* (Cambridge: Joint Center for Urban Studies, Harvard and MIT Press, 1963); Edward M. Levine, *The Irish and the Irish Politicians* (Notre Dame, Ind.: University of Notre Dame Press, 1966); and Milton Rakove, *Don't Make No Waves, Don't Back No Losers: An Insider's Analysis of the Daley Machine* (Bloomington: Indiana University Press, 1975).
5. Sandra Featherman and William Rosenberg, *Jews, Blacks, and Ethnics: The 1978 "Vote White" Charter Campaign in Philadelphia* (New York: American Jewish Committee, 1979).

6. Largely because of Mayor Rizzo's anti-black positions, the charter reform campaign, which would have allowed Rizzo to seek a third term, was viewed as an anti-black proposal. When the issue was raised, black leaders so defined it and Rizzo responded by referring to a pro-charter reform stance as a "white vote." Although the vote substantially split along racial lines (96 percent of the black voters in the election opposed it), there was significant white opposition; 48 percent of the white voters opposed it. Some of this opposition was in response to the racial overtones (69 percent of the Jewish vote was opposed, which was largely a function of the liberal attitudes of Jewish voters toward minorities), but part of the white opposition was a reaction to the additional power that Rizzo was seeking. Featherman and Rosenberg, *Jews, Blacks, and Ethnics.*

7. Lee had just won his second mayoral election (1957) by a 2 to 1 margin. For a good account of the charter reform campaign, see Raymond Wolfinger, *The Politics of Progress* (Englewood Cliffs, N.J.: Prentice-Hall, 1973), esp. chap. 11.

8. Ibid., pp. 368, 378.

9. Mayor Lee was one of the pioneers of urban renewal. Through his projects in New Haven, he achieved widespread popularity within the city and national recognition. Lee operated, however, from a formally weak mayor's office. He strengthened his influence through the urban renewal money, which he used to create a powerful redevelopment authority under the strong direction Ed Logue. The charter changes sought by Lee would have given formal recognition to these institutional relationships that Lee and Logue developed. In the end, there were 18,411 votes against the measure and 9,915 votes for it. Wolfinger, *The Politics of Progress*, p. 382.

10. Interviews with leading proponents and opponents, 4 Feb. 1981 and 16 Feb. 1981.

11. For a discussion of LaGuardia and education, see Charles Garrett, *The LaGuardia Years: Machine and Reform Politics in New York City* (New Brunswick, N.J.: Rutgers University Press, 1961); for Lindsay, see Marilyn Gittell, *Participants and Participation: A Study of School Policy in New York City* (New York City: Praeger, 1967).

12. Martha Wagner Weinberg and Philip B. Heymann, "The Paradox of Power: Mayoral Leadership on Charter Reform in Boston," in Walter Dean Burnham and Martha Wagner Weinberg, eds., *American Politics and Public Policy* (Cambridge: MIT Press, 1978), pp. 280–303.

13. Ibid.

14. Ibid. and interviews with state representatives, 18 Feb. 1981.

15. Ibid., p. 290. Timilty unsuccessfully ran against White for mayor in 1975 and 1979.

16. Daniel Pool, "Politics in the New Boston, 1960–1970," Ph.D. diss., Brandeis University, 1974.

17. In New Haven, a charter committee was used, but the selection process

involved a careful screening by Ed Logue, which included agreements from members that they would go along with Lee's proposals for charter revisions. See Wolfinger, *The Politics of Progress,* p. 364.

18. Interview with James Haas, 15 June 1981.
19. Election Department records.
20. Theodore J. Lowi develops this argument in *The End of Liberalism* (New York: W. W. Norton, 1969).
21. Interview with member of charter reform commission, 15 June 1981.
22. Ibid.
23. Election Department records.
24. Frederick M. Wirt, *Power in the City: Decision Making in San Francisco* (Berkeley and Los Angeles: University of California Press, 1974).

CHAPTER 7

1. James L. Sundquist, *Making Federalism Work* (Washington, D.C.: Brookings Institution, 1969), p. 27.
2. For a good development of this point, see Richard Cloward and Francis Fox Piven, *Regulating the Poor* (New York City: Random House, 1972).
3. Sundquist, *Making Federalism Work*, and Terry Sanford, *Storm Over the States* (New York City: McGraw-Hill, 1967). The theme is also implicit in the literature on federal programs that emphasizes the intergovernmental aspect rather than local government. See Jeffrey Pressman and Aaron Wildavsky, *Implementation* (Berkeley and Los Angeles: University of California Press, 1973), and Bernard Frieden and Marshall Kaplan, *The Politics of Neglect* (Cambridge: MIT Press, 1977).
4. Philip Rutledge, "Federal-Local Relations and the Mission of the City," *The Annals of the American Academy of Political and Social Science* 416 (Nov. 1974): 77–90.
5. Senator Edmund Muskie, an expert on intergovernmental affairs, described local administration as "lacking in quality and experience, unimaginative, and too subject to negative political and bureaucratic pressures." Quoted in Richard H. Leach, *American Federalism* (New York City: W. W. Norton, 1970), p. 186.
6. The 1967 Green Amendment was a legislative attempt to change this by giving local governments the option to become the CAA or to designate one. Sundquist found, however, that less than 5 percent of the local governments took this option. He cited the strength of the existing CAAs and mayoral weariness over the uncertainty of federal funding as the major reasons for local government's failure to act. *Making Federalism Work,* pp. 38–39.
7. Jeffrey Pressman, *Federal Programs and City Politics* (Berkeley and Los Angeles: University of California Press, 1975).
8. David Greenstone and Paul Peterson, *Race and Authority in Urban Politics* (New York City: Russell Sage Foundation, 1973).

9. Sundquist studied two to four localities in each of the following states: California, Pennsylvania, Georgia, Minnesota, Kentucky, West Virginia, New Mexico, and New Hampshire. He also visited one locality in Tennessee and one in Florida. *Making Federalism Work*, p. 28.

10. Pressman, *Federal Programs and City Politics*.

11. James Q. Wilson, "Mayors vs. the Cities," *The Public Interest* 16 (Summer 1969): 25–37.

12. The term "rising politico" is from Fred Wirt, "San Francisco: The Politics of Hyperpluralism," *Transaction* 6 (April 1970): 46–55. Alioto's early arrival on the national scene also attracted the attention of the Republicans. In 1970 Alioto faced federal charges of fee splitting in Washington State, an indictment which was engineered by U.S. Attorney General John Mitchell and which several informants suggested was part of Nixon's overall strategy of eliminating potential competition. The charges against Alioto were never proven.

13. Interviews with journalists, 5 May 1981 and 7 May 1981; and Alioto's deputy mayor, 1 June 1981.

14. Frieden and Kaplan, *The Politics of Neglect*, p. 211.

15. *National Journal* 4 (16 Dec. 1972): 1924.

16. Reprinted in Donald H. Haider, *When Governments Come to Washington* (New York City: Free Press, 1974), p. 98.

17. Interview with member of Federal Relations Office, 27 Feb. 1981.

18. Ibid.

19. Interviews with member of Federal Relations Office, 27 Feb. 1981; and White's press secretary, 10 Feb. 1981.

20. Interview, 17 Feb. 1981.

21. The Boston Plan produced only a public works project at the time, but since then projects have begun in the areas outlined in the proposal.

22. The totals were compiled from figures supplied by the Department of Labor, the Manpower Demonstration Research Corporation (MDRC), HUD, and the Department of Commerce.

23. This term is from Eugene Bardach, *The Implementation Game* (Cambridge: MIT Press, 1977).

24. Ibid., p. 90.

25. Ibid.

26. For a detailed history of this relationship, see Haider, *When Governments Come to Washington*.

27. James Q. Wilson, *Political Organizations* (New York City: Basic Books, 1973), chap. 16.

28. Pressman, *Federal Programs and City Politics*, p. 69.

29. For a full discussion of the importance of a favorable context, see Martin A. Levin, "Conditions Contributing to Effective Implementation and Their Limits," paper delivered at the American Public Policy and Management Conference, Chicago, Oct. 19, 1979.

30. Massachusetts Commission Against Discrimination (MCAD) report.

31. Poll conducted by Jack Walsh, 1972.
32. *Boston's Fiscal Crisis: Origins and Solutions*, special report prepared by the Boston Municipal Research Bureau, Dec. 1976, p. 24.
33. Interviews with EEPA (Employment Economic Policy Administration, umbrella agency for all CETA funds) personnel, 6 Jan. 1981 and 9 Jan. 1981.
34. The money came from a combination of CETA Titles II and VI and NIMH. Interviews with YAC personnel, 20 Feb. 1981.
35. Interviews with EEPA personnel, 6 Jan. 1981 and 9 Jan. 1981.
36. Lecture by David Mundell (former EEPA director), Florence Heller Graduate School, Brandeis University, April 1981.
37. Greenstone and Peterson, *Race and Authority in Urban Politics*.
38. Sundquist, *Making Federalism Work*.
39. Interview, 10 Feb. 1981.
40. Civil Service Department records.
41. Greenstone and Peterson, *Race and Authority in Urban Politics*.
42. Interviews with black community leaders, 18 May 1981 and 8 June 1981; and with member of Community Development Office, 20 May 1981.
43. Interviews with ILWU and SFRA members, 5 June 1981 and 22 May 1981.
44. Interview, 1 June 1981.
45. Interviews with Alioto's deputy mayor, 1 June 1981; and former members of Community Development Office, 20 May 1981.
46. Interview with former member of Community Development Office, 20 May 1981.
47. Chester Hartman, *Yerba Buena* (San Francisco: Glide Publications, 1974).
48. Interview with ILWU representative, 1 June 1981.
49. Frank Levy, Arnold Meltsner, and Aaron Wildavsky, *Urban Outcomes* (Berkeley and Los Angeles: University of California Press, 1974), p. 232.
50. Interview, 20 May 1981.
51. Ibid.
52. Natale Cipollina, *No Past and No Future: The Politics of Accountability and Structure in New York City* (forthcoming). Cipollina demonstrates how Lindsay's use of federal programs put him in such a weak position that he was unable to say no to his constituents, even when the resources were not there.
53. Interview, 20 May 1981. Chinatown was a relatively small area: it covered less than half a square mile and had a population of 30,000. By contrast, the Mission district had almost two square miles and a population of 50,000; Hunter's Point/Bayview had over five and a half square miles and a population of 31,000. *District Handbook*, Coro Foundation.
54. Interview, 11 May 1981.
55. Sanford, *Storm over the States*.
56. Interview with former member of Community Development Office, 21 May 1981.

57. Pressman, *Federal Programs and City Politics*, p. 69.
58. Pressman and Wildavsky, *Implementation*.
59. Martha Derthick, *New Towns—In Town: Why a Federal Program Failed* (Washington, D.C.: Brookings Institution, 1972); Sundquist, *Making Federalism Work*. New Towns was a major program planned by the federal government to build new communities in seven localities; in only one city did a project begin. National Emphasis Programs included Head Start, legal services, comprehensive health services, foster grandparents, and Upward Bound.
60. Paul E. Peterson, *City Limits* (Chicago: University of Chicago Press, 1981).

CHAPTER 8

1. Douglas Yates, *The Ungovernable City* (Cambridge: MIT Press, 1977), p. 152.
2. John Mollenkopf, *The Contested City* (Princeton, N.J.: Princeton University Press, 1983).
3. Yates, *The Ungovernable City*, p. 147.
4. Zuckerman also purchased the Boston-based *Altantic Monthly* in 1980.
5. Quoted in Jean Gogolin, "Politics of Property," *Boston Magazine,* July 1980.
6. Interview, 25 Nov. 1980.
7. Interview with journalist, 6 Jan. 1981.
8. Dahl and Wolfinger both discuss this at length. Robert A. Dahl, *Who Governs?* (New Haven, Conn.: Yale University Press, 1966), and Raymond Wolfinger, *The Politics of Progress* (Englewood Cliffs, N.J.: Prentice-Hall, 1973).
9. *New York Times,* 5 Mar. 1974.
10. Blakely and Zuckerman were involved in a court suit over the interests in 60 State Street, a major building in the financial district, where Cabot, Cabot and Forbes are located.
11. Interview with journalist, 6 Jan. 1981.
12. Eugene Bardach, *The Skill Factor in Politics* (Berkeley and Los Angeles: University of California Press, 1972).
13. Interview with *Boston Globe* reporter, 6 Jan. 1981.
14. Mahoney obtained an injunction that temporarily delayed the Department of Community Affairs hearings, but he was not successful when he requested that the DCA hearings be judicial rather than administrative. Interview with BRA personnel, 8 Dec. 1981.
15. Interview with *Boston Globe* reporter, 6 Jan. 1981.
16. Lindy, Zuckerman's partner, felt that the project was straining their resources and the rest of their business. Interview with BRA personnel, 11 Feb. 1981.
17. Interview, 11 Feb. 1981.
18. Ibid.

19. Jack Cole brought suit against WBZ-TV (Channel 4) in 1975 and was awarded $100,000 in damages. The Massachusetts Supreme Judicial Court, however, overturned this verdict. Their ruling was upheld by the U.S. Supreme Court in November 1982.
20. *Boston Globe*, 2 Jan. 1983, p. 14.
21. Kucinich served during the 1970s, but his crusading reformer pattern of leadership resembled that of 1960s mayors.
22. See Dahl, *Who Governs?;* Wolfinger, *The Politics of Progress;* and Yates, *The Ungovernable City.*
23. The planning director, Paul Opperman, claimed that the absence of significant blight in the area made the plans contrary to the intent of federal urban renewal legislation. Chester Hartman, *Yerba Buena* (San Francisco: Glide Publications, 1974), p. 28.
24. Bardach, *The Skill Factor in Politics.*
25. *San Francisco Chronicle*, 14 Apr. 1963.
26. Hartman, *Yerba Buena.*
27. For a discussion of how these concepts relate to implementation, see Martin A. Levin and Barbara Ferman, *The Political Hand: Policy Implementation and Youth Employment Programs* (Elmsford, N.Y.: Pergamon Press, 1985).
28. Hartman, *Yerba Buena*, p. 67.
29. The *Chronicle* and the *Examiner* are located in the South of Market area. YBC's potential to increase real estate values there gave both papers a major financial stake in the project.
30. There were more than 700 merchants in the area at the time and more than 4,000 residents. Hartman, *Yerba Buena*, p. 19.
31. Interviews with SFRA members, 22 May 1981; and journalists, 8 May 1981.
32. Hartman, *Yerba Buena.*
33. Ibid.
34. Quoted in *San Francisco Chronicle*, 25 Feb. 1972.
35. *Examiner*, 25 Feb. 1972.
36. *San Francisco Chronicle*, 24 Feb. 1972.
37. Report to the Court, by U.S. Department of HUD, *TOOR v. HUD*, No. C-69 324 (N.D. Cal. filed 24 Aug. 1971). See Hartman, *Yerba Buena*, chap. 5.
38. Interviews with SFRA personnel, 22 May 1981; and Alioto's deputy mayor, 1 June 1981.
39. The project was finally implemented during Moscone's administration after Moscone established a committee to review the plans and a public vote was taken. The original plans were scaled down to a convention center that was built underground. The facility was renamed the George Moscone Convention Center.
40. Interviews with former commissioner, 21 May 1981; former director, 10 June 1981; and current director, 12 June 1981.
41. The architectural firm was Skidmore, Owings and Merrill. For back-

ground on this firm and U.S. Steel, see Bruce Brugmann and Greggar Sletteland, eds., *The Ultimate Highrise: San Francisco's Mad Rush to the Sky* (San Francisco: San Francisco Bay Guardian Books, 1971). For the height controversy, see p. 113.

42. Interview with planning commissioner, 21 May 1981.
43. Supervisor's records.
44. Brugmann and Sletteland, eds., *The Ultimate Highrise.*
45. Ibid., p. 123.
46. Jeffrey Pressman and Aaron Wildavsky, *Implementation* (Berkeley and Los Angeles: University of California Press, 1973).

CHAPTER 9

1. Charles Levine, *Racial Conflict and the American Mayor* (Lexington, Mass.: D. C. Heath, 1974), p. 127.
2. Ibid. Levine presents a strong argument for this approach.
3. Alexander George, "Political Leadership and Social Change in American Cities," *Daedalus,* Fall 1968, p. 1197.
4. For an analysis of Mayor Lee's use of the executive-centered coalition strategy, see Robert Dahl, *Who Governs?* (New Haven, Conn.: Yale University Press, 1961).
5. Douglas Yates makes this argument in *The Ungovernable City* (Cambridge: MIT Press, 1977). See also James Q. Wilson, "Mayors vs. the Cities," *Public Interest* 16 (Summer 1969): 25–37.
6. See Mayer N. Zald, ed., *Power in Organizations* (Nashville, Tenn.: Vanderbilt University Press, 1970).
7. Eugene Bardach, *The Skill Factor in Politics* (Berkeley and Los Angeles: University of California Press, 1970), pp. 241–42.
8. These models include "Executive as Manager," "Policy Expert," and "Public Executive." For a discussion of these models, see John P. Kotter and Paul R. Lawrence, *Mayors in Action* (New York City: John Wiley and Sons, 1974). See also Douglas Yates, "The Roots of American Leadership: Political Style and Policy Consequences," in Walter Dean Burnham and Martha Wagner Weinberg, eds., *American Politics and Public Policy* (Cambridge: MIT Press, 1978), pp. 140–68.
9. Yates, "The Roots of American Leadership," p. 149.
10. For a rich discussion of the comparative strategies of Lindsay and Beame, see Natale Cipollina, *No Past and No Future: The Politics of Accountability and Structure in New York City* (forthcoming).
11. White made two previous unsuccessful attempts to gain control over the School Committee: Proposition 3, Question 7 and Charter Reform. White successfully used the public fervor for fiscal austerity surrounding Proposition 2½ to connect the "fiscal crisis" with the School Committee's excessive spending. As a result, the School Committee's budget was frozen at the previous year's level and powers were shifted from the committee to the superintendent. New revenue raising sources for Boston

were gained in the Tregor Bill which was finally passed by the state legislature in 1983.

12. See Eugene J. Meehan, *The Quality of Federal Policy Making: Programmed Failure in Public Housing* (St. Louis: University of Missouri Press, 1979). Also see Roger Starr, "The Public Housing Quagmire," *Public Interest 59* (Spring 1980): 110–17.

13. Interviews with mayoral aides and leading figures in the busing controversy, 6 Jan. 1981 and 22 Jan. 1981.

14. Cipollina, *No Past and No Future.*

15. *New York Times,* 5 June 1980.

16. Interviews with ILWU and SEIU representatives, 5 June 1981 and 11 June 1981.

17. Chester Hartman, *Yerba Buena* (San Francisco: Glide Publications, 1974).

18. Martin Meyerson and Edward C. Banfield, *Politics, Planning and the Public Interest* (Glencoe, Ill.: Free Press, 1955).

19. Jeffrey Pressman, *Federal Programs and City Politics* (Berkeley and Los Angeles: University of California Press, 1975).

20. Willis D. Hawley, *Nonpartisan Elections and the Case for Party Politics* (New York City: John Wiley and Sons, 1973), p. 129.

21. Quoted in Frank Levy, Arnold Meltsner, and Aaron Wildavsky, *Urban Outcomes* (Berkeley and Los Angeles: University of California Press, 1974).

22. Hawley, *Nonpartisan Elections and the Case for Party Politics.* Hawley argued that when issues are decided in the administrative rather than the political arena, poor people and minorities suffer the most because they lack the time, information, and resources to pursue administrative matters. For a more specific version of this argument, see Francis Fox Piven, "The Urban Crises: Who Got What and Why," in Robert Paul Wolff, ed., *1984 Revisited* (New York City: Knopf, 1973); and Martin A. Levin and Barbara Ferman, *The Political Hand: Policy Implementation and Youth Employment Programs* (Elmsford, N.Y.: Pergamon Press, 1985). These authors demonstrate that middle-class groups benefited the most from social welfare policies directed to the poor. Their examples include OEO programs, public higher education subsidies, and food stamps for students.

23. E. E. Schattschneider, *The Semisovereign People* (Hinsdale, Ill.: Dryden Press, 1975), p. 34.

24. Robert Crain, Elihu Katz, and Donald B. Rosenthal, *The Politics of Community Conflict: The Fluoridation Decision* (Indianapolis: Bobbs-Merrill, 1969).

25. There appears to be a positive correlation between strong mayors and the control exercised by the mayor over urban renewal. Boston under Collins and White, New Haven under Lee, Chicago under Daley, and Philadelphia under Dillworth and Clark were cities with strong mayors and significant mayoral control of urban renewal programs. By contrast, in cities

with highly decentralized power, the mayors had less control over urban renewal, as in New York City, San Francisco, and Weekaugen, Illinois.

26. See Zald, ed., *Power in Organizations.*

27. Michael Parenti, "Power and Pluralism: A View from the Bottom," *Journal of Politics* 32, no. 3 (Aug. 1970): 501–30; Sharon Perlman Krefetz, *Welfare Policymaking and City Politics* (New York City: Praeger, 1976).

28. Michael Lipsky, "Protest as a Political Resource," *American Political Science Review* 62 (Dec. 1968): 1144–58.

29. Gabriel Almond and Sidney Verba, *The Civic Culture* (Boston: Little, Brown, 1965).

30. Theodore Lowi, "Gosnell's Chicago Revisited via Lindsay's New York," in Stephen David and Paul Peterson, eds., *Urban Politics and Public Policy* (New York: Praeger, 1973), p. 25.

31. The argument of the reformers was that nonpartisan elections would remove the influence of corrupt political parties and that at-large elections would force legislators to appeal to citywide interests. These two factors would permit voters to select officials on the basis of their expertise. See David and Peterson, eds., *Urban Politics and Public Policy,* for a full discussion of this argument, pp. 12–15.

32. Lowi, "Gosnell's Chicago Revisited via Lindsay's New York," p. 25.

33. Thomas Sowell, *Knowledge and Decisions* (New York City: Basic Books, 1980), pp. 131–32.

34. V. O. Key, *Southern Politics* (New York City: Vintage Books, 1949), p. 304.

35. Schattschneider, *The Semisovereign People,* esp. p. 138.

36. Examples of personality politicians include Hicks in Boston, Rizzo in Philadelphia, Cobb and Nichols in Detroit, Yorty in Los Angeles, and, to a lesser extent, Stenvig in Minneapolis. See Schattschneider, *The Semisovereign People,* and Levin, *Political Dilemmas of Social Policymaking.*

37. For a discussion of these programs, see Dahl, *Who Governs?*

38. Meyerson and Banfield, *Politics, Planning and the Public Interest.*

39. James Reichley, *The Art of Government* (New York City: Irvington Publications, 1972).

40. Morris P. Fiorina, *Congress: Keystone of the Washington Establishment* (New Haven, Conn.: Yale University Press, 1977); and Richard Fenno, *Home Style: House Members in Their Districts* (Boston: Little, Brown and Company, 1978).

41. George E. Berkeley, "Flaws in At-Large Voting," *National Civic Review* 55 (July 1966): 372.

42. Sowell, *Knowledge and Decisions.*

43. Ibid., p. 121.

44. Hawley, *Nonpartisan Elections and the Case for Party Politics.*

45. James Q. Wilson, "We Need to Shift Focus," in Edward Banfield, ed., *Urban Government,* rev. ed. (Glencoe, Ill.: Free Press, 1969), pp. 21–33.

46. Douglas Arnold, "Overtilled and Undertilled Fields in American Poli-

tics," *Political Science Quarterly* 5 (Spring 1982): 91–103; Nelson Polsby, "Contemporary Transformations of American Politics: Thoughts on the Research Agendas of Political Scientists," *Political Science Quarterly* 4 (Winter 1981–1982): 551–70.

47. John Rawls, *A Theory of Justice* (Cambridge: Harvard University Press, 1971).

48. Martin A. Levin, "A Politics of Institutions," in Vincent Davis, ed., *The Post-Imperial Presidency* (New Brunswick, N.J.: Transaction Books, 1980).

49. Aaron Wildavsky, "The Past and Future Presidency," *Public Interest* 41 (Fall 1975): 56–76.

# Selected Bibliography

Abrams, Richard M. *Conservatism in a Progressive Era: Massachusetts Politics, 1900–1912*. Cambridge: Harvard University Press, 1964.

Adams, Russell B. *The Boston Money Tree*. New York City: Thomas Y. Crowell Company, 1977.

Almond, Gabriel, and Sydney Verba. *The Civic Culture*. Boston: Little, Brown, and Company, 1965.

Altshuler, Alan A. *Community Control: The Black Demand for Participation in Large American Cities*. New York City: Pegasus, 1970.

Arnold, Douglas. "Overtilled and Undertilled Fields in American Politics." *Political Science Quarterly* 5 (Spring 1982): 91–103.

Bachrach, Peter, and Morton S. Baratz. "Two Faces of Power." *American Political Science Review* 56 (Dec. 1962): 947–52.

Banfield, Edward C. *Political Influence: A New Theory of Urban Politics*. New York City: Free Press, 1961.

Banfield, Edward C., ed. *Urban Government*. rev. ed. Glencoe, Ill.: Free Press, 1969.

Banfield, Edward C., and James Q. Wilson. *City Politics*. New York City: Vintage Books, 1963.

Bardach, Eugene. *The Implementation Game*. Cambridge: MIT Press, 1977.

_____. *The Skill Factor in Politics*. Berkeley and Los Angeles: University of California Press, 1972.

Bean, Walter. *Boss Reuf's San Francisco: The Story of the Union Labor Party, Big Business and the Graft Prosecution*. Berkeley and Los Angeles: University of California Press, 1967.

Bellush, Jewel, and Stephen M. David, eds. *Race and Politics in New York City*. New York City: Praeger Publishers, 1971.

Bellush, Jewel, and Murray Hausknecht, eds. *Urban Renewal: People, Politics and Planning*. New York City: Anchor Books, 1967.

Berkeley, George E. "Flaws in At-Large Voting." *National Civic Review* 55 (July 1966).

Broder, David S. *Changing of the Guard: Power and Leadership in America*. New York City: Simon and Schuster, 1980.

_____. *The Party's Over: The Failure of Politics in America*. New York City: Harper and Row, 1971.

Brugmann, Bruce, and Greggar Sletteland, eds. *The Ultimate Highrise: San Francisco's Mad Rush to the Sky*. San Francisco: San Francisco Bay Guardian Books, 1971.

Burns, James MacGregor. *Leadership*. New York City: Harper and Row, 1979.

Caro, Robert. *The Power Broker: Robert Moses and the Fall of New York*. New York City: Random House, 1975.

Castells, Manuel, and Karen Murphy. "Cultural Identity and Urban Structure: The Spatial Organization of San Francisco's Gay Community." Working Paper, San Francisco, 1980.

Chambers, William Nisbet, and Walter Dean Burnham, eds. *The American Party Systems: Stages of Political Development*. New York City: Oxford University Press, 1967.

Cipollina, Natale. *No Past and No Future: The Politics of Accountability and Structure in New York City*. (Forthcoming).

Cloward, Richard A., and Francis Fox Piven. *Regulating the Poor*. New York City: Random House, 1972.

Costikyan, Edward N. *Behind Closed Doors*. New York City: Harcourt, Brace and World, 1966.

Crain, Robert L. *Politics of School Desegregation: Comparative Case Studies of Community Structure and Policy-Making*. Chicago: Aldine Publishing Company, 1968.

Crain, Robert L., et al. *The Politics of Community Conflict: The Fluoridation Decision*. Indianapolis: Bobbs-Merrill, 1968.

Dahl, Robert A. *Who Governs?*. New Haven, Conn.: Yale University Press, 1966.

Dalin, David. "Public Affairs and the Jewish Community: The Changing Political World of San Francisco Jews." Brandeis University, Ph.D diss., 1977.

David, Stephen, and Paul Peterson, eds. *Urban Politics and Public Policy: The City in Crisis*. New York City: Praeger Publishers, 1973.

Derthick, Martha. *New Towns—In Town: Why a Federal Program Failed*. Washington, D.C.: Brookings Institution, 1972.

Downs, Anthony. *Inside Bureaucracy*. Boston: Little, Brown and Company, 1967.

Fairlie, Henry. *The Kennedy Promise: The Politics of Expectation*. 1st ed. New York City: Doubleday and Company, 1973.

Featherman, Sandra, and William Rosenberg. *Jews, Blacks and Ethnics: The 1978 "Vote White" Charter Campaign in Philadelphia*. New York City: American Jewish Committee, 1979.

Fenno, Richard. *Home Style: House Members in Their Districts*. Boston: Little, Brown, and Company, 1978.

Fiorina, Morris. *Congress: Keystone of the Washington Establishment*. New Haven, Conn.: Yale University Press, 1977.

Frieden, Bernard, and Marshall Kaplan. *The Politics of Neglect*. Cambridge: MIT Press, 1977.

Friedman, Robert S., et al. "Administrative Agencies and the Publics They Serve." *Public Administration Review* 26 (1966): 192–204.

Garrett, Charles. *The LaGuardia Years: Machine and Reform Politics in New York City*. New Brunswick, N.J.: Rutgers University Press, 1961.

George, Alexander. "Case Studies and Theory Development: The Method of Structured, Focused Comparison." In *Diplomacy: New Approaches in History, Theory and Policy,* edited by Paul Gordon Lauren, 43–68 (New York City: Free Press, 1979).

——. "Political Leadership and Social Change in American Cities." *Daedalus* 97 (Fall 1968): 1194–1217.

Gittell, Marilyn. *Participants and Participation: A Study of School Policy in New York City*. New York City: Praeger Publishers, 1967.

Gogolin, Jean. "Politics of Property." *Boston Magazine*, July 1980.

Gordon, Diana. *City Limits: Barriers to Change in Urban Government*. New York City: Charterhouse, 1973.

Green, James R., and Hugh Carter Donahue. *Boston's Workers: A Labor History*. Boston: Boston Public Library, 1979.

Greenstein, Fred. "Eisenhower as an Activist President: A Look at New Evidence." *Political Science Quarterly* 4 (Winter 1979–1980): 577–99.

Greenstone, J. David, and Paul Peterson. *Race and Authority in Urban Politics*. New York City: Russell Sage Foundation, 1973.

Haider, Donald H. *When Governments Come to Washington*. New York City: Free Press, 1974.

Hartman, Chester. *Yerba Buena: Land Grab and Community Resistance in San Francisco*. San Francisco: Glide Publications, 1974.

Hawley, Willis D. *Non-Partisan Elections and the Case for Party Politics*. New York City: John Wiley and Sons, 1973.

Hawley, Willis D., and Michael Lipsky, eds. *Theoretical Perspectives in Urban Politics*. Englewood Cliffs, N.J.: Prentice-Hall, 1974.

Heclo, Hugh. "Issue Networks and the Executive Establishment." In *The New American Political System,* edited by Anthony King, 87–124. Washington, D.C.: American Enterprise Institute, 1979.

Holden, Mathew, Jr. "'Imperialism' in Bureaucracy." *American Political Science Review* 60 (1966): 943–51.

Huntington, Samuel. *American Politics: The Promise of Disharmony*. Cambridge: Harvard University Press, 1981.

Jacobs, Allan B. *Making City Planning Work*. Chicago: Planners Press, 1978.

Key, V. O. *Politics, Parties and Pressure Groups*. New York City: Thomas Y. Crowell, 1949.

——. *Southern Politics in State and Nation*. 4th ed. New York City: Vintage Books, 1963.

King, Anthony, ed. *The New American Political System*. Washington, D.C.: American Enterprise Institute, 1979.

Kotter, John P., and Paul R. Lawrence. *Mayors in Action: Five Approaches to Urban Governance*. New York City: John Wiley and Sons, 1974.

Krefetz, Sharon Perlman. *Welfare Policy Making and City Politics*. New York City: Praeger Publishers, 1976.

Levin, Martin A. "Conditions Contributing to Effective Implementatio Their Limits," Paper presented at Association of Public Policy An: and Management Conference, 19 Oct. 1979.

———. *Political Dilemmas of Social Policymaking.* (Forthcoming.)

———. "A Politics of Institutions." In *The Post-Imperial Presidency,* edi by Vincent Davis. New Brunswick, N.J.: Transaction Books, 1980.

Levin, Martin A., and Barbara Ferman. *The Political Hand: Policy Implemen tation and Youth Employment Programs.* Elmsford, N.Y.: Pergamon Press, 1985.

Levin, Murray B. *The Alienated Voter: Politics in Boston.* New York City: Holt, Rinehart and Winston, 1960.

Levine, Charles. *Racial Conflict and the American Mayor.* Lexington, Mass.: D.C. Heath and Company, 1974.

Levine, Edward M. *The Irish and Irish Politicians.* Notre Dame, Ind.: University of Notre Dame Press, 1966.

Levy, Frank. *Northern Schools and Civil Rights: The Racial Imbalance Act of Massachusetts.* Chicago: Markham, 1971.

Levy, Frank, et. al. *Urban Outcomes.* Berkeley and Los Angeles: University of California Press, 1974.

Levy, Mark R., and Michael S. Kramer. *The Ethnic Factor: How America's Minorities Decide Elections.* New York City: Simon and Schuster, 1973.

Lindsay, John V. *The City.* New York City: W. W. Norton and Company, 1969.

Lipsky, Michael. "Protest as a Political Resource." *American Political Science Review* 62 (Dec. 1968): 1144–58.

Litt, Edgar. *The Political Cultures of Massachusetts.* Cambridge: MIT Press, 1965.

Long, Norton. "The City as Reservation." *Public Interest* 25 (Fall 1971): 22–38.

Lowi, Theodore J. *The End of Liberalism: Ideology, Policy and the Crisis of Public Authority.* New York City: W. W. Norton and Company, 1969.

———. "Gosnell's Chicago Revisited via Lindsay's New York." In *Urban Politics and Public Policy: The City in Crisis,* edited by Stephen David and Paul Peterson, 19–26. New York City: Praeger Publishers, 1973.

———. "Machine Politics . . . Old and New." *Public Interest* 9 (Fall 1967).

Lupo, Alan. *Liberty's Chosen Home: The Politics of Violence in Boston.* 1st ed. Boston: Little, Brown and Company, 1977.

Lupo, Alan, et al. *Rites of Way: The Politics of Transportation in Boston and the U.S. City.* Boston: Little, Brown and Company, 1971.

Mann, Arthur. *LaGuardia Comes to Power, 1933.* Philadelphia: J. B. Lippincott Company, 1965.

McFarland, Andrew. *Power and Leadership in Pluralist Systems.* Stanford, Calif.: Stanford University Press, 1969.

Meyerson, Martin, and Edward Banfield. *Boston: The Job Ahead.* Cambridge: Harvard University Press, 1966.

————. *Politics, Planning and the Public Interest: The Case of Public Housing in Chicago.* Glencoe, Ill.: Free Press, 1955.

Michels, Robert. *Political Parties: A Sociological Study of the Oligarchical Tendencies of Modern Democracy.* New York City: Free Press, 1962.

Mollenkopf, John. *The Contested City.* Princeton, N.J.: Princeton University Press, 1983.

————. "The Post War Politics of Urban Development." *Politics and Society* 5:3 (Winter, 1975) 247–95.

Neustadt, Richard E. *Presidential Power: The Politics of Leadership.* New York City: John Wiley and Sons, 1960.

O'Connor, Len. *Clout: Mayor Daley and His City.* Chicago: Henry Regnery Company, 1975.

O'Connor, Thomas H. *Bibles, Brahmins and Bosses: A Short History of Boston.* Boston: Boston Public Library, 1976.

Orren, Gary. "The Cycle of Black Political Impotence: School Politics in Boston." Paper presented at annual meeting of Midwest Political Science Association, 1978.

Parenti, Michael. "Power and Pluralism: A View from the Bottom." *Journal of Politics* 32 (August 1970): 501–30.

Paul, Dianne. *Politics of the Property Tax.* Lexington, Mass.: D.C. Heath, 1975.

Piven, Francis Fox. "The Urban Crises: Who Got What and Why." in *1984 Revisited*, edited by Robert Paul Wolff. New York City: Alfred A. Knopf, 1973.

Polsby, Nelson. "Contemporary Transformations of American Politics: Thoughts on the Research Agendas of Political Scientists." *Political Science Quarterly* 4 (Winter 1981–1982): 551–70.

Pool, Daniel. "Politics in the New Boston, 1960–1970: A Study of Mayoral Policymaking." Ph.D diss., Brandeis University, 1974.

Pressman, Jeffrey. *Federal Programs and City Politics.* Berkeley and Los Angeles: University of California Press, 1975.

————. "Preconditions of Mayoral Leadership." *American Political Science Review* 66 (1972): 511–24.

Pressman, Jeffrey, and Aaron Wildavsky. *Implementation.* Berkeley and Los Angeles: University of California Press, 1973.

Rakove, Milton. *Don't Make No Waves, Don't Back No Losers: An Insider's Analysis of the Daley Machine.* Bloomington: Indiana University Press, 1975.

Ravitch, Diane. *The Great School Wars: New York City, 1805–1973.* New York City: Basic Books, 1974.

Reichley, James. *The Art of Government.* New York City: Irvington Publications, 1972.

Riordon, William L. *Plunkitt of Tammany Hall.* New York City: E. P. Dutton and Company, 1963.

Royko, Mike. *Boss: Richard J. Daley of Chicago.* New York City: Signet, 1971.

lge, Philip. "Federal-Local Relations and the Mission of the City." *Annals of the American Academy of Political and Social Science* 416 (Nov. 974): 77–90.

ary, Robert. "Urban Politics: The New Convergence of Power." *Journal f Politics* 26 (Nov. 1964).

d, Terry. *Storm over the States.* New York City: McGraw-Hill, 1967.

Wallace, and Herbert Kaufman. *Governing New York City.* New York ity: Russell Sage Foundation, 1965.

schneider, E. E. *The Semisovereign People: A Realist's View of Democracy in America.* rev. ed., Hinsdale, Ill.: Dryden Press, 1975.

an, Harold. *Politics, Position and Power: The Dynamics of Federal Organization.* 2d ed. New York City: Oxford University Press, 1975.

n, Tom. "Bossism by the Book." *Boston Phoenix*, 18 Nov. 1980.

___. "Faces of Change." *Boston Phoenix*, 2 May 1978.

Thomas. *Knowledge and Decisions.* New York City: Basic Books, 1980.

Sternlieb, George. "The City as Sandbox." *Public Interest* 25 (Fall 1971): 14–21.

Stokes, Carl B. *Promises of Power.* New York City: Simon and Schuster, 1973.

Sundquist, James L. *Making Federalism Work.* Washington, D.C.: Brookings Institution, 1969.

Teune, Henry, and Adam Przeworski. *The Logic of Comparative Social Inquiry.* New York City: Wiley Interscience, 1970.

Tocqueville, Alexis de. *Democracy in America.* New York City: Mentor, 1956.

Tolchin, Martin, and Susan Tolchin. *To the Victor: Political Patronage from the Clubhouse to the White House.* New York City: Vintage, 1972.

Weinberg, Martha Wagner. "Boston's Kevin White: A Mayor Who Survives." *Political Science Quarterly*, 96 (Spring 1981): 87–106.

Weinberg, Martha Wagner, and Philip B. Heymann. "The Paradox of Power: Mayoral Leadership on Charter Reform in Boston." In *American Politics and Public Policy*, edited by Walter Dean Burnham and Martha Wagner Weinberg, 280–303. Cambridge: MIT Press, 1978.

Wildavsky, Aaron. "Government and the People." *Commentary*, Aug. 1973.

___. "The Past and Future Presidency." *Public Interest* 41 (Fall 1975): 56–76.

___. *Politics of the Budgetary Process.* 2d ed. Boston: Little, Brown and Company, 1974.

___. *Speaking Truth to Power: The Art and Craft of Policy Analysis.* Boston: Little, Brown and Company, 1979.

Wildavsky, Aaron, ed. *Perspectives on the Presidency.* Boston: Little, Brown and Company, 1975.

Wildavsky, Aaron, and Jack Knott, "Jimmy Carter's Theory of Governing." In *American Politics and Public Policy*, edited by Walter Dean Burnham and Martha Wagner Weinberg. Cambridge: MIT Press, 1978.

Wilson, James Q. *The Amateur Democrat: Club Politics in Three Cities*. Chicago: University of Chicago Press, 1966.

————. "Mayors vs. the Cities." *Public Interest* 16 (Summer 1969): 25–37.

————. *Political Organizations*. New York City: Basic Books, 1973.

————. "We Need to Shift Focus." In *Urban Government*, edited by Edward Banfield, 21–33. Glencoe, Ill.: Free Press, 1969.

Wirt, Fred. *Power in the City: Decision-Making in San Francisco*. Berkeley and Los Angeles: University of California Press, 1974.

————. "San Francisco: The Politics of Hyperpluralism." *Transaction* 6 (April 1970): 46–55.

Wolfinger, Raymond. *The Politics of Progress*. Englewood Cliffs, N.J.: Prentice-Hall, 1973.

Wood, Robert. "Professionals at Bay: Managing Boston's Public Schools." *Journal of Policy Analysis and Management* 4 (1982): 454–68.

Yates, Douglas. "The Mayor's Eight-Ring Circus: The Shape of Urban Politics in its Evolving Policy Arenas." Paper presented at annual meeting of American Political Science Association, 1978.

————. "The Roots of American Leadership: Political Style and Policy Consequences." In *American Politics and Public Policy*, edited by Walter Dean Burnham and Martha Wagner Weinberg, 140–68. Cambridge: MIT Press, 1978.

————. *The Ungovernable City*. Cambridge: MIT Press, 1977.

Young, James Sterling. *The Washington Community 1800–1828*. New York City: Harcourt, Brace and World, 1966.

# Index

Index

Index

261

Index

Index

Index